REFLECTIONS IN THE MIRROR OF LIFE

REFLECTIONS IN THE MIRROR OF LIFE

A Philosopher's Notebook

Stephen L. Weber

San Diego State University Press

2023

Reflections in the Mirror of Life: A Philosopher's Notebook by
Stephen L. Weber, and edited by Ralph Villanueva,
Seth Mallios, and William Nericcio, is published by
San Diego State University Press.

No part of this book may be used or reproduced in any
manner whatsoever without prior permission from
San Diego State University Press. These permissions are
waived in the case of brief quotations embodied in
critical articles and reviews.

San Diego State University Press publications may be purchased at discount for educational, business, or sales promotional use. For information write:

SDSU PRESS
San Diego State University
San Diego, California 92182-6020

Copyright © 2023 Stephen L. Weber

All rights reserved.

sdsupress.sdsu.edu   facebook.com/sdsu.press
hype.sdsu.edu   amatlcomx.sdsu.edu

Cover and Book Design by Guillermo Nericcio García
for memogr@phics designcasa, memo@sdsu.edu

ISBN: 978-1-938537-74-5

FIRST EDITION

PRINTED IN THE UNITED STATES OF AMERICA

SAN DIEGO STATE

Dedication

To the strong, wise, and caring women who have enriched my life, some of whom include:

Catherine, Helen, Susan, Deborah, Nancy, Sally, Mary Ruth, Darlene, and Stephanie

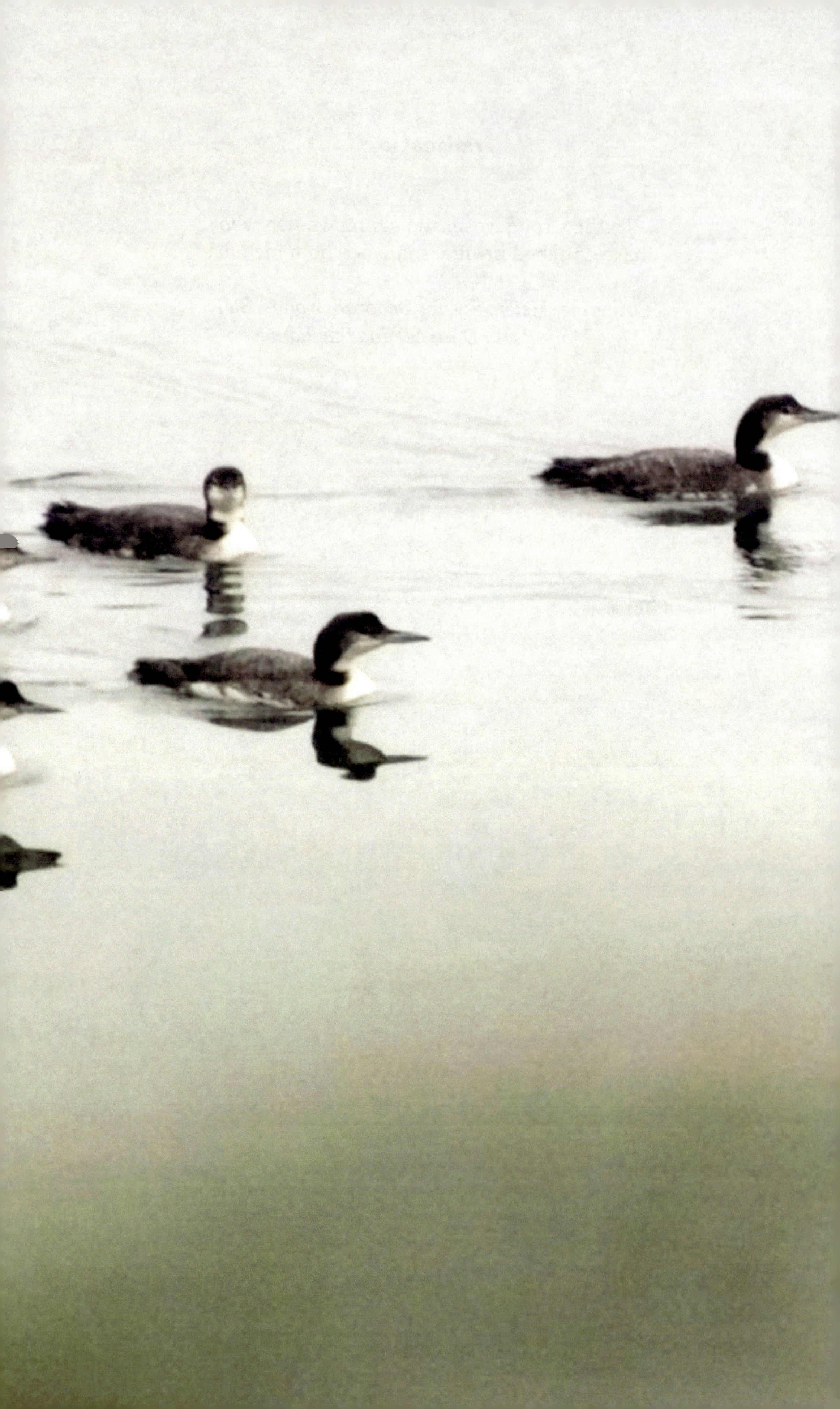

Table of Contents

Foreword by Seth Mallios	13
Preface	17
1. Place and Moment	19
One Morning in Maine	20
A Walk Through History	24
Fog 1	27
Stuck Behind a School Bus	29
End of Summer	30
Fog 2	31
Visitors From Away	33
First Light	36
Fall 2016	40
Arachnophobes, Beware:	43
1. Deadly Courtship	43
2. A Second Web	45
3. The Spider and the Wasp	48
Tragedy of the Commons	49
You'll Shoot Your Eye Out	53
Fog 3	58
The Maine Woods	59
I Couldn't Make This Up	63
Rainy Day	65
It was a Cold and Snowy night	67
2. Childhood: Everybody Has One	73
Part 1: The Barn	74
Part 2: Basketball	77
The Eat'em Bug	79
Culture Shock	81
Labor Day	83
3. Not All Politics are Politic	86
Immigrants	87
Democracy	89
Women	91
Iraq War	94
Political Views	95
July 4th	97
Norway	101
Save our Bay	103

Memories	105
A Guest Essay by my Son, Matt	107

4. Chasing Sophia — 110

Philosophic Essay	111
Reflections on 75	113
Hallelujah	116
Under the surface	117
Veterans	119
An "Ingrown" Lecture, March 2002	121
Home	122
Love: A Triptych	124
Philosophia	127
The Mystery that is Woman	130
Goodness, Truth and Beauty	131
Tidal Falls	134
Life	135
Thoughts While Dying	137

5. San Diego State — 140

Aristotle	141
Pride and Praise	142
Courage	145
Radio, recollections of an Old Man	146
Celebration	147
Weeds	148
A Good Word Gone Bad	150
Beyond "Price"	152
Anonymous	154
Charge to Graduates	155

6. Love — 156

Not Nostalgia	157
Neatness	159
A Halloween Memory	160
Poem for Susan – scanned	162
Compact of the Heart	164
Picnics	166
Yesterday	169
Home Alone	174
Grief	174
Yes	179
Intimacy	180
Sons, Brothers, Friends...	182

Embracing the Bad with the Good	184
To Life: You've Made it Very Good for Me	185
Goodbye	186

7. Reflections of an Old Man — 187

Simple Gifts	188
Emmett Till	189
Seventy	191
Retirement Reflection	193
Visitors	195
Overheard in the Jacuzzi	196
Attraction	198
Shallow	200
West Texas	201
Lobster Fest	205
Retirement, Jim and Sally	208
Sick	209
Hospitality	210
Welcome Home	211
Sea Jewels	213
Mothers and Daughters	215
Rabbi Ben Ezra	216

Acknowledgments — 220

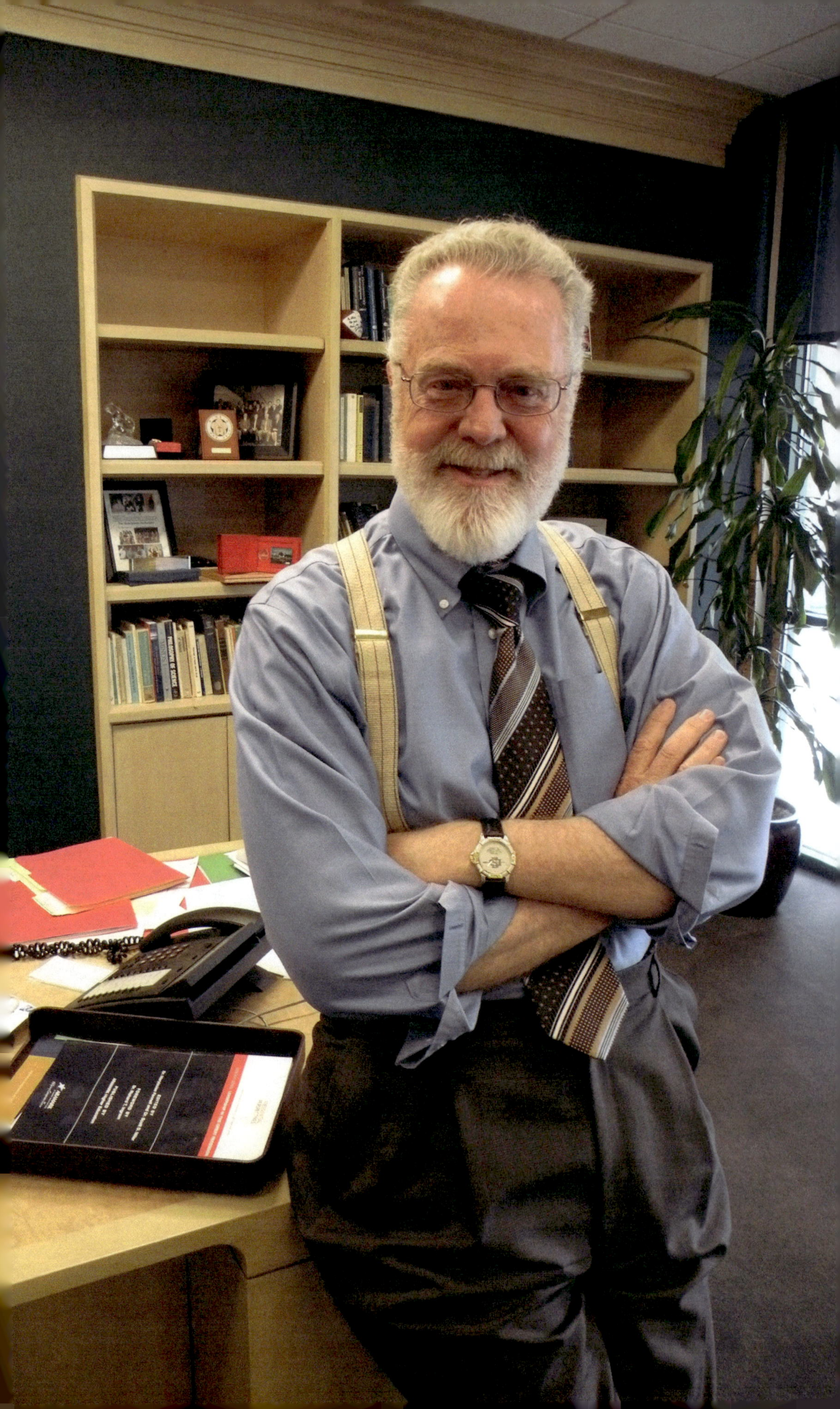

Foreword

Stephen L. Weber served as president of San Diego State University from 1996-2011; his writings intersect many of SDSU's important transitions and transformations during his time as administrative lead (a role he liked to refer to in typical self-deprecating fashion as "Institutional Hood Ornament"). The kernels of wisdom sprinkled in Dr. Weber's *Reflections in the Mirror of Life: A Philosopher's Notebooks* are timeless, uplifting, and reflective of a life well-lived. These short compositions include keen insights into higher education, natural philosophy, and relationships.

Ask Steve Weber about his achievements at San Diego State University and he beams about the nation-leading surge in student graduation rates, the many successful community partnerships that set the stage for spectacular growth in the 21st century, and the rejuvenation of cooperative and mutually respectful relations with the University Senate. But if you pose the same question to those of us who worked closely with President Weber during his decade and a half on Montezuma Mesa, a strikingly different answer emerges. While the aforementioned accomplishments are undoubtedly impressive, they pale in comparison to the sincerity, integrity, and compassion with which he routinely approached tasks at the university. Dr. Weber insisted on putting SDSU students first and went to great lengths to avoid trampling the personal experiences of others in pursuit of institutional progress. Steve *cared* about San Diego State.

When Steve Weber was hired by SDSU as its seventh president, the San Diego State community was fractured, fragmented, and frustrated. The institution's draconian budget cuts of 1992—resulting in what was at the time the largest-ever termination of tenured faculty members (111) in U.S. higher education history, the deletion of 662 classes from the upcoming academic schedule, and the dissolution of majors for over 1,100 enrolled students—started a chain reaction of fervent protest and political upheaval that left the campus reeling. Like all university presidents, Dr. Weber was expected to be an intelligent and adept leader, but the task that lay before Steve at San Diego State required significant restorative skills as well.

Then, the worst tragedy in university history struck SDSU. In President Weber's first weeks in office, there was a premeditated, on-campus triple homicide during a graduate thesis defense. Faced with a traumatized SDSU community, Steve embarked on an extended campaign to heal his new home with empathy, kindness, and inclusion. With tears in his eyes, Dr. Weber spoke at the campus-wide memorial for the three slain faculty members on September 3, 1996, and told the thousands of people assembled: "***We*** have suffered a great loss. But it is nothing compared to the human loss which this senseless tragedy has inflicted on the families of our fallen colleagues... ***Our university*** community speaks ***as one*** in this expression of our deep sadness."

These guiding principles—***we***, ***our university***, and ***as one***—were the building blocks by which President Weber slowly led a broken-hearted university back to health. The "Shared Vision" he convened became a blueprint for rebuilding SDSU together. At its core was an ethos of caring, respect, and inclusion.

Dr. Weber would be the first to credit this renaissance of SDSU to the positive, constructive instincts of faculty, staff, and students; to a great team of administrative colleagues; and to the guidance/wisdom/engagement of his beloved wife, Susan. Nonetheless, Steve Weber excelled in "staying present" long before it was a trite administrator buzzword; he repeatedly demonstrated extraordinary patience, insisted on listening before speaking, and managed to find hope in many difficult situations during the late 1990s and 2000s.

It is these traits that repeatedly surface in this personal collection of essays. Regardless of whether the particular topic is the natural beauty and bounty of Hancock Point, Maine, his unwavering dedication to and affinity for philosophy, or on the role of the modern university, Steve's narrative trademarks are a comfortable pace and inclusive style, keen insight through unhurried observations, and an optimistic embrace of the world in which we live.

It is worth noting that Dr. Weber's patient focus on the positive should not be equated with an easy life or lack of engagement with pressing hardships. Trials and tragedies have not spared Stephen L. Weber; and yet, in the face of loss—even his own—Steve first and foremost chooses to comfort others. I believe this made him an outstanding president and an even better person.

Seth Mallios
Professor of Anthropology and University History Curator, SDSU

Steve Weber's delightful sense of humor is one of his defining traits and includes an infectious laugh, a heartwarming Cheshire grin, and an unbridled love of wordplay. (Illustration courtesy of Seth Mallios)

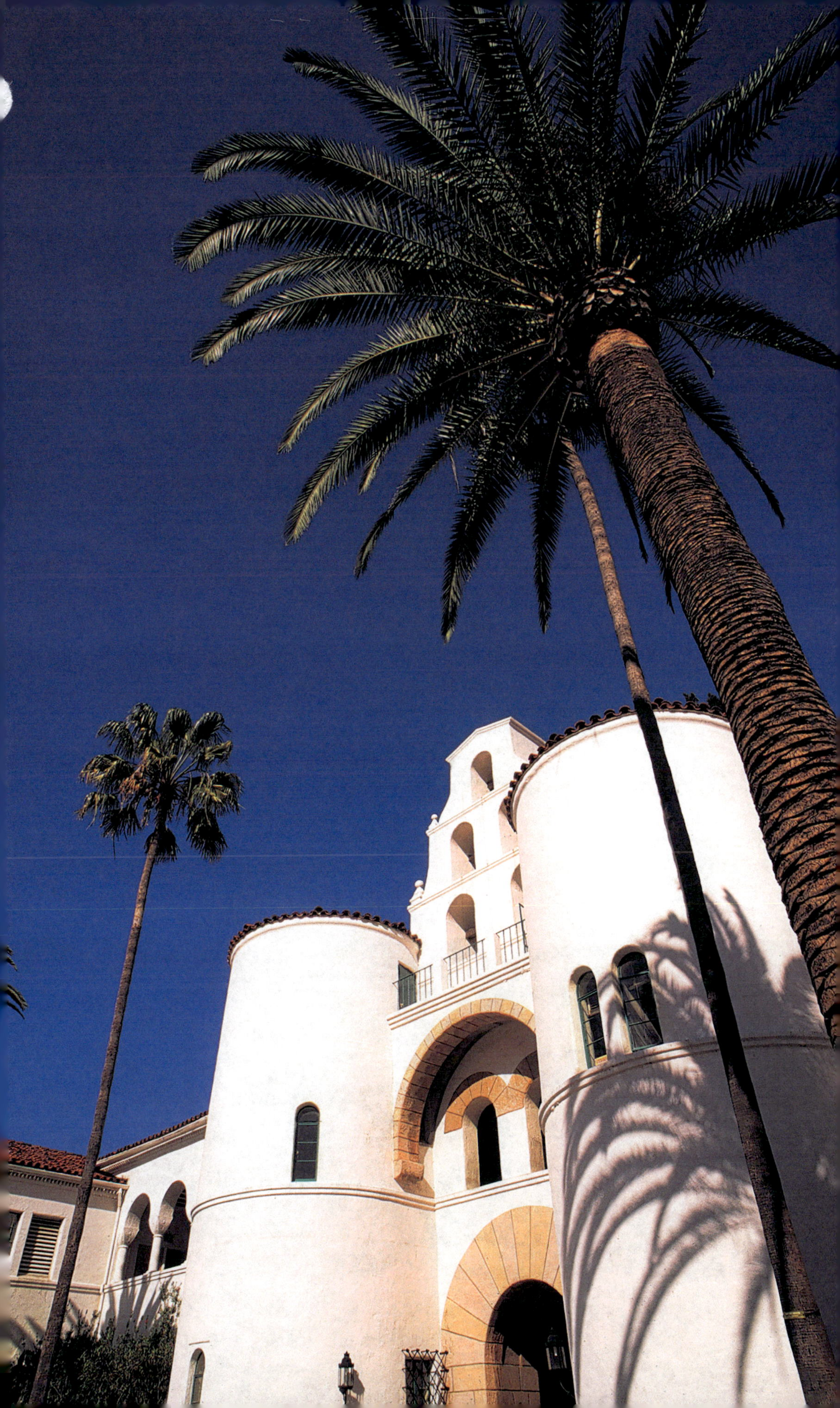

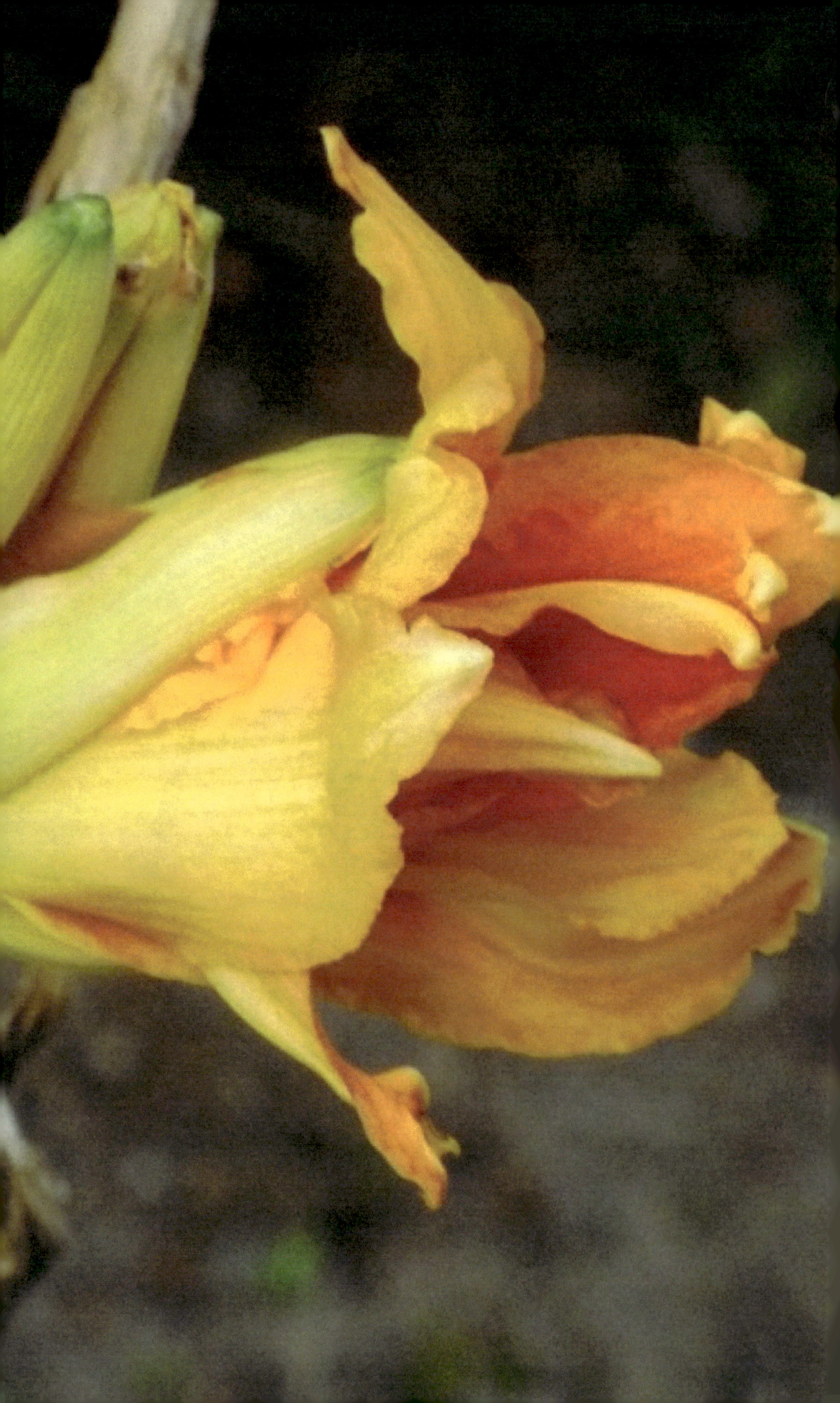

Preface

Dear Reader, I enjoy writing. For years I have imposed random essays on family and friends. Some of the better ones are collected here for your pleasure. The topics vary, but the "voice" remains constant throughout. The essays were not originally written in the order in which you now encounter them, nor were they arranged under their present headings which have been added so that, if your interest is piqued, you may pursue other essays of a similar kind. Each essay is intended to stand on its own; they may be read in any order. I hope you find as much enjoyment, amusement, and perhaps even occasional edification in reading these essays as I found in writing them.

21

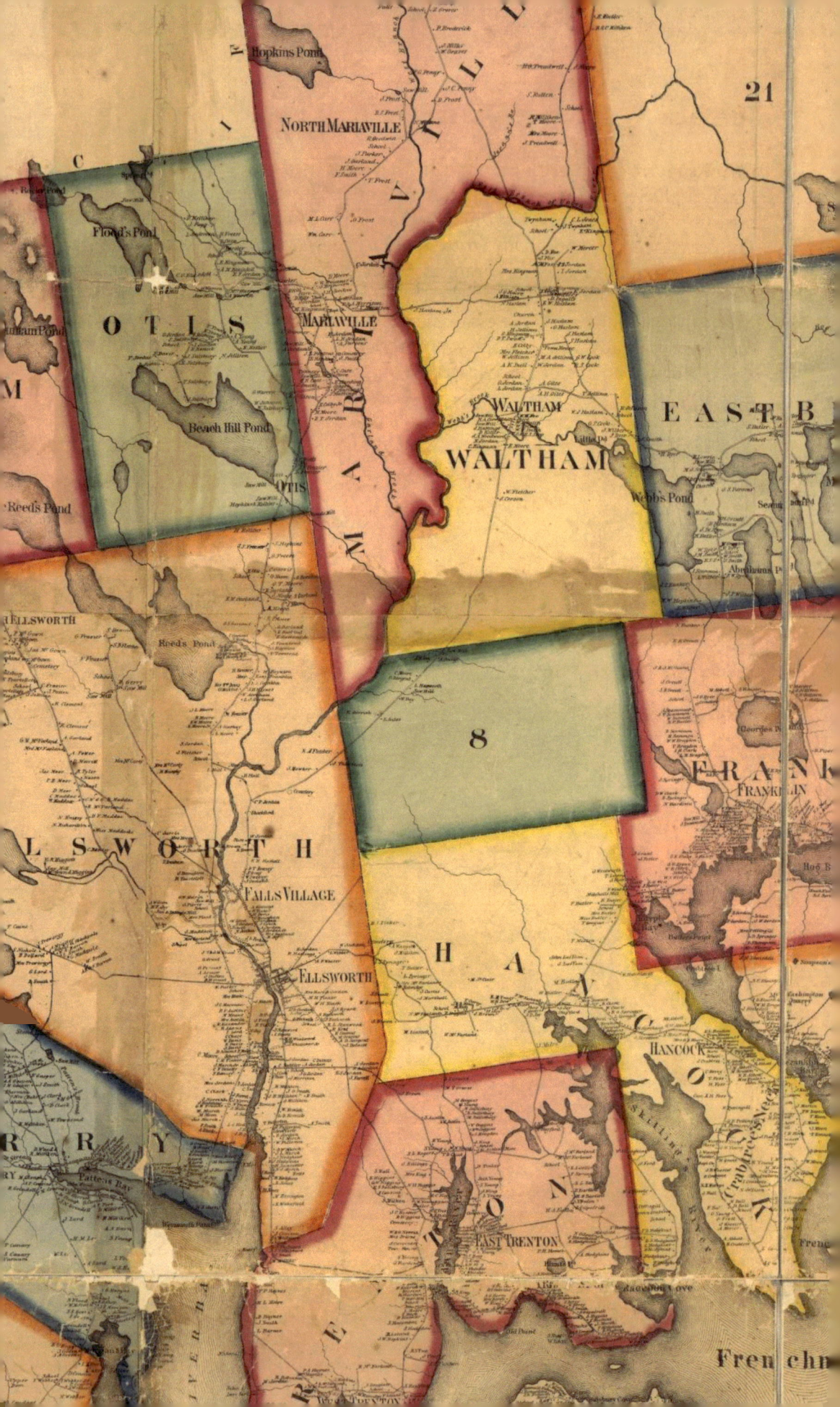

Hopkins Pond

NORTH MARIAVILLE

Floyd's Pond

OTIS

Beach Hill Pond

MARIAVILLE

WALTHAM
WALTHAM

EAST B

Reed's Pond

Webb's Pond

ELLSWORTH

Reed's Pond

8

FRAN
FRANKLIN

ELLSWORTH

FALLS VILLAGE

ELLSWORTH

HANCOCK

H A N G O

RRY

EAST TRENTON

Frenchm

1. PLACE AND MOMENT

This first group of essays is about a place that releases its beauty easily and its significance quietly. It is a bony finger of land called "Hancock Point" stretching south into Frenchman Bay. I trust you have such places of your own and hope that in reading of this place and these moments your mind will happily return to your own special place and times.

One Morning in Maine (September 1, 2015)

I used to say that being a university president was a good job for a person with a short attention span: each day is different. There are so many competing constituencies that any day can change on a dime from the one you anticipated, which is after all part of what made the job such fun. Now my life is considerably more predictable. Typically, the day I anticipate is the one I live. And because today is Tuesday, I predictably found myself at 6:30 this morning out on the deck doing my thrice-weekly Tai Chi, wearing my SDSU sweat suit as defense against the cool morning air. This indulgence of exercising outside cannot last much longer, perhaps another month. Already the early morning temperature is in the upper 50s. But what a beautiful morning — so beautiful that I must share some photos. First, however, let me set the scene. The deck is one quarter of a twenty- foot radius circle, wedged between the two wings, if single rooms can be wings, of our small house. Two Adirondack chairs and a low table (all home-built) are pulled toward the northwest corner where petunia-filled window boxes (also self-built) mark the deck's edge. Kayak paddles stand at the ready against the "crotch" of the deck. Except for a railing descending the steps, the deck is bare.

My Tai Chi routine begins with warm up exercises, including some deep breathing. The air I take in is so clean it tastes of pine and sea salt. This may sound contradictory; those smells suggest what in other circumstances might be called pollutants. But this is Maine and they're natural, and, well you get the idea. Those pine and sea salt "flavors" are enhanced by the fact that it is still early. The cool humidity makes the air rich and heavy with scents that the sun, still hiding itself behind the trees, will soon drive away.

While warming up I was buzzed by a hummingbird and then another, hurrying towards their feeder which is perhaps fifteen feet away. Since my sweat suit is black I dismissed the usual attraction of color and assumed they just resented my intrusion into their world. But then, it became clear that, as is so often the case in life, it was not about me at all, but rather that I was simply the post about which they were sparring to claim ownership of the feeder.

The morning was so perfect, under clear, still-cool skies, that I resolved to share the experience with you. Then, of course, everything called out in its post card voice, "Take a picture of ME. I am what the mornings in Maine are all about." And so it was that my usually 30-minute Tai Chi session stretched to 45. Why? Because I paused to go inside and retrieve the camera, take the photo, then put the camera back inside since I was afraid I might forget and leave it on the deck, though there is no threat of rain and theft is not in our forecast either. So, Tai Chi complete, predicted morning errands run, I am now at the computer downloading this morning's photos. I wish you could have been here to enjoy the morning with me, but as you could not, having lives and cameras and special experiences of your own, I share these photos as glimpses of what Robert McCloskey entitled, "One Morning in Maine."

The recently-full moon still floats across the Bay...

...even though the sun is already painting the slopes of Mt. Cadillac with its morning rays.

Lobstermen and women are already hard at work ... racing from buoy to buoy, each illuminated by the early morning sun.

On the other side of the house the flowers prepare for their (also predictable) day. The Oriental Lilies lord it over the others.

The Monkshood kowtow in deference.

The Cosmos, being annuals, do not understand the hierarchy and hence just bubble forth in their private oblivion. While the hollyhocks stand, shy and reserved, in the background.

And the day lilies, being fundamentally clueless, are just struggling to wake up.

As I turn toward my predictable breakfast I feel sorry for the day lilies. They have already missed so much.

*   *   *

A Walk Through History (October 2013)

Mount Desert Island rises across the Bay. At 1,528 feet it is the highest coastal peak on the eastern seaboard of the U.S. For perhaps 6,000 years this was the land of the Wabanaki, translated fittingly as "People of the Dawnlands." Their discarded shell heaps remain, as do they.

If you discount, as most experts do, the Viking coin found in Brooklin, Maine (about 40 miles from here), the first European to see these shores was probably the French explorer Samuel de Champlain who sailed/mapped this coast in 1604 which is why it is not an accident that our bay is named "Frenchman." Sixteen years before the Pilgrims, Champlain scrambled ashore on September 5, declaring that, "The mountain summits are all bare and rocky, I name it *Ile des Monts Desert*." I like to imagine his 40-foot *patache* floating at anchor on the Bay over 400 years ago.

Not surprisingly, French Jesuits followed within 10 years and began construction of a settlement on *Monts Desert*. Two months later, on July 2, 1613, Captain Samuel Argall of Virginia arrived on board the *Treasurer* to destroy their mission. Killing three of the missionaries, wounding three others, and capturing twenty or so to be taken back to Jamestown as prisoners was insufficient to quell his Protestant passion. On a subsequent voyage Argall returned to *Mont Dessert* to cut down the cross the Jesuits had erected and to burn the remaining buildings. I find it interesting that Native Americans persisted here for 6,000 years while Europeans were killing each other within ten.

Working on the firm principle that, "there is no one to whom we will not surrender," French, Dutch, British and, finally, American flags have all flown over our region. So, this is a place of history, but it is a different history through which I walk this morning. It is our lived/remembered history of Hancock Point.

As I climb the steps up to our drive to begin my walk I look to the right to the spot where we pitched a tent shortly after buying the property in an effort to get to know it better and to begin thinking about siting a future house. Woodsman that I am, I managed to pitch our tent on a prodigiously uncomfortable root. We climbed out the next morning as stiff and bent in our youth as we are now in old age. There are, as you might suspect, many kinds of conifers here: pine, spruce, fir, larch, etc... There is also balsam. As I walk past one at the top of our driveway I'm reminded of the Thanksgiving, soon after the house was built when we drove up for a weekend and brought back some greens for the fireplace mantle in Connecticut. They were lovely, soft balsam boughs. But of all the conifers, balsams are wired to drop their needles almost immediately. After placing our sentimental treasures on the mantle, we came down the next morning to find a collection of twigs sheltering piles of brown needles beneath them.

A half-mile along our dirt road, down the slope to my right is the home of the venerable Oliver Crosby, a former diplomat, serving mostly in Africa and the Middle East. Oliver, who recently asked me to suggest a philosophy book, is now in his 90s and is very much "all there," still sharp and wise, still engaged, and still possessed of a natural charm and grace that must have stood him well in our diplomatic service. I turn left on Bragg Road and walk up the hill to the main road. I'm on pavement now. I turn right, toward the library and recently abandoned one room 10'x12' post office. Almost immediately Robert Waldner's foursquare, white frame colonial rises on my left. Bob died less than a year ago; it will be hard for any of us to think of the Point without him. Bob was a sailor who moored two of the most beautiful day sailors in our little harbor. I served with him on the library committee and was regularly the recipient of his advice.

A hundred yards or so further on, our tiny library is set back to my right. I cannot pass without recalling its damp mustiness on rainy summer afternoons. But I turn left instead, down Wharf Road to the harbor where on this October day only about a fifth of the summer boats still float at their moorings. There, still below me as I descend the hill, slightly to my left are the boathouse and wharf where Rick and Matt took their summer sailing lessons, where Matt almost ran us aground speeding wing-and–wing past our mooring. This is also the place where on a hot summer day while watching kids dive from the wharf, Susan uncharacteristically declared a bobbing head to be, "the ugliest kid she had ever seen," only to have Rick point out that the swimmer in question was a seal. I smile. The boathouse is where, for over thirty years we have enjoyed (perhaps that was not always true), the sailing program's annual blueberry breakfast. The kids would pick wild blueberries on Bean Island which I now see floating a half-mile offshore to my left as I continue my walk, now on east side, toward the tip of our Peninsula.

Almost immediately I see Bill O'Tool's house on my right with its gold-lettered "Tool Box" sign proudly displayed. Bob was a colleague at the University of Maine, an engineer considerably senior to myself. Philosophers and engineers don't mix much in the natural world, but I got to know him when I served as a liaison from the College of Arts and Sciences to the College of Engineering. Some say that Bill is suffering from Alzheimer's which is probable, but I think he might just be **HARD OF HEARING**.

Another academic memory lies a few hundred yards ahead. My morning walk now takes me past Connie Carlson's craftsman cottage on the east side of the Point. She was also a colleague at the University of Maine. I knew her as the Dean of Bangor Community College, at that time a part of the University of Maine. She went on to be the President of the University of Maine at *Presque Isle*. Note the lingering French tradition. When Susan and I were thinking about buying this property I called Connie to ask if the price was reasonable. Connie has long since died, but I think of her whenever I pass her snug little craftsman cottage. There is a bench on the library porch in Connie's memory.

A still earlier memory lies only a few hundred yards farther along the road, on the tip where we visited Hancock Point for the first time. We had come down with Bob, who was our Department Chair, and Judy Tredwell who were closing up a large "cottage" for friends, a great old turreted house that persists today under the name "Finistere," meaning *end of the earth.*" Between Connie's house and Finistere, I walk past the grand "Bell View" tutor house, so named because it looks out on the bell buoy marking a ledge at the entrance to our harbor. When Susan and I were walking this same ground 42 years ago, we stopped to look at and listen to the buoy. Susan said she was not feeling well. Later we realized it was morning sickness: she was pregnant with Rick.

Now on the way back home, I pass Eliott Cutler's home. He is the independent candidate for governor of Maine. When I pass his house I think of Kay Cutler, his mother, whose husband, Lawrence, was Chair of the Board of the University of Maine System. He was an excellent board chair. One afternoon Bob Treadwell and I sailed a Rhodes 19 around from Southwest Harbor to the Point. It was a long, rolling, pitching sail. At the end we met up with Susan and Judy at the Cutler's for some much-needed hot chocolate and tea. Kay and Larry have long since passed on, but Susan and I (having no idea that we would someday be playing similar roles), learned a lot from their example and their hospitality. Ironically, about a half mile further on we pass the summer home of former governor, John McKernan and his wife, Olympia Snowe. We don't see Olympia on the Point much anymore, perhaps once a summer. She is a small, now somewhat stooped woman, whose independence has always reminded me of a previously strong Maine woman: Senator Margaret Chase Smith. Now that Olympia's left the Senate, now that her book has appeared, I am hoping we will see more of her.

Moving closer to home I pass Jean O'meara's salt box on the right. It's a solid, properly-Maine house that, like several other homes on the Point, was built by Jeff Smith. It pleases me to think that ours was the first— a place entrusted then to a hard-working young man recommended by Paul Petrell who had done some quality work for us when we lived in Orono. About a half mile farther along the dirt road, now for the first time repeating my steps as I have completed the Point loop and head back along West Shore road, I once more pass by Oliver's house, and walking up a slight slope, arrive at Arnold and Peggy Amstutz' compound. After an awkward first meeting and some adolescent posturing, our two boys and their two girls got to know each other in the sailing program. They have continued to be good friends ever since. Matt still visits Ann occasionally when he is in New York while Rick and Kath occasionally see Alice when she visits her friend on Skaneateles Lake. They all try to align their summer visits to the point to allow an annual reunion. I remember when, having been caught up, like everyone else, in the phenomenon of "The Phantom," our families once met in New York City where we treated the kids to an opportunity to enjoy the operatic performance.

The Point has a continuity from generation to generation. Sometimes history is prospective. It's already clear that that Rick and Matt as well as Alice and Ann will be spending future summers on the Point and unless I miss my guess the following generation will do so as well. That also pleases me. Sometimes history is little things — an ancient Norse coin pretending to have been left a thousand years ago; sometimes history is big things — the long tradition of the Wabanaki on this coast. Sometimes history is foolish things — Protestant/Catholic wars carried to a distant shore. Always it is human things.

* * *

Fog 1

There are mornings like this one when I think clarity is over-rated. As the sun rose, a dense fog hung at the mouth of Frenchman Bay. It was obstructed by Mount Dessert Island and the Porcupines, but you could see the fog loitering, not quite risen from its nocturnal slumber. That fog has now slipped silently through the gaps between the Porcupines, over their hills and slowly filled our Bay from south to north. For a while, as the fog worked its way up the Bay, you could still see the peak of Cadillac Mountain protruding in its rounded permanence. Then Cadillac was gone but the far shore still visible. The distant pines along our shore and the reef to our south soon slipped away. Before long I lost sight of our own woods. The trail shortened until it vanished at the edge of our deck. The sun retreated from a bright patch of sky to a dull smudge. It has now vanished in the uniform gray.

Fog hangs on our garden plants in spheric, reflective bubbles of water, especially on the Lady's Mantel. The deck is darkened with wetness. Tiny droplets have condensed on the Adirondack chairs. Yesterday's warm spring sun on my face has given way to a cool dampness — not unwelcome. Now the fog has deepened to envelop us in its gray quiet. We see only it. But sounds persist: gulls fighting over a treasure on the rocks — perhaps an urchin or a mussel. A loon calls, another answers.

There is no wind and the trees are still. The gently undulating waves are sufficient to send the sound of shuffling pebbles our way with the occasional drops of water which fall from our roof with an audible "plop"... "plop"... "plop." A chickadee calls from our nearby feeder — perhaps letting its mate know where it is. The fog slides in closer still. The proverbial "hand in front of your face," is there no more, though I confess I am not looking. I feel pleasantly alone, drifting like the fog: I am Descartes' "disembodied mind." The retreat is now inward toward the self that is so easily distracted by the chatter of sunshine. Strangely enough, being afloat in this interior, the fog brings clarity and dullness sparkles with reflection. The inner fog lifts as the outer one descends.

I think how peaceful this is, how peaceful I am. What a pleasure it is, after a life filled with busyness and distractions, with real and imagined emergencies, that I have nowhere to go — not even indoors. I can just sit here as the fog fills my beard, as my wool sweater dampens. I think about life's many satisfactions, one of which is place, another time. Neither cost anything. Indeed, neither can be avoided, yet both are elusive. This fog has captured them for a moment, and me as well. Like this fog, life comes and goes — silently slips away, becomes a memory, then vanishes into oblivion. That is not an unpleasant prospect. After a while we do not need the illusion that we will leave a trace — any more than this fog will leave a trace. Perhaps, like the fog, we have provided some moisture for life to swell, perhaps some nutrition. That is enough. This sounds like melancholy, but it is the fog-bound clarity of stillness. Camus asks that we live without illusion, counsels that life is fuller, more immediate, without the chimera of progress or purpose. Like this fog it makes for clarity — and a strange kind of appreciation that you have had a moment to play the game.

* * *

Stuck Behind a School Bus (May 2014)

It is a foggy, drizzled spring morning in Maine. I am driving home from an early workout at the Y. Just past Chipper's restaurant and Merchant's Auto Service I come upon a school bus. My first thought is that I am going to be late. Upon reflecting, I am reminded that I will not be late for anything, that Susan is probably not even up yet, and on the plus side, this will slow me down enough to hear the 8:00 a.m. news on public radio. So I relax and begin to appreciate the scene.

The first thing I notice is a father and daughter, I would guess her to be in the fourth grade, waiting at the end of a drive I had not previously noted even though I have driven past it for over thirty years. The drive has no visible house connected to it. I suspect it winds back about a quarter mile north to the shore of Hogs Head Bay. But what is most striking is that the father has made the walk to wait for the bus with his daughter. All clear: he places what I imagine to be a melancholy hand on her shoulder as she sets off purposefully in her bright pink jacket with blue lunchbox in hand, across US Route 1 to begin her day. He turns back to walk to the invisible house alone.

We pass the General Store on our right and then the Post Office, also on our right. Two more school pick-ups on Route 1. We are approaching the turnoff to Hancock Point. Perhaps the bus will go straight and I can speed home. I cannot help myself, in my red Audi. But no, the bus turns to the right and lumbers down the Point Road in front of me. I am now immediately behind, not third or fourth in line. All the better to watch the early morning drama.

The next stop has two kids and a mother holding a large coffee cup. The older climbs aboard resolutely; the younger turns home, his hand in hers saying to himself, "at last, I thought he would never leave."

A mile or so on, the bus groans to a halt, its left arm stop sign swings awkwardly forward shepherding what is clearly a multi-family embarkation. Five kids cross the street in various stages of conversation. The mothers, having done their duty, remain behind captured by their own conversation. Lights blink again. A solitary high school girl/woman boards the bus, earbuds installed, carefully showing no emotion. She carries a small case that I take to be a flute. Her father, who I presume has driven up from Young's Cove, watches from the car.

Finally, the bus turns left on Cross Road and I am free to speed home -- arriving so early that I have to sit in my parked car to listen to the news before carrying my gym clothes down the stairs and into our still-quiet house. When I was riding school busses parents never accompanied their kids to the roadside. Some did wave from the house, in which case we would torment our school mate if he/she returned the distant wave.

There is something sad about this turn of events: the necessary concern even rural parents must have for their children's safety. But there is also something positive in this human accommodation to a changing world. Here is a father and daughter enjoying, I would like to imagine, a morning walk together and perhaps a chat while waiting for the bus. There a younger brother seeing off his older brother and then clasping Mom's hand for the walk back to the house as well as two or three families chatting, waving, beginning their day together. The more things change...

Kids still board school buses. Here in Maine in the spring they cruise past scraggly birch and fir trees along still-sanded roads. When I rode these vehicles, they cruised deep-ditched, Ohio roads past rows of corn and wheat stubble. But somehow I am confident that they haul the same developing dramas; the same older, top dogs wise-cracking in the back; the same younger ones slightly apprehensive, mostly silent in the front.

Sometimes it is good to slow down, even involuntarily. To see that not all the spring buds are on willows and birch trees. That some of those buds carry blue lunchboxes or flutes and ride, just as we once did, in big yellow futuremobiles.

* * *

End of Summer (August 2013)

Summer is fading; Labor Day weekend is here. Fall clichés have appeared: occasional V's of geese headed south, leaves losing their grip, rose hips glowing orange on our Rugosas. In meadows the broad, flat, white heads of Queen Ann's Lace are drooping from their tall stocks — alongside Goldenrod and the last of the daisies. Eiders, presumably up in the high Artic for a summer of sex and chick-raising, are back in the Bay, cruising the shore in small groups looking for mussels. Boat trailers, groaning with just-pulled boats, head inland where marinas are telling them, "We shrink wrap." Our local weekly paper, <u>The Ellsworth American</u>, is printing school bus routes.

Our gardens are beginning to look a bit worn, though the Phlox and Monkshood are still doing their bit for the team. A pile of split firewood lies drying by the garage, waiting to be stacked to which I will get to when we come back from Newfoundland. Hancock Point seems to have done its summer work. Walkers I encounter are moving more slowly, with a greater sense of reflection. I see fewer blackberries being scanned, more blackberries being picked. Our summer library here on the Point closes for the season this morning. I returned my last library book of the summer a few days ago. Our Chapel's final service will be Sunday. Fathers are strapping bikes and kayaks and sailboards to car roof racks, assuring families that these ornaments are well-secured for the trip home.

For many years Susan and I were part of this late-summer exodus. Now we observe it, trying not to appear smug although truth be told, Susan tries harder than I do! When we were in their condition, i.e. forced to leave by the call of responsibilities elsewhere, our melancholy came not from a reluctance to return to work and our lives in Fairfield, St. Cloud, Oswego, or San Diego, but rather a sadness at giving up the Point. The sadness following an end to long summer days, to cool breezes off the Bay. To summer cocktail parties with old friends. Now we stay to enjoy the coming fall. End-of-summer pensiveness has given way to a guilty anticipation such as fewer traffic jams in Ellsworth, or shorter lines at the grocery.

So, what is it that makes end-of-summer so bittersweet? Is it that we do not like our various labors? Alas, for some that is true, but it never was for Susan or me. Is it the quickening pace of fall? No, I liked the faster pace. Perhaps it is the self-indulgence of summer; the chance to read what you want, to sleep in a bit, to play with family members? Maybe, but winters snuggled together in front of a fire offer their own indulgences. I wonder if the melancholy could be a holdover from our first years of going to school? Being broken to the reins, seated in rows, shushed? Being taken off the range and put into a corral? In short: being civilized. There is in each of us a yearning to be free, to be self-directed, to feel the prairie under our hoofs and the wind in our mane. Summer recalls all of those feelings.

If we are lucky we can be engaged in important work, grow to love it and our companions, but there should always be a little corner of ourselves, even in retirement, yearning to be free and hence mourning the passage of still another summer. I hope that you have had as full-of-wonders a summer as we and that the corral to which you return does not cramp but allows you the opportunity to be who you are.

* * *

Fog 2

I have written about fog before. No matter, I am moved to do so again. Lately the Bay has treated us to the most lovely fogs: banks of opacity rolling in and out over otherwise clear waters. This gives you a sense of the scene:

Can you feel the quiet? The stillness? The fog will burn/blow off soon, but now, in the early morning light, it hangs over the Bay and over me. This is not the enveloping fog that dampens your face and brings the smell of pine and balsam closer. It is distant, remote — the unknown "out there." What we have been struggling against since we swung from Acacia trees onto the plains of Africa. Rather than coming in, it bids us outward, bids us to venture beyond ourselves.

The knowledgeable among us will say that the fog is caused by cold air hovering over the still-warm Bay. Perhaps. But I think fog is part of the world's mystery, its delightful, unknown strangeness, its sense of foreboding. This fog is just one of the many mysteries in my bay-side meadow this morning. There is something inherently poetic about fog, its changing shapes, its multiple meanings, the way it beckons us forward — both into it and into ourselves.

One thinks of fog as supremely solitary, forcing us into a welcome aloneness. But that aloneness is full of courage. Look again, more closely. The human struggle for clarity continues. The courage to turn into the unknown, into the fog. Life goes on, in spite of the fog. Such has it always been, the human need to move forward, even with a lack of clarity. To acknowledge the fog, to know that we do not know — and still to throttle ahead.

Magnificent.

* * *

Visitors From Away (October 2016)

No matter how much we love our friends there is no guarantee they will like one another. We introduce friends with a certain trepidation. Will he see in her what I do? Will she appreciate his wit? We think about how to make the introduction, when and where. How can I give this meeting the best chance of success? So it was recently for me. An old friend and her sister were visiting. I was eager to introduce them to my friend: Maine.

But then Maine can be somewhat temperamental, a bit pouty at times. She can hunch her shoulders and turn her back. Sometimes she can be harsh and forbidding. My visitors had grown up in California, surfing its beaches with their brothers. You can see why I was concerned.

I had bragged about my friend Maine and her beauty. I had made promises that they would like each other. But would they? Moreover, it was that autumnal time when Maine could show any of a number of faces: warm, sunny days with crimson and amber flecking her pine forests or cold grey days with sleet slanting into your face. Which would it be? To make matters worse, fall colors were waning. Would my visiting friends be confronted with a landscape of grey-brown twigs trembling over roadsides slick with fallen leaves? I studied weather forecasts, 10-day forecasts, 5-day forecasts, tomorrow...

My friend and her sister would be staying in the almost-heatless guest apartment over the garage. Would they freeze? I imagined the headline: "California women freeze in Maine hovel." Would Maine wake my friend and her sister up to see their breath vaporizing in the mirror as they washed their faces with ice-cold water? I wrote warning letters about Maine's legendary coolness. Bring warm clothes, I implored; gloves and hats — and that's just for sleeping! Slowly their visit and my friend-to-friend introduction approached. As much as I love her dearly I could only think of the many ways in which Maine might disappoint. She, Maine, is after-all an acquired taste.

My friend and her sister rendezvoused in Boston and began their journey north. It did not begin well: a late flight brought them to Kennebunkport, a necessary stop for Republicans, at 11:00 p.m. Not an auspicious beginning, but perhaps they would blame the darkness on the airlines and not on friend Maine. But then Maine began to revert to form, began to reveal the Maine I know and love. My friend and her sister rose to clear skies and sun. Leaves were still on the trees and seemed to be especially charming. There was the obligatory stop at L.L. Bean's, fun and impressive followed by a long drive north on I-95 through rolling hills just undulating enough to provide stretching vistas of color dancing in the sun light. I think my friends were beginning to like one another.

My visiting friend and her sister arrived here on the Point around six in the evening. The guest apartment had been warmed by Indian-summer sun. I had chili warming on the stove, just in case Maine had given them her cold shoulder. My gardens had held on to produce a few surviving flowers for the kitchen table, and for the apartment. Some wine. A few of Maine's local artists on display. My friends were becoming comfortable with one another. I was so pleased. But it was early in the visit, Maine might still become surly. Not so. My guests passed, or so they said, a relatively comfortable night in the garage apartment. It was warm enough for them to sit up and watch the third presidential debate — doubtless with comforters tucked up under their chins, but that might be interpreted, I told myself, as charming. When they came down the next morning I had blueberry pancakes waiting in the oven's warming drawer and fresh Maine syrup on the table. I think my friend and her sister were still a bit wary of Maine — justifiably so — but they were warming to one another.

Now came the test. It was time to leave my visiting friends alone with Maine. They were off to Acadia National Park, across the Bay on Mt. Desert Island. But first, did I mention the Bay? It was picture perfect, lobster buoys rolling on barely-rippled waters, loons and cormorants diving, lobster boats working, seagulls circling. Across the Bay's placid surface Cadillac Mountain rose to the morning sun wearing red, yellow and green. Perhaps preening just a bit, Maine sent her signature chickadees, her black-masked nuthatches and her now-dulling Gold Finches to ply my feeder as we ate our pancakes. A fall hatch of ladybugs, bejeweled the screens, shiny hemispheres of red and black. Oh, my! Maine had decided she liked my friends, resolved to show off a bit.

They drove to the park, motored up the mountain, explored the park loop road, hiked Acadia's trails, ate its famous popovers at Jordan Pond House. They poked around Bar Harbor. This is the time of year when cruise ships are double-parked outside the harbor bringing stir-crazed tourists to fill her streets. But today, to accommodate my friends, friend Maine had shooed the cruise ships away. Bar Harbor was almost its charming self. Our visitors returned to my humble Maine home in the late afternoon, the fading sun had warmed the house so over-well that I had to open doors to make it comfortable. We shared a glass of wine while Maine danced on the Bay beyond.

My friend and her sister praised the glories of friend Maine: the sea was so...., the leaves were like...., the trails were...., I smiled and began to feel more comfortable. A contented sigh escaped my previously pursed lips, the sort of sigh that escapes when you think friends might see in one another what you see in them. Perhaps this would work out.

Then we were off to the Crocker House, here on the Point, for dinner. Maine scallops were on the menu. Mainers on their best behavior took our orders, brought our food and drink. When my guests commented on the potatoes au gratin the wait staff brought the recipe. Nice touch. When I asked if the owner, Rich Malaby, was here tonight I was told that he was the evening's cook. Not wanting to pass up an opportunity I asked whether "he could come out and meet some fellow Republicans?" The response was, "well, the kitchen is warm and he is working over the stove dressed just in a tee shirt as he serves our guests." My friends and I understood.

Not one to disappoint, five minutes later there was Rich, full of Maine charm and hospitality, taking time to talk with these kindred spirits about his legislative duties. He has now served three terms in Maine's legislature and is running for his fourth, after which he will, I suspect gratefully, be termed out. By now Maine and my visiting friends could let their hair down. Rich could talk about Maine's poverty, about its opioid epidemic, about its struggles to address issues of mental health. Maine being Maine, we left with boxes of delicious food left over from Rich's too-generous portions.

We returned to the house, nicely full not only of Rich's food but also of Maine. A glass of wine and my friends adjourned to the amazingly still-warm apartment for a good night's sleep before an early departure. Now my concerns had begun to shift. Had Maine been deceptively nice, not quite herself? Might my guests like her for the wrong reasons? Might they think her sunny, charming and friendly when Maine is not always so? Had I been perpetrating a hoax? But once again, Maine came through. The morning broke with wind and rain while the Bay was a shambles of whitecaps peaked by a cold north wind over dark-gray waters. Maine was confident enough in the strength of her new-found friends — now hers and not just mine — that she could turn a bit grumpy. A last hug, my thanks for their coming, their thanks for my introduction to Maine and they were off. At last, I could relax; my work was done.

* * *

First Light (June 2015)

I awoke at first light — about 4:30 — not because of the light, but due to the rattling of windows that signaled arrival of a weather front and its predicted rain. I had no desire to rise so early, but I had to go to the bathroom, as old men too-frequently do, and then my still-groggy mind began filling up with lists. Soon my mind needed to summon its memory, so the lists would not be forgotten, and I was awake. Still, my mind irretrievably engaged, I could have wrapped myself in blankets against the chill morning air and indulged some daydreaming, composed some essays, imagined some woodworking projects, or …. Problem was, one of the lists included, things to do before the rain.

For instance, years ago I was told that fireplace ashes ought to be scattered around lilac trees. Mine, the ashes that is, are well-cooled. There is no threat of fire but still in an abundance of caution I like to spread them before a rain. And my bulbs having now finished their spring display are dying back. I need to spread some bone meal on them before they disappear and I lose track of just where they are. Moreover, the wisteria also craves bone meal — that this coming rain will slowly percolate through its eager soil. So, I am up: tinkled, brushed, scrubbed, combed, dressed. A closer look, with glasses now employed, reveals that the rain has begun. But it is still soft and gentle — not too late for this morning's chores. So, raincoat donned, hat atop my head, I am out the early morning door: just the mosquitoes, deer and me. Duties complete, ashes and bone meal scattered, I put some water on the stove for tea and report to my keyboard to compose this note.

The Point is a symphony of rhythms: seasons, moons, tides, arriving and departing birds. One of those rhythms is expressed in the cycle of blooming plants. And in that cycle is a moment of supreme fecundity. The season is short; we northerners must, "make hay (or rhododendrons) while the sun shines." And so we are. Daffodils have past, as has the Red-bud; Lilacs are fading; Ornamental Allium, Iris and Rhododendron are at their peaks. This Rhododendron is almost 35 years old, probably 40 if you count its time at the nursery. You can get a sense of its size from the large construction wheelbarrow at its base.

Comparatively, these naturalized Iris are mere children.

Dog woods are just beginning their night, make that day, at the prom. The woods are full of blooming bunchberry. Wild blueberry and cranberry are hiding their modest, low-to-the-ground blooms. Pollen fills the air and floats along the shore of the Bay — like cheap perfume at a high school dance. Among the rhythms, let me share the calliope of our spring — the ubiquitous Lupin. Susan used to say that, "If crows weren't so common we could see how beautiful they are." So, too, with Lupin. They are everywhere at this time of year: fields, road-sides, pastures, etc...

Their blossoms each start out something like this...

... tight little heads, perhaps 3 inches high, above lush foliage.

Within days, the head begins to elongate into this:

A few more days and they are splendid specimens in (primarily) blue or salmon, each blossom a foot long, buzzing with bees.

Each is lovely, but it is their massed color that most excites.

So, too, it is with us. We are pretty enough as individuals, but John Wayne to the contrary not-withstanding, it is together that we accomplish most.

* * *

Fall (2016)

Fall is perhaps the loveliest of times: not full of spring-like hope or summer warmth, or winter snows, but a spectacular finale, a fireworks display, before the grey sets in. We still have eleven or so hours of sunlight. Weather is cool, but not painfully so. And the color!!! When I look across the Bay I see dabs of yellow, and red amidst the persisting green.

The Point road is ablaze.

What's going on here? Weakening sunlight and cooler temperatures are inhibiting the production of Chlorophyll, the source of photosynthesis and of the green we have seen all summer. Now Carotene (yellow) which has been hidden by the vibrant green, along with anthocyanins which produces the reds, emerge. I say reds (plural) because if the tree's sap is highly acidic it produces bright reds, if less so, then darker purples. These colors have been there all the time, but hidden by the verdant Chlorophyll.

Leaves are everywhere.

But there are other things going on as well on a smaller, but no less interesting scale. I have been smitten by a spider, holding on until the frost. Were a wall of glass not separating us I would have long since tumbled into her web.

She is an Cross Orbweaver, (Araneus diadematus), so named for the pattern of white spots on her abdomen that form a cross.

She is of European descent and spins a classic wheel-like orb web. Usually, she sits, head-down in the center of her web waiting for dinner guests. Note her Dr. Seuss stockings. I advised against them, arguing that two were a stretch (no pun intended), but that eight would be chaotic. As you can see, she ignored my advice.

She has spun her web on a south-facing window of our living room, precisely opposite where my evening light glows (is that an accident?). Her web is about a half inch out from the glass, strung across the window frame. She sits on the inside, between the web and the glass, facing outward, her back to me, her mouth to visitors.

She has been my evening companion, standing watch as I view the evening news, lingering until I turn out the light.

I know it is sexist, and I approached the matter delicately, but I have urged her to shave her legs; still to no avail.

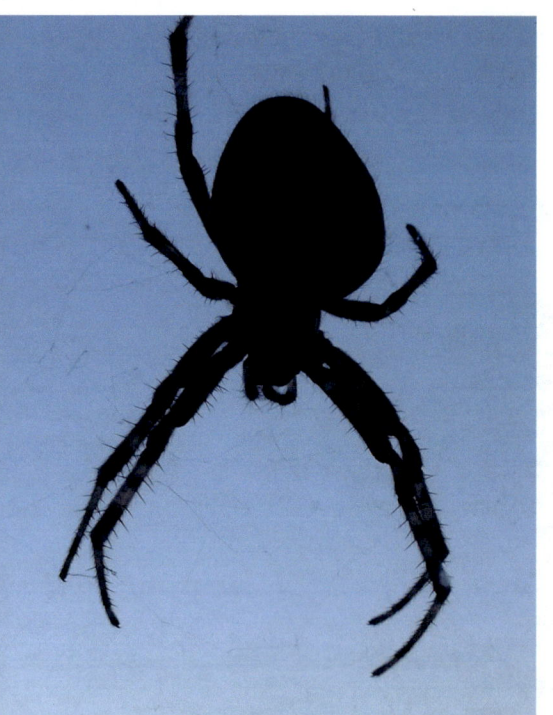

She will die shortly, but not before laying anywhere from 100 to 800 eggs secreted away from her web in a yellowish egg sac.

Autumn is not unlike these later years of life — full of quiet beauty, tenacity and the discovery of hidden/latent qualities. As with the leaves, there are aspects of our character that lie hidden, covered up by the getting and spending of youth, only finding expression in these later years, sans work, sans youngsters, sans, sans, sans. It is not as if these qualities are new to the scene, as if they have just been invented; rather, they have persisted through time, like Carotene and anthocyanins, have done their quiet work and only now have become visible. I hope life and family and friends and work and beauty and goodness have filled you with brilliant reds and yellows and that life will give those wonders a chance to shine forth.

* * *

Arachnophobes, Beware

1. Deadly courtship

We are once again in the season of spiders here on Hancock Point. Those of you who have followed my earlier chronicling of this phenomenon will recognize that they hold a special place in our annual cycle.

Perhaps my fascination is due in part to the fact that it is in September that the winners emerge from the nooks and crannies of their world into the sunlight, with big, bold, round spiral webs trembling in the autumn breeze.

It is the hourglass-backed orb spiders that most attract my attention, so named because of their round webs. We have one beauty at the far end of our back porch, its web anchored to the overhanging green spruce and to our railing just as it disappears under the rhododendron. She (it is the large females that you see riding the quivering webs), is right there.

I greet her every morning as I head out of the house. As has often been my experience with females, she pretty much ignores me, but that is another matter.

This year, however, a second web struggled to establish itself, also by our back door, this one to the left, just beyond the opening screen door. I say struggling because it is attached to the railing above the stairs that lead down to the ground and to the faucet, to which I often have recourse as I water our gardens in this drought. That means that I often forgetfully disrupt the web, brushing its strong strands from my thinning hair. This time, however, I have a drama to report.

Coming back from some work in the garage I passed the first web, spider patiently waiting in its center, and came to the second one closer to our back door. What caught my eye was another, smaller spider on the periphery of the web. It moved gingerly toward the large female in the center. She moved; it retreated. My suspicion, since webs do not typically contain two spiders, was that the intruder was a horny male. I opened the kitchen door and called Steph, my partner, to come take a look. Steph came out just as the second spider was once again venturing out onto the web. Slowly. Tentatively. But there she was with all her round curves, legs that would not quit, eight (not two) eyes into which a male could tumble helplessly. Perhaps she was as eager as he? Hard to say, but this time she did not flinch. He moved closer still. She remained in the center of the web/target. He was five inches away, now three, now paused at an inch. Steph and I stood as still as did the female spider.

Then he was on her. Legs, and legs and legs entwined. There was a trembling. And then, quicker than you could say "was it good for you?" still in their clinch, she turned from lover to diner. We could not discern the precise moment that she bit him, but now she was wrapping him in a tight package for a later snack in front of the TV. All was suddenly still, even the new package secured just above the center of her web.

Steph and I had just observed far more genuine drama than might ever be encountered on a daytime soap opera. Of course, I immediately turned to my computer for an interpretation of what we had just seen and found this on Wikipedia:

> *Spiders: In the <u>cannibalistic</u> and <u>polyandrous</u> orb-web spider <u>Argiope bruennichi</u>, the much smaller males are attacked during their first copulation and are cannibalized in up to 80% of the cases. All surviving males die after their second copulation, a pattern observed on other Argiope species. Whether a male survives his first copulation depends on the duration of the genital contact: males that jump off early (before 5 seconds) have a chance of surviving, while males that copulate longer (greater than 10 seconds) invariably die. Prolonged copulation, although associated with cannibalism, enhances sperm transfer and relative paternity.*

Tough choices! But the species will survive another Maine winter, tucked safely in a crack beneath our railing, where a baluster intersects.

2. A Second Web (October 11, 2018)

Yesterday afternoon, as I walked to the garage to continue working on the cherry trestle table I am building for our kitchen, I happened to look up. There on the south-facing eave, was Eve. And who was that other spider at the edge of her web? Could it be Adam? I grabbed the camera and went out on the garage deck, above the spiders. Sure enough, there were two. Female ...

And male—he was toward the periphery of the web, perhaps half way between its center and the garage where the web was attached. He strummed several filaments headed into the center of the web, like Neil Diamond at the Hollywood Bowl. Usually courting her with two legs strumming; sometimes with three of four. Occasionally, when she was not paying attention he would lurch on a fiber moving himself a full half inch and visibly shaking the still-centered female. Strum, strum. Lurch, lurch.

Gradually, I am talking about a period almost extending a full hour, he won her attention. She turned and advanced. They came within about two inches of one another.

He strummed harder, she strummed in return. Then she retreated to the center, turned her back on him and pulled down the protein shake that hung just above her head.

This happened again and again. I tired of the wait— as perhaps did she. Some work in the garage; return; still no progress. Watch awhile, go down and work on the compost, come back and still two spiders separated like middle schoolers at a Saturday night dance. But then they reengaged.

Now, they moved closer than ever before... and closer, still. First base!!!

Quickly, he stole second. Each becoming more vulnerable to the other.

And then, like Angelica Huston and Jack Nicholson in "Prizzi's Honor," they did it.

Talk about "restless leg syndrome"!!! I have blurred the focus out of respect for their privacy. Most extraordinary of all, he walked away unscathed. When last I looked, Eve was back at the center of her web smoking her signature brand of cigarette; Adam was munching on an apple.

3. The Spider and the Wasp (October 2012)

Fall is the season of spiders: big winners of Darwin's carnival in survival. For the past month we have been admiring one whose web spreads across an upper (outside) corner of our porch window. When we first began observing she was a large, nickel-sized spider who would appear in the evenings. At first, we thought nothing of it and would casually notice her as we looked out on the sunset across the bay. But over time we became attached. There is something impressive about this night hunter.

The spider's web is about fourteen inches in diameter, radiating spokes join roughly concentric circles about three eighths of an inch apart. She rarely appears in the day, but occasionally ventures out if some unwary flyer falls into her web. Usually we say hello in the evening and congratulate her in the morning as we note the detritus of a night's hunt hanging limp in the web.

The Point is a still and quiet place, so there is time for spider watching; life is close enough at hand that there is constant occasion for fascination and respect. So we watched her grow through September and then into October wondering when she would finally succumb to Maine's increasing cold.

And all the time she grew, and grew, and grew almost noticeably every morning. The nickel-sized spider gradually became a magnificent quarter-sized spider with legs that stretched an inch beyond in eight different directions. She is now so big that occasionally, as evening descends I am reminded to look by her shadow falling on our wall. I must add that she is a beautiful beast. White spots run down the back of her taupe/tan abdomen that dwarfs the rest of her body; her legs are striped with alternating bands of Dr. Seuss socks.

So, a few days ago it was unusual when I noticed her out of the corner of my eye in mid-morning. I turned and immediately saw what had brought her out of hiding and had subliminally caught my attention. A huge wasp was caught in her web. Susan and I were about to watch a titanic battle.

At first the wasp seemed to be caught only by the spurs on its rear legs. It held its body high from the web buzzing furiously to free itself. The spider stood off to the side, about an inch away waiting for the wasp to tire. This standoff persisted for a few minutes until the wasp began to quiet. At that point the spider moved in, gingerly fending off the wasp's sting with its long legs. The wasp was surprisingly agile, able to keep the spider at bay by rotating its stinger. Finally, the spider saw an opening and quickly moved in, appeared to bite the wasp and began to roll the wasp in its silk. One wing was now pinned, but still the wasp fought bravely. Then the wasp gained the upper hand and began stinging the spider's huge abdomen. The spider backed off an inch or two. Five minutes had elapsed. Now the spider reengaged; the wasp contorted itself into a position in which it could sting the spider's thorax and head. Sting. Sting. Sting. Each time a visible shudder shook the spider.

The spider disengaged and retreated out of sight into its crevasse at the edge of the web. Had the wasp won? Was the spider through? We watched intently. The wasp was now alone in the web working to free itself. Again, its flexibility was prodigious. It contorted itself to either break or slide strands of the web from its bound wing and its legs. Still no sign of the spider.

The wasp was making progress: one wing free, both wings free, four legs lose, five.... Finally, the wasp buzzed itself loose and flew/fell to the deck about six feet below. There it seemed to lie in exhaustion, close to the ground, seeming to be rubbing itself on the wood of the deck. Then it grew still, resting we assumed. But no, it was dying. Soon it was still, occasionally tipping as the breeze caught its motionless wings. One minute, two, three: still no movement. The wasp was dead.

But what of the spider? We could not tell since its retreat had taken it out of our sight. We did not see her all day, nor that evening when we would have expected her to emerge. The next morning the spider's web remained mangled and unattended. Nor did we see her that afternoon or evening. We assumed she had succumbed to the wasp's sting, as it had evidently succumbed to her bite. But then, on the second morning we awoke to find a repaired web. That evening we saw her once again on patrol. We have seen her rarely since, but it is getting cold here in Maine. Soon the frost will do what the wasp could not.

* * *

Tragedy of the Commons (December 2014)

It is perhaps hard for those of you who live in the outside world, with your paved roads and superstores to imagine our small town of Hancock, ME. Hancock is officially a town; "village" would be more appropriate. There are 2,394 of us — 80 per square mile. We are 96.6% white. I suspect French Canadians are counted as the other 3.4%. When Susan and I arrived in Maine in 1969 it was not uncommon to see signs in store windows proclaiming, "French Canadians, sometimes 'Canucks,' not served here".

The median income for a Hancock household is $32,778 earned by hard-working, generally impoverished, survivalists who pull lobster traps, cut pulpwood, dig clams, and do other hard manual labor to make ends not-quite-meet. Our downtown consists of a small general store, a Congregationalist church and a post office. Farther afield are an auto repair garage, three restaurants and a garden shop.

The "Tragedy of the Commons" is displaying itself just beyond my semi-frosted window. You will remember that Garrett Hardin's "Tragedy of the Commons" maintains that rational people, acting in accordance with their own self-interest can actually be acting against their long-term self-interest by depleting a common/shared resource, "the commons." In this essay the commons is Frenchman Bay and the resource is scallops.

I awoke about 6:30 on December 1st — more-or-less my usual time. A sound was disturbing the stillness. What was I hearing? As I lay in bed I heard a boat motor on the Bay. Lobsters have pretty much migrated to deeper water for the winter — about 5–10 miles off shore — and so I rarely hear lobster or any boats this time of year. It is just not worth the fuel to go after the stragglers. Most lobster traps are now stacked in yards and most lobster boats hauled out for winter repairs and maintenance. If not a lobster boat, then what? Answer: December 1st, was opening day of scallop season. The sound I heard was a Scallop dragger right off our shore, perhaps 100 yards or less, making GPS-guided circles.

These draggers look like extra-large lobster boats with a rear superstructure from which they drag a heavy steel trap that scrapes along the bottom and picks up pretty-much everything in its path — scallops to be sure, but also clams, urchins, star-fish, crabs, sea cucumbers, etc. Soon this dragger was joined by two more, mowing the Bay as if it were their back yard. By noon there were five draggers within my range of vision working our bay. In Maine the scallop season is limited to 70 days spread over six months. Specific zones are established, each with their own schedule. December 1st was the first of those permitted days in our bay, provoking a gold rush of sorts.

A recent article in the Bangor Daily News quotes Rob Bauer, General Manager of Beal's Lobster Pier in Southwest Harbor, where most of "our" Scallops are headed, saying that, "There were reports of good hauls Monday off Harrington and Machiasport, and of several boats fishing the tidal Skillings River, between the towns of Lamoine and Hancock." (That's us). And those "hauls" were profitable. Dock prices," i.e. what the fisherman is paid at the dock, are unusually high, approximately $14 per pound, a strong incentive in a poor state. The catch-limit, is three five-gallon buckets, just the meats, at about 40 pounds each. That is 120 pounds of Scallops. At $14 per pound those three buckets are worth $1,680, not bad for a day's work in a poor state. And the cost of diesel fuel that propels most of these draggers is down, making the net (pun intended) even more attractive.

Bauer continues, "At $13 to $14 per pound, an extra 40 pounds of scallops could net an additional $500 or so for each fisherman every time he or she, (yes, there are slicker-clad, intrepid females piloting some of the draggers), goes out if the supply holds up. The extra bucket is definitely an incentive around here," he said. "It's a chunk of money." The operative words are, "if the supply holds up." And that is a concern. In 1981 Maine produced 3.8 million pounds of scallops; last year we produced 424,500 pounds, about a ninth of the former harvest. The "Tragedy of the Commons" is typically aided and abetted by a "Comedy of Greed." And so, it has been in Maine. As the stock dwindles, prices climb. As prices climb fishermen ply our bays more intensely. Stocks decline further. Fishermen scrape the bottom of our bay still more intently.

My conservative friends, of whom I have a disconcertingly large number, are opposed to regulation. "Let the free market prevail," they say. But, of course, in this and many similar instances, were we to let the free market prevail it would soon implode of its own unsustainability. Don't believe me? There is now no fishing for Cod in the Gulf of Maine. Why? The fishery had to be shut down for lack of fish. In 1991 Maine fisherman pulled 21,179,886 pounds of Cod from Maine waters; in 2001 2,941,934 pounds; last year, 286,299 pounds, only 1.3% of the harvest 23 years ago. See a pattern here? The Feds do. NOAA has determined that the cod population in the Gulf of Maine, "has dwindled to as little as 3 percent of what it would take to sustain a healthy population."

On November 10 the Boston Globe reported: "In an effort to halt dramatic declines in the cod population, federal officials overseeing the fishing industry on Monday announced unprecedented measures that effectively ban all commercial fishing of the region's iconic species in the Gulf of Maine.... The new rules, which fishermen say will be devastating for their livelihood, will take effect this week and last for at least the next six months." Continuing the Globe article: "Not surprisingly, fishermen throughout the region questioned the need for the emergency measures and said, (doubtless correctly), they will have dire impacts on their livelihood. 'It's all over,' said Joseph Orlando, who has been fishing for cod for more than 40 years out of Gloucester. 'We can't go fishing. We can't leave the dock.' He said he doesn't know how he will feed his family. 'If you can't go fishing, what do you do?' he said. 'I'm 60. Who's going to hire me? I have no backup plan.'"

The solution, of course, would/should have been better management, which is to say better regulation. That is not only my conclusion, but that of the Pew Charitable Trust: "The cod collapse is largely due to a long history of risky management decisions that failed to rein in chronic overfishing...." So, moving on to the perfect trifecta: we have the "Tragedy of the Commons"; we have the "Comedy of Greed"; what is missing? Obviously, an attack on the science behind the regulations. And there it is! "David Goethel, who has been fishing for cod out of Hampton, N.H., since 1967, blamed the cuts on faulty science..." Also, Jackie Odell: "She and other fishermen argued that the government has improperly counted cod."

Sigh. Back to Scallops: The Maine Department of Marine resources has proclaimed that "two-thirds of the fishing areas between eastern Penobscot Bay and West Quoddy Head have been open to scallop fishing in each of the past two seasons, but only one-third will be open this winter. Closures will rotate among three sets of scallop fishing areas in eastern Maine each year through early 2022, with only one set open each year."

Their regulation reads in part: "This season is undertaken with the understanding that the length of the season as presented likely far exceeds what the resource can sustain, and that the Department may need to use emergency rulemaking authority during the season to prevent overfishing. Another reason for the December 1, stampede. The industry, through the Scallop Advisory Council, has requested that the Department provide the fishing opportunity up front, and make adjustments in season as necessary. The Department is willing to take this approach in part because this fishery is prosecuted in the winter months, and proposing a very limited season could create an incentive to fish in unsafe conditions. The Department will take action to continue to rebuild the scallop resource, as well as provide stability and predictability for the industry into the future."

It is sometimes said (by people who have never watched squirrels bury acorns) that a distinguishing feature of our species is its ability for delayed gratification. I see little evidence of that. Our fishermen have not been "done in" by regulations, but by a short-sighted lack of them. It is an irony of our language that people who resist such regulations are called "conservatives".

* * *

"You'll Shoot Your Eye Out" (July 2012)

You will remember Jean Shepherd's wonderful, "A Christmas Story," in which Ralphie dreams of getting a Red Ryder BB gun for Christmas. When Ralphie expresses this wish he is constantly confronted by concerned adults who respond to a person: "You'll shoot your eye out." I say this because, like Ralphie, I have had a dream: a boat with which to explore/enjoy Frenchman Bay. There is, however, an adult in my life whose constant refrain when I talk about buying a boat is: "You'll shoot your eye out."

When I expressed my wish to a friend she wondered if Susan's objection might stem from the fact that the boat I have settled on is old, a 1989 Four Winns bow-rider, and used. "Perhaps," she suggested, "Susan's concern is that it is unsafe?" But that is not it. "You'll shoot your eye out," refers not to any uncertainty about the boat, but to a certainty about my competence. So why would my otherwise fair and objective friend and lover of over 47 years arrive at this concern?

Was it the time I strapped our new Samsonite luggage onto the roof of our Saab, assuring Susan that it would be fine, only to watch in the rear-view mirror as it bounced along the highway behind us? Or the time when I confidently predicted the path of a large pine we were felling here on the Point, "It will fall right in the direction of those two lobster buoys," only to have it fall in precisely the opposite direction crashing to the ground six inches from the house? Or was it when my friend Clark and I showed up at our front door in Orono soaking wet, after capsizing Clark's kayak in the Stillwater River, but still clutching fresh fiddlehead ferns? Or was it when I determined to give Susan a load of manure for our vegetable garden only to mire the trailer deep in the still-soft spring soil of our back yard? Oh, yes, it was Mother's Day. So, admittedly Susan has cause for concern.

Some attribute this klutziness to my philosophic proclivities, but there are many extraordinarily competent philosophers who are more than capable of making their way in the world.

What is the attraction of a boat? Partially it is evenings like this one, quiet, pink, the Bay glassy smooth. And I like the idea of expanding our "turf" now that we are in more permanent residence on the Point. We have built stairs to the "beach," paths into the woods; we hope to soon add a shore-side perch above the rocks looking down the Bay and out to the Atlantic.

I want to explore up bay to the mouth of the Skillings River, and the east side of the Point up to Tidal Falls. I'd like to cruise over to Bar Harbor and visit Sorrento, perhaps stopping at Bean Island on the way. And I like the thought of having the grandkids in the bow as we explore. When conditions allow, I would like to get out into the open ocean for some whale watching and visit Petit Manan Island, east of Schoodic peninsula looking for Puffins near the southern-most extremity of their range.

All this has led me to do something I very rarely do, to proceed without Susan's approval. It is not that she does not have some legitimate concerns, but I know the risks and I am pretty much an adult, so... Actually, it is the legitimate concerns that draw me. I fear what John Adams called, "*dying from the top*." Not Alzheimer's, that I imagine to be worse for those of us on the outside watching than for the plaque-filled grayness within, so much as the atrophy of non-use. That is why I am out in the shop mastering new tools and techniques. It is good for me to wake up thinking about how to build a jig that will allow me to make splined miters, or how to set up my new joiner. In recent weeks it has been the selection and purchase of a boat that has kept my mind moving. And, once bought, has driven me back to my old Chapman's to brush up on seamanship.

Now instead of waking early to compose letters or arguments I am going over launching protocol, lists of safety equipment I need on board, the proper lines to buy, tying up at our mooring etc... It helps that these are not just idle thoughts and dreams, but that there are real consequences for getting it wrong. Consequences for screwing up with my new joiner, or after hours of work, botching the mirror frame I have been building for Susan, or for failing to make the boat secure on its mooring. It is not just our geographic "turf" I seek to expand, but myself through the stimulus of new challenges. So, I say again, competence is not out of reach for philosophers, we just have to keep at it.

P.S. Old salts tell me that it is bad luck to rename a boat. Perhaps, but I will (re)name the boat, "You'll Shoot Your Eye Out." Why? Because the prospect of my boat on a reef somewhere with a photo of those words on the stern is potentially embarrassing enough to keep me thinking as I explore the Bay.

P.P.S. Time passes.

Before I could launch "You'll Shoot Your Eye Out," I had to master some advanced seamanship, like how to grease the "bearing buddies" that keep salt water out of my trailer bearings, how to splice an eye in the end of my mooring line (notice that I did not say rope), and most importantly how to detach the trailer from Susan's car — which I did with the help of a neighbor who is an English Literature Ph.D. I also had to have a second person to help me launch. This problem was solved when our son Rick and his family came to join us for a week on the Point. I had done everything I could do vacuuming, cleaning, polishing, mounting a new name on the stern, etc. without actually getting the boat wet. The moment of truth was approaching.

My plan was to launch at the village wharf, about a mile and a half away on the other side of the Point. But if I was to do that, fill up the gas tank at nearby Hancock Marina, and return to my mooring off our beach, I would need to solve the question of how I would then get from the moored boat to shore.

I solved this by buying a used inflatable dingy. Now I needed to tie the dingy on the mooring so it could await my triumphal return. To do so I tied the inflatable's pinter to the stern of my kayak and paddled out to the mooring in a stiff wind with choppy seas. Alas, when I arrived I found, predictably, that I could not reach the stern of my kayak (from its cockpit) to untie the dingy. So, back to the beach; retie the dingy to the side of the kayak and head back to the still-empty mooring. The pinter is long enough that I could paddle, but not so long that it did not influence my ability to turn which was difficult with the wind and waves. I spiraled in on the mooring and finally captured it. I untied the pinter, brought it across to meet the eye at the end of the mooring line, and proceeded to tie up — two loops through the eye followed by two half hitches. I had officially begun my new life as a seaman.

But, there was a problem: I had in effect also tied up myself. The pinter stretched off to my right, the mooring line to my left. I could not back my kayak out from under because the newly-tied lines caught on the bow of my kayak, (which is too far away to reach even with the extended paddle). I could not raise the lines over my head and paddle forward because, again, they would snag on the stern of my kayak. What to do?

I was sitting there contemplating this dilemma, knowing that if necessary I could always untie the lines and start over, when a power boat with two people slowly made its way toward me. Help had arrived. My strategy in life, like Blanche's, is to "rely on the goodness of strangers"; once again, it had paid off. They pulled up ever so slowly and carefully, saw my predicament and carefully reached over their freeboard to lift the lines from my bow and drop them into the deep. So far, so good. But then they asked me to, "back up and pull along-side." That's when I noticed they were each wearing guns. They were the Maine Marine Patrol and I was pulling alongside so that they could write me a citation for "Insufficient PFD." For those of you who do not know, PFD means Personal Floatation Device. And since none is pretty clearly "insufficient," I had little ground upon which to object.

As they wrote the citation and interrogated me, asking everything but my SAT's, we drifted with the wind and tide so that when complete we were now some distance from my mooring and our beach. They kindly towed me back. I thanked them for the citation and the reminder that a PDF would have made sense. Then I told them of Susan's, "You'll shoot your eye out." They saw immediately the appropriateness of Susan's concern, but being men kindly suggested that I did not have to tell her about the citation. I responded that it would mean so much to her that I did not have the heart to keep it a secret.

P.P.P.S. "Failure to Launch"

Eager as I was to launch "You'll Shoot Your Eye Out," the stiff breeze and ocean chop made me think that tomorrow might be better. But, as it usually does in the late afternoon, the wind died down, as did my memory of the recent citation, so Rick and I set off to launch the boat. When I rehearsed this in my mind (countless times) it is always a perfect half tide, with calm seas: admiring children watch from the wharf; seals beckon me to come and frolic with them. But such was not the case this Saturday afternoon. Now it was within an hour of high tide. That meant that we were high on the shore or the steepest part. To launch the boat, I had to back it down a narrow gap, about twice the width of "You'll Shoot Your Eye Out," between the wharf and the boat house. I must confess that I missed the class on downhill trailer backing in graduate school.

However, after several false attempts and with excellent prompting from Rick, I got lined up (more or less), and began to back down the narrow, steep slope. All was going well until it became apparent that the trailer, not I, was driving. All I could do was press on the brake and pull on the knock-off, emergency brake. I managed to skid to a stop, perilously close to the wharf, unable to go forward or back. But then my life strategy kicked in again: another stranger arrived. This time in the guise of a burly 18-wheel truck driver named Don who had a humungous black pickup truck with a built-in winch in its grill. He hooked a cable on to the tow hook of Susan's Isuzu and pulled me and the trailer far enough up the hill that I could re-align and continue sliding down the slope to the shore and my launch.

By now a crowd had gathered. In Maine six constitutes a crowd, and there were at least eight. The London Olympics were on television, but this was better. As I loosened the tie downs, turned on the blower, deployed fenders and prepared to release the boat from the trailer to slide gracefully into its proper home, one helpful spectator suggested that it might be best if the boat were backed up far enough to actually be over the water. Now from the boat, I allowed as that was a good idea and Rick, safely on shore, backed us up another eight or nine feet. I lowered the stern drive far enough into the water to submerge the water intakes that cool its huge V-8 engine and to give propulsion for my triumphant cruise to the dock.

All was in readiness, the crowd's attention was fixed like sixteen lasers as I moved to the Captain's chair and turned the key. BUT there was no response, absolutely nothing. Before I could reason that the blower and trim had been working so I obviously had power, the crowd told me so. In fact, they were full of suggestions: "Is it in neutral?" Yes. "Try the release neutral, not just the regular one." "Is the master switch on?" You get the idea. Meanwhile, the tide was rising and soon Susan's car would also be at sea. In fact, there was a chance that we might succeed in the rare feat of launching the car while the boat stayed ashore. Then, as if by magic, the man who sold me this boat appeared; he had been fishing. He climbed aboard, checked the engine, the connections, and officially pronounced the boat dead. Rick pointed out that in New York, where he lives, anyone who sold someone such a boat would, upon seeing this scene, flee in the opposite direction, rather than offering assistance.

Now the rising water was half way up Susan's tires to the rear axle. I re-secured the boat to the trailer. But we still could not go forward. I might have had traction without the boat, but together the boat and trailer were simply too heavy. Fortunately, Don was still there, waiting for the rising tide to go fishing. With the surf lapping at Susan's rear axial, for the second time this summer — but that is a different story, Don reattached the winch and, accompanied by the cheers of the crowd, majestically towed me, the Isuzu, the trailer and "You'll Shoot Your Eye Out" up the slope to safety. So, though I originally named the boat, "You'll Shoot Your Eye Out," as a prophylactic and as a paean to Susan, it turns out it earned its name before we had even put out to sea.

P.P.P.P.S. Addendum from son Rick.

This essay is, indeed, an accurate portrayal of the events of the first boat launch attempt. In fact, if anything, dad has undersold the sheer spectacle of this event. For one thing, the individual who yelled "put it in neutral, Steve" and who recommended that we put the trailer in the water before de-trailering the boat is long time Hancock Point resident. This is significant because it means that those on the Point who may have missed the show will hear a highly embellished and not quite accurate version for years to come. Dad also failed to mention that I returned to the scene of the crime with a shovel to fill in the ruts we had left in the boat launch area. But from my perspective, none of these events were the most surprising part of the exercise. (After all, I was the kid with the axe when the tree fell toward the house -- adverse results are always within the realm of possibility when one undertakes to do great things...). As it became apparent that this exercise was becoming a truly epic failure, I took solace in the fact that no one I know outside of Maine would ever hear of this. And as I was feeling good about this, I struck up a conversation with two of the spectators. Who, I learned, were from Syracuse. And who, it happens, had sent their son to the University of Buffalo. (My alma mater). "Oh", said I, "what year did he graduate?" Bear in mind, there are 6,000 graduates a year from that school, and plenty of those students come from the Syracuse area. No worries. The woman paused for a moment, then looked to her husband, "Cooper graduated in 1994, right?" Uh-oh. "What's your last name?" I asked. "Gilbert." Of course! The parents of one of my college housemates! Why not! We had a great chat. They were genuinely entertained by the whole event. I saw them days later at the annual Point square dance, and reassured them that we had in fact successfully launched the boat. Finally, it should be noted for the record that we took the boat to the other side of the bay for our second launch attempt, far away from anyone with knowledge of our first attempt. And though it did not go as scripted, the smiles we got out of Colin and Aaron on the inaugural voyage made it all worth it!

* * *

Fog 3

We are approaching the longest day of the year; sunrise is officially at 4:49, though it is light considerably earlier. Indeed, I was awakened about 5:30 with insistent daylight flooding my bedroom. The light was bright with fog — the visual equivalent of white noise. I did not begrudge the early hour, but rather lay-a-bed remembering early mornings of summer camp when dampness would infuse our log cabins. If you listened closely you could hear the wire springs beneath us rusting. This morning's dampness filled my solitary room in a similar way. It was warm and humid last night. As I went to bed the arms of my Anderson windows were cranked wide.

Question: what is it you can hear coming but not leaving? Answer: a Black-backed Gull on your roof. Mine arrived about 5:40, dropping with an audible thud, not as graceful as they appear from a distance, followed by a few steps to secure its balance/perch. Then, with a sound that could have come from an adjacent bed, it announced its ownership to the world. The world being indifferent, it had to repeat its claim again, and again and.... It's now about 9:30 in the morning. I am sitting on the deck in one of our large green Adirondack chairs, taking a break, sipping tea in the lingering fog. Clouds of damp gently sweep past. The sun is brightening as the fog burns off. There is something seductive about fog, escaping from the sharp edges of true and false, relaxing into grey. There is not much to look at, but lots to hear — most off all, the silence.

Out of that silence occasionally burst sharp, raucous calls. Invisible gulls gliding by — close. I can distinguish their voices enough to recognize that there are several. They have perhaps twenty feet of visibility, and yet they fly confident that even in such a short distance they can avoid a pine tree, a house, or a tea drinker. Sounds as if other gulls are below, down on the beach — more constant conversation from there. Up here, the gliders are singular. In jeans and a worn canvas shirt, I sip my tea and lean back in the wet chair. I cannot see the edge of our woods; can just barely make out the shapes of large trees between me and the shore. But then, a Herring Gull emerges from the fog. Silent, wings extended, feathers adjusted to provide just enough motion to prevent a stall. It banks away and disappears back into the fog. May your day provide some silence... and be no more foggy than you wish.

* * *

The Maine Woods (October 2015)

It is a country full of evergreen trees, of mossy silver birches and watery maples, the ground dotted with insipid, small, red berries, and strewn with damp and moss-grown rocks, — a country diversified with innumerable lakes and rapid streams, peopled with trout and various species of leucisci, with salmon, shad, and pickerel, and other fishes; the forest resounding at rare intervals with the note of the chicadee, the blue-jay, and the woodpecker, the scream of the fish-hawk and the eagle, the laugh of the loon, and the whistle of ducks along the solitary streams; at night, with the hooting of owls and howling of wolves.... Such is the home of the moose, the bear, the caribou, the wolf, [Alas, we have now lost the caribou and the wolf.], the beaver, and the Indian. Who shall describe the inexpressible tenderness and immortal life of the grim forest, where Nature, though it be mid-winter, is ever in her spring, where the moss-grown and decaying trees are not old, but seem to enjoy a perpetual youth; and blissful, innocent Nature, like a serene infant, is too happy to make a noise, except by a few tinkling, lisping birds and trickling rills?

— H.D. Thoreau, *The Maine Woods*, 1864

So, ya up for a walk in the Maine woods? Perfect morning; temperature's about 45; clouds cleared out last night; still a bit breezy, but when the woods close in around us we'll be snug as a bug in a rug. Got some good hikin' boots? Maybe a light jacket and a hat? OK then, we're off. Some friends of mine are just opening a new trail in Mariaville, about 30 miles from here. We can be there for the grand opening at 10:00. It should not be far now. Just past this blueberry barren, held in place by these ancient glacier-rounded, granite boulders. Isn't that great fall color?

There's the sign; now about a quarter mile farther down this rough road. There they are. It's like they were waiting for us, fellow hikers, eager for a new trail to explore. Yeah, we have to listen to a few words of introduction, but it won't be long. It's just the Director of Frenchman Bay Conservancy telling us about the tiny snapping turtle his son caught down by the river this morning and will soon release. And, of course, the former Director needs to give us a bit of history. Did you know that back in logging days Mariaville was the financial hub between Ellsworth and Eddington? I thought not.

See, I told you it would not be long. Yes, too long but not THAT long. This first part of the path is an old logging trail. We're gradually dropping down to the river. Watch your step; lots of tree roots to snag a toe on.

The deciduous trees are still mostly green, the ferns are also still green though curling a bit; some are brown around the edges. Looks to me (philosophers know about these things), as if frost has not yet penetrated these woods.

Yes, that new bridge over the creek was just put in.

You're right; one of Thoreau's "damp and moss-grown rocks."

What we are walking toward is the Union River, about 20 miles north of Ellsworth. The river is perhaps fifteen yards wide — except where it is wider, or for that matter, where it is narrower.

This is a legendary fly-fishing stream, but now that the trail has been made so easy, (watch that root; step over this log. Yes, another of Thoreau's "moss-grown and decaying trees"), it will soon be less productive. Our former Director, who used to be an executive for L.L. Bean, is an avid fly fisherman. He tells me, and anyone else who will listen, that he once caught over 20 small-mouthed bass here in less than an hour without changing a fly. Used a "Woolly Bugger." No, it's really called that.

Was that a deer?

LOOK at those eyelashes!!!

Hear the falls? We're getting close. The rain we had Wednesday has it running pretty strong. There're the falls, through those trees. Yeah, I know it's not Niagara, but still well worth the walk.

We'll walk out by a different trail — more along the river, and across another creek on the way back. It's about a mile to the trailhead.

> *I looked with awe at the ground I trod on, to see what the Powers had made there, the form and fashion and material of their work. This was that Earth of which we have heard, made out of Chaos and Old Night. Here was no man's garden, but the unhandselled globe. It was not lawn, nor pasture, nor mead, nor woodland, nor lea, nor arable, nor waste-land. It was the fresh and natural surface of the planet Earth, as it was made for ever and ever, — to be the dwelling of man, we say, — so Nature made it, and man may use it if he can. Man was not to be associated with it. It was Matter, vast, terrific, — not his Mother Earth that we have heard of, not for him to tread on, or be buried in, — no, it were being too familiar even to let his bones lie there, — the home, this, of Necessity and Fate. There was there felt the presence of a force not bound to be kind to man. It was a place for heathenism and superstitious rites, — to be inhabited by men nearer of kin to the rocks and to wild animals than we. We walked over it with a certain awe, stopping, from time to time, to pick the blueberries which grew there, and had a smart and spicy taste.* _ H.D. Thoreau

Can you feel it too? Thoreau's "force not bound to be kind to man." Perhaps it is that force that provides the sense of awe.

* * *

I Couldn't Make This Up!!! (May 2014)

It's Sunday morning. What to read as I eat my Sunday morning bagel and await Susan's rising??? I know, the May issue of <u>Down East</u>. Good companion when the best one is still sleeping. I soon arrive at an article entitled, "A Reverberating [sad pun] Question." Being a philosopher, I am a sucker for reverberating questions so I read on. Turns out the question is the perennial one: whether or not we can trust the Canadians!!! Even Aristotle would find this of interest. In the instant case, the question is occasioned by nearby Gouldsboro's possession of a 158-year-old brass bell. Should it be loaned back to the slippery Canadians as they celebrate the birth of their nation?

Perhaps a bit of history is in order. Canada's "Declaration of Independence" was forged in Charlottetown on Prince Edward Island. The conference that turned into their 1776 took place between September 1–9, 1864. (Canadians were a bit slow to the party.) Delegates were transported to the convening aboard the SS Queen Victoria. Because there was a circus in town, the first in more than 20 years, few accommodations were available. Most delegates stayed aboard the Queen. Indeed, the agreement to declare independence seems to have been forged during a champagne-soaked luncheon in the stateroom of the Queen. A Canadian friend of mine gently reminds me that Canada did not literally declare "independence" from Great Britain in 1864-7. I should have suspected that Canadians were too civil to do so. They simply formed a federation that eventually in 1982, became the independent nation of Canada.

Two years later, on October 4, 1866, the SS Queen Victoria was caught in a hurricane off Cape Hatteras and lost at sea, but not before the hardy crew of the Gouldsboro-based (and built) Ponvert, under the command of Captain Rufus Allen, rescued its Canadian captain and 41 crew members — as well as its almost 80-pound bell. In gratitude—a typically Canadian sentiment—the Canadian crew presented the bell to Captain Allen, not anticipating what jerks Allen's descendants would be.

Upon his retirement in 1875, Rufus having, in the best American tradition, no clue as to its historic significance gave the bell to the Prospect Harbor School where it was used for many years to signal the start of the school day. Used until, that is, "It was removed when the building and belfry were considered too unstable [foreshadowing] to support its weight." After which time it was entrusted to the good ladies of the Prospect Harbor Woman's Club and displayed in a proper glass case.

In the 1980's several unofficial attempts were made to regain possession of the bell by Canadian interests that styled themselves as "patriots." This led to concern among Gouldsboro townsfolk about the possibility of a clandestine Canadian raid by the crack Canadian special force "Beavers," analogous to our Navy Seals. Tempers flared and, as one stout Gouldsboroian,

Selectman Hammond, said at the time: "That bell's gonna stay here. I don't think the Canadian government has any right to ask for the bell back." That sentiment was echoed by Sylvia Smith, President of the Prospect Harbor Woman's Club who recalled, "I used to ring that bell when I went to school as a girl. I don't see where they think we should give it to them. It was a gift to us." Speaking in 1988 about those who could see some merit in the Canadian request, Sylvia was succinct: "They're not natives of this village. They just don't feel the same way about it."

To forestall any such raid, the bell was deeded to the town of Gouldsboro and locked up in the safe at the town office. Meanwhile, Gouldsboro residents came up with a fiendish plan to fool the gullible Canadians by giving them a fake reproduction of the bell.

An ugly international crisis was averted. Hold that thought: Mainers defending their rightful treasure against misguided Canadians.

Now, roll the clock forward 26 years to a new generation of Gouldsboroians defending the bell. The Canadians, thinking there is something of significance in the founding of their preternaturally civilized country want Gouldsboro to loan them the bell for their sesquicentennial celebration of independence. Note: the request is no longer to give, just to *loan*. Nonetheless, as you might imagine, the good citizens of Gouldsboro are alarmed. Rumors once again circulate of a Canadian "plot to steal the bell." The used-to-be British are coming; "One if by land..."

One of Gouldsboro's latter-day minutemen, whose clock works are perhaps a second or two short of a full minute, complains, "We have a selectmen who comes from out-of-state, (i.e. who cannot be trusted and whose judgment is flawed), who doesn't give a hoot about our history, and he doesn't see why the bell cannot be loaned for nine months…. I don't want them to have it for as much as nine hours. The bell is a prominent symbol of Gouldsboro's seafaring and shipbuilding heritage," she said. "We won't get it back."

Upon reading this I immediately deduce, that this carpet-bagging selectman must be my friend, Roger. So it is. And, sure enough, the next line, (<u>Down East</u> being dedicated to balanced journalism), has Roger's response: "Yes, I am in favor of lending the bell," Bowen said. "I think it is the neighborly thing to do. It costs us nothing, and in return it generates enormous goodwill…. I sometimes think people are accusing me of having a logic attack … and I plead guilty." <u>Down East</u> tells us that Roger is inclined to believe Jean-Francois Lozier, curator at the Canadian Museum of History when he writes, "I can assure the people of Gouldsboro that neither the museum, nor the Canadian government, would try to confiscate the bell. It will be returned."

<u>Down East</u> further points out that our U.S. National Archives will be lending the original Webster-Ashburton Treaty, the one that established the boundary between Maine and New Brunswick in 1842. But then, that generosity is perhaps easy for the National Archives since as part of the federal government, they have access to tanks, cruise missiles and Navy Seals, just in case.

* * *

Rainy Day (April 2012)

As refugees from San Diego, Susan and I are readily seduced by the magic of a rainy day. There is something womb-like and "snugifying" about the white noise of rain that encourages inwardness, a pause for quiet and reflection. The weather has been so good and so warm that we have been hard at work preparing the gardens. Rainy day jobs, e.g. hanging window shades, filing a winter's worth of stacked papers, have had to wait. Now those pleasures seem a perfect fit for this rainy day. When they are done we look forward to a nap, a fireside read, some hot chocolate and then a good movie.

It's been an uncharacteristically dry spring; until now there has been no water standing in the woods. But the rains began yesterday and promise to continue through tonight. We went to sleep with the sound of a steady, gentle rain on the roof and skylights. This morning the rain is more earnest -- as if determined to reach the prognosticator's projection that we will receive three inches of this precious moisture for which our gardens, like we, have been yearning. If their predictions are accurate we will receive in these 36 hours a third of San Diego's annual rainfall. Gusty winds out of the northeast are predicted momentarily. Now there are whitecaps on the bay.

The rain shortens our view, obliterating Mt. Dessert Island and Cadillac Mountain. The horizon is gone; we are adrift in the rain.

When the sky occasionally lightens, intrepid chickadees and gold finches dart to and from our feeders while the song sparrow stands watch over its seaside tangle of huckleberry and juniper. Soil that was rendered light and fluffy by the winter freeze will be battered back down by this soaker — but not before we have safely planted our morning glories and sweet peas. Ferns have emerged in the woods, thrusting up, but not yet unfurling their fiddlehead tops. They are three inches taller this morning than yesterday; they will grow another three inches today and tonight. Incidentally, fiddleheads are a local delicacy that can be purchased in the supermarket this time of year. Some await us even now in the refrigerator. They are typically harvested by Native Americans who know the right type (not all emerging ferns are fiddleheads) and locations. A quick boil, drained, served with melted butter and a pinch of salt: to me they taste like something between lettuce and cabbage with a hint of brussel sprouts, but to Susan they taste like spring.

Hancock Point and its surrounds are ablaze with forsythia. Because we have not previously been on the Point in April, we have never before seen these otherwise sedate, plain bushes in their party garb. They are perfect harbingers of spring as they blaze against an evergreen background. Yesterday Susan was on Gouldsboro peninsula where she noted a gray frame house with a bright yellow door that she and I have seen many times before. What we had not known is that the plain bushes framing that door in the summer are in fact forsythia. Now, for these few weeks it is absolutely arresting. Such discoveries are part of the joy about being here both earlier in the year, April, and later in the year, November: we see sights that enrich our vision during the summer. We will never again see that yellow door, even in August, without seeing the forsythia in bloom.

The world is always more complex than our first view reveals. We have to watch awhile, see the whole cycle. I used to say the same thing to my academic colleagues as they undertook new assignments: step back, be patient, see the whole board. **Our polyvalent world reveals itself only when we have seen it from many angles. Once comprehended, each facet reflects/reveals/enriches the whole.**

We had a similar experience this past winter in San Diego. We had lived there for 15 years, but had never before seen people walking on the beaches on weekday mornings, or mothers with their children in the parks, or old folks like us walking dogs. Turns out, not everyone is dressed in business attire and sitting in conference rooms! Who knew?

The same principle guides the discovery of marriage. After the initial wonder of a second toothbrush in the bathroom and the sexual intoxication, a significant "other" (apt though awkward phrase) begins to emerge. How does he or she disagree? Does he play fair? Does she sulk? What art does she like? What does he read? Does he have a capacity for silence? Can she paddle a canoe? How will he handle disappointments? And then there is the revelation of parenthood. Where did that come from??? How did she know what to do? To be so calm in the face of emergency? These are facets of self that are unknown, even to oneself, in the beginning, let alone to a spouse. But through it all a fuller, richer, more complex human being emerges. Once grasped, the silliness of an afternoon giggle is made even more precious by the now-glimpsed depths/complexity that lie behind it. **Our polyvalent world will reveal itself only when we have seen it from many angles. Once comprehended, each facet reflects/reveals/enriches the whole.**

The day after, the weather gurus were right. The closest weather station to us reported 4.12 inches. As I walked around the Point this morning brooks that usually murmur a friendly gurgle were in full-throated roar. They had been joined by other streams invented just for the occasion. A few branches had been blown down onto the dirt road, but my favorite find was a handfull of Spanish moss, actually a lichen, that had been blown off one of the still-bare trees. I took it home to Susan. Like us, the lichen is symbiotic. Unlike our symbiosis, its mutual dependency is one of fungus and algae — a complexity that was not grasped until the time of the Civil War. It takes time to fully see what is right in front of you. **Our polyvalent world will reveal itself only when we have seen it from many angles. Once comprehended, each facet reflects/reveals/enriches the whole.**

* * *

It Was a Cold and Snowy Night... (November 2015)

This story has many beginnings: a high school dance, a card game, but I am going to begin in Nazi Germany in 1944. Joachim von Ribbentrop, Germany's Foreign Minister, was seeking ways to learn more about America. In particular, he wanted to know how German propaganda was being received. Toward that end, he turned to the Schutzstaffel (the infamous SS) which, in turn, selected a German citizen, Erich Gimpel, alias Edward George Green, and an American defector, William Curtis Colepaugh, for a spy mission.

Gimpel, born March 25, 1910, had served as a radio engineer for seven years in South America before being tapped for service as a spy and saboteur. William Curtis Colepaugh, alias William C. Caldwell, was a disillusioned American, born in Connecticut in 1918, who had dropped out of MIT after three years. He had briefly served in the US Navy before being honorably discharged on suspicion of German sympathies. He then joined the Merchant Marine, sailed to Lisbon, Portugal where he jumped ship and presented himself for duty at the German Consulate. Following special training at The Hague, the cool German professional and the eager

American amateur had an assignment, code name: Untermehmen Elster, or "Operation Magpie." Originally intended to gather information gauging the effectiveness of Nazi propaganda in the United States, the objective was later widened to include the gathering of technical engineering information, generally from public sources.

Of particular interest was intelligence on shipyards, airplane factories, and rocket-testing facilities. Gimpel and Colepaugh were to sail from Kiel, Germany aboard a German submarine bound for the east coast of the U.S. where they would be secreted ashore.

To set some context, in 1944 the war in Europe was beginning to shift in favor of the Allies:

>-Allied troops landed in Anzio in January and freed Rome on June 4th.

>-The invasion of Normandy took place on June 6th and by late July the Allies had broken out of the beachhead and were racing toward Paris.

>-On June 22nd the Russians launched a massive counter-offensive in eastern Belarus.

>-Allied forces landed in southern France on August 14 near Nice and advanced rapidly to the northeast.

You get the idea: not a good time to be wearing a swastika. That was the state of the war as Gimpel and Colepaugh's submarine, U-1230, slipped out of Kiel harbor on September 24, 1944 and laid quietly on the ocean floor just outside the harbor, perhaps testing systems?

On Sept 26 she then headed for Horten, Norway where she arrived at about 7:00 a.m. on the 27th. There additional tests were run. On Oct 3, she sailed to Kristianand, arriving early the following morning. On October 6, she headed out into the north Atlantic, separated from her escort, submerged and set course for the banks of Newfoundland. She made the crossing typically submerged but for four to six hours spent on the surface each night. Averaging only 6 knots, it was a long 5-week crossing. As they approached Newfoundland U-1230 began running entirely submerged, except for "Schnorcheling," i.e. snorkeling, to recharge batteries. They acquired the banks of Newfoundland on November 20.

From there they headed due south for Sable Island, from which they headed west for the Nova Scotia light. Not being able to spot the light the Captain surfaced to take bearings — in this case from commercial radio stations — only to find that they were off Maine, close to Bar Harbor, just south of Mt. Desert Rock, to which they proceeded. For the next six days the crew worked on ship repairs. The humidity of the long, largely submerged, crossing had damaged many of the electronics. They would schnorchel at night and lay on the bottom, in about 100 meters of water, during the day. In particular, they were paying close attention to tides and currents which would be critical for their landing.

On the evening of November 29, 71 years ago today, U-1230 rose to periscope depth and headed into Frenchman Bay entering between Porcupine and Ironbound Islands. At approximately 10:30 p.m., she was a few hundred yards off shore. She surfaced with her decks awash. A rubber raft was brought up and inflated. Gimpel and Colepaugh, dressed in civilian clothes — light trench coat, fedoras, suitcase— boarded the small craft; two uniformed members of the ship's crew rowed them ashore. They landed at: 44°28'25"N 68°14'41"W — a finger of rock known to locals as "Sunset Ledge"—protruding westward into the Bay. [Digression: if you call up Google Maps and enter those coordinates your little red pin will drop on the western shore of Crabtree Neck. Move in closer and you will see West Shore Road tracing the western coast, past Bragg Lane and Adleman Way. Switch to satellite (what a wonder!), and move closer still: a right-angled house will appear, next to it a separate garage by the drive, and curving paths to the shore. Whose house is that? OURS!!! Indeed, 44°28'25"N 68°14'41"W puts you just off our southern pocket beach where you can see, to the north the inviting rocks. The house, garage, paths, etc. were obviously not there in 1944 when I would have been about two and a half years old. There is a puzzlement in this. Locals, myself included, associate Sunset Ledge with the rocks at the northern end of our northern pocket beach (also visible on the Google satellite photo), which would be our neighbor's ledge, not ours. But I ask you? Would Germans lie? Would they get their coordinates wrong? Pardon my self-centered digression. Back to our story.]

The two uniformed crew members handed Gimpel and Colepaugh their luggage, stood on the shore themselves to give a "Heil Hitler" salute just so they could later brag that they had, and returned to the waiting sub. Gimpel and Colepaugh were on their own. Well, not entirely. The SS had provided them with two loaded revolvers, forged birth and draft certificates, secret inks as well as $60,000 in small bills (almost $700,000 today) and 99 small diamonds to sell if the US currency had changed by the time they arrived or if they eventually needed additional funds. Clearly, the Germans had made a major investment in this mission — in addition to committing a submarine and crew.

The two spies set off through the woods to the Point Road and proceeded to walk north approximately four and a half miles to US Route 1. Enter the high school dance; seventeen-year-old, Boy Scout, Harvard Hopkins (is that a great name or what!) was driving home from a high school dance when he spotted two strange men walking through the night's snow who were obviously "not from around here," i.e. city-garb, suitcases and most-telling-of-all: topcoats! Shortly thereafter Harvard's neighbor, Mary Forni was driving home from a card game and saw them as well (more on this later).

After they reached US Route 1 the spies hailed a cab!!! Yes, a cab at what must have been about midnight on a cold and snowy night in late November in rural Maine. If you were to attempt that today, i.e. stand by US Route 1 at the junction with the Point Road and wait for a cab you might be there for the better part of a day, but they hailed a cab! How is that possible?

This was war time. Navy officers on their way back to their Winter Harbor base, about fifteen miles farther east on Route 1, had just occupied the seats of the returning cab that would soon pick up the German spies and, in exchange for $6.00, take them to Bangor. From Bangor the spies caught a 2:00 a.m. train to Portland. Alas, we have no such train service from Bangor today. Think of that: landing in a rubber raft at approximately 10:30 p.m., a four-and-a-half-mile walk, securing a cab, driving to Bangor (probably 90 minutes then), and catching a 2:00 a.m. train!!! Talk about a string of serendipity.

A 7:00 a.m. train took the spies from Portland to Boston where Gimpel attempted to buy a tie. Upon subsequent interrogation by the FBI the salesman said he had recognized the cloth and cut of Gimpel's trench coat as not being American. The next day they trained on to Grand Central Station and the Big Apple.

Meanwhile things were "moving on" in Maine. U-1230, was once again lying low off the Maine coast. Two days after dropping off Gimpel and Colepaugh the German sub sighted and sank a 5,548-ton Canadian freighter, the Cornwallis, once again a loser (think Yorktown) carrying sugar and molasses from Barbados to St. John, New Brunswick. Alarmed by the possibility that this U-boat might have dropped off enemy agents, the Boston FBI office sent men north to Maine to investigate. The agents soon located 29-year-old Mary Forni and her next-door neighbor, 17-year-old Harvard Hodgkins, the two Hancock residents who had driven past the spies walking in the snow.

When interviewed Mary explained that, "They stood out like sore thumbs because they were so overdressed," she said. "We knew everybody in town, and these strange fellows you couldn't help but notice with their expensive looking topcoats, fedoras, and attache' case. They didn't have that Down East look. It was much like Wall Street." Mary then proceeded to throw her husband under the bus, "When I arrived home, I described the sighting to my husband, Dante. He told me not to be so nosy." But, ignoring the noseless gentleman, as Maine wives often do, Mary alerted the deputy sheriff, Dana Hodgkins, the next day. The FBI was called in and interviewed her. Given Mary's description the spies' tracks were followed back to where they left the road and then through the woods to the landing site.

It is not known what Harvard Hodgkins said to the FBI, but there is no truth to the persistent rumors that he asked if there might be a merit badge in it for him. In any event, the hunt was on. It is not clear that Eliot Ness and the boys could have found the spies had if not been that Colepaugh decided to give up spying and abscond with the money-stuffed suitcases. Not being from Maine, and having a male need to brag, he ran into an old friend and introduced himself as a spy. Not smart! The FBI was alerted; Colepaugh was taken into custody and sang like a canary; Gimpel, still in New York, was arrested on December 30.

Indications were that the-Newly arrived pair had not yet affected any sabotage. Since landing on American soil on November 29 they were said to have been making a round of New York City's night clubs and bars in an effort to get information which they planned to transmit to Germany by short wave radio. When seized they had $56,574 left of the $60,000 -provided them by the German government.

Our tale is not yet over. The Office of Naval Operations described Gimpel as follows: "Prisoner GIMPEL is a very difficult subject for interrogation. He was a professional German espionage agent, thoroughly indoctrinated in security. He believes that the death penalty awaits him and that nothing he can do will mitigate his sentence. He was untruthful on several occasions with his interrogators and told them only what he believed they already knew. His statements are of very little value." Of Colepaugh they write: "Prisoner COLEPAUGH's statements are much more valuable. He is a somewhat unstable New Englander (almost a contradiction in terms), but impressed his interrogators as attempting to tell the truth. He is intelligent, very observant, and has an extraordinary visual memory for details. His attitude toward the interrogators was friendly and cooperative. He was always careful to distinguish between eye witness evidence and hearsay. The interrogators were under the impression that his helpfulness was inspired by the hope of escaping the death penalty." (You can read the account of Gimpel and Colepaugh's interrogation at http://ibiblio.org/hyperwar/USN/rep/U-1230/index.html)

In early February 1945, Gimpel and Colepaugh were tried by a military court at Fort Jay on Governors Island, New York. They were convicted and sentenced to death by hanging on Valentine's Day. Before their sentence was carried out however, President Franklin D. Roosevelt died, and all federal executions were suspended for four weeks. Isn't that quaint!? By the time that month was up, the war had ended in Europe. On June 23, the new president, Harry S. Truman, announced that he was commuting the two sentences to life in prison — Gimpel's because the United States and Germany were no longer at war, and Colepaugh's because he had given himself up and provided the FBI with the information needed to arrest Gimpel.

Colepaugh served 17 years in prison, then moved to the Philadelphia area where he operated a business in King of Prussia, Pennsylvania before he retired to Florida. Gimpel served 10 years at Leavenworth, Alcatraz, and Atlanta before he was released and deported to Germany in 1955. He later moved to Brazil, where he celebrated his 94th birthday in 2004. Forni continued to live in the Hancock area and was one of the guests of honor at a June 2005 party to celebrate the birthdays of some local residents. Sixty years earlier, she had been honored at another local party; shortly after the spy incident, when her friends organized an event to honor her for her role in providing information that helped capture Gimpel and Colepaugh and to present her with a $100 war bond.

Americans ate up the story of Hodgkins, the Hancock Boy Scout (We were just as shallow then as we are now). The New York Journal-American sponsored the high school senior's first ride in an airplane, bringing him and his family to New York for a week in January 1945, where he was given a key to the city. He saw the Statue of Liberty, Radio City Music Hall, and some Broadway shows, and met Governor Thomas Dewey, boxing champion Joe Louis, and Babe Ruth. After he graduated from Ellsworth High School, Hodgkins received a full scholarship to the Maine Maritime Academy for his anti-spy efforts. He died in May 1984.

So, other than the pleasure of telling a good story, why do I share this essay with you? First, because it reminds me that history is all around us. Second, because that history can often provide context and perspective. At a time when Chicken Littles are seeing enemy agents behind every Syrian refugee it might be wise to remember that real enemy agents have walked among us before — and that they were frustrated by a card-playing Maine housewife and a 17-year-old Boy Scout.

P.S. This wintry tale was compiled with some help from the internet.

2. CHILDHOOD: WE ALL HAD ONE

It takes a long time and many experiences to build a human being. Often those experiences rush by in a blur; it's only later that we recognize the formative ones.

Part 1: The Barn

After our father died, Mom, a registered nurse, moved my two brothers and me back to the farm in northern Ohio where her aging parents still lived. Her three farmer brothers were nearby. She rightly thought it would be a good place to raise her sons while she dutifully cared for her aging parents. Some context: our mother had grown up on this farm, had left it to go to nursing school, then to be an airline stewardess and a Powers model in New York City. Her first husband was a basketball coach whom she lost to an infection after less than a year of marriage; her second, my dad, died at age 40 leaving her three sons to raise — the youngest of whom was only two weeks old. She gave up the friends and society of a Boston suburb to return to the farm and to provide a life for us kids. In short, she was unreasonably fond of us and invested in our success.

My grandparents' old farmhouse, originally built without indoor plumbing, and in which my mother was raised, was at the junction of US Route 20 and Luckey (Yes, it is spelled with an "e".) Road. Their small farm spread out to the south and east. There were, as was typical of mid-western farms of that time, a number of surrounding structures: a milk house, the garage that housed a Chrysler sedan grandma, (a pusher of candy corn), referred to as, "the machine," a workshop complete with forge (farmers were self-reliant), a corn crib/storage shed and, about 75 yards south of the house, a large barn. Between the milk house and the garage, both close by the road for obvious reasons, was 2.5" diameter pipe that rose from the ground about three feet, turned 90 degrees, ran about five or six feet and turned back into the ground. It was a hitching rail that once welcomed horses and carriages but that now supported grandkids as they swung by their knees and did other acrobatic feats.

Barns are wonderful structures. This one was particularly large and handsome. It was a major part of growing up for my brothers and me. From the north (house) side of the barn a sliding door hanging from rollers on an overhead track, opened into what might best be called a cement-floored, tack room, half of it a step lower than the entrance level. A rack, on which equipment hung, separated the 2 levels. If you looked closely you could see that the dividing rack was in fact stanchions that formerly held cows as they were milked. We used the space largely to store grain supplements for livestock as well as equipment such as shovels and pitchforks. Below that foyer we stepped down two steps to a still cement-floored area, an extension to the original barn, where we usually kept pigs, including occasionally 400-pound sows with their litters of 10 to 12 piglets. Beyond that, through another roiling door, was a connecting space that once housed chickens and beyond that a seldom used low, flat-roofed pig shed. Farther to the east was a fenced-in pasture.

There would inevitably come a time, usually when the piglets had grown to 20 to 30 pounds, when we would herd the young males, not an easy task, up into the tack room where I would help my uncles confine them in a small space, grab them one by one, and castrate them. I remember my nausea as a young adolescent male the first time I witnessed this procedure. I slid away to the other side of the barn to vomit. Also, on that lower level there was a large cement water tank, I would guess about 6' by 3' and 3 feet high. My grandfather, who was both an inventor and entrepreneur, designed it so that it was automatically filled, originally by windmill, later by an electric pump. A toilet-like float regulated the water level. At one end of the tank a bent pipe, serving as a siphon, delivered the water to two built-up bowls at floor level where the livestock could drink. On top of the tank there were wooden planks to keep out dust, feathers and other barn detritus.

In the winter a heat lamp hung over the syphon keeping it from freezing. But the water in the tank would freeze over and if left unattended eventually disrupt the syphon that was not easily re-established. Consequently, in cold weather once or twice a day my brothers or I would use an axe to cut through the 2–4-inch-thick ice on the tank. We would chop through the ice last thing, before we went to bed and then again early in the morning. This was a cold, unpleasant job, made no better by the spooky dark barn. A single bare bulb, even 100 or 150 watts, has little purchase against the dark of a cavernous barn. I would proceed tentatively from island of light to distant light switch, to new island of light, to..., you get the idea.

Walking into this cement-floored section of the barn the first thing you might notice was its thinly whitewashed, walls, windows, and straw-lined loft where selfish chickens occasionally hid their eggs. In fact, the thin white film was not whitewash, but rather dried DDT — the miracle cure-all of the fifties. Above this cement-floored section of the barn ran a track on which a bathtub-sized bucket, raised and lowered with chains and ratchets, could be filled with manure, lifted up and sent out through a window-sized opening to a waiting (steaming in the winter) manure pile. Approaching the front of the barn from the west there was a pair of large sliding doors at the top of the "barn bridge" that brought equipment, trucks, wagons, tractors, etc., up to the raised floor level. Lower and to the right was another sliding door through which manure could be loaded by a tractor and scoop into a manure spreader for dispersal on our fields of corn, wheat, oats or soy beans. Did you know that if you take a handful of freshly harvested wheat, put it in your mouth and chew, it becomes a perfectly serviceable gum? I thought not! But I digress.

Inside the main barn doors, to the left of the barn floor were granaries. Ahead and far enough overhead for large trucks to pull under, was one of my grandfather's proudest contraptions: a huge bin for storing grain, usually wheat, oats or corn. I would estimate that the bin was approximately 20x20x20. That's a lot of grain. Grandpa had a conveyer belt with cups attached, built into the floor that would carry the grain aloft. We would just shovel the grain over a hole in the floor where the conveyer belt would pick it up and carry it aloft. When the time came to take the stored grain to market, presumably now commanding a higher price, a simple gravity-fed chute unloaded the grain into waiting trucks below. To the right of the barn floor was another sliding door that opened into the dirt-floored livestock area — about four feet below. A large, probably three feet wide, manger jutted out into the livestock area connecting in a "T" with another large manger that ran to the right and left. Most of the time we would be feeding sheep, sometimes cattle in this area. We would walk through the mangers spreading grain and baled hay. If memory serves, we put down fresh straw bedding once a week.

In retrospect I think the responsibility of having 150 sheep or 50 cattle depending on you played a large part in the future dependability of my brothers and me. But, for us the glory of this grand, already old, barn was literally above all this. About eight or nine feet above the barn floor, reachable by ladder, were haymows on each side. A single mow to the left and a doublewide mow to the right. Of course, their purpose was to store straw and/or hay — originally loose, later baled. In fact, we could store all the hay/straw we needed in the single mow and in the front half of the double mow — which left the back mow for the basketball court about which I will write presently.

As kids this was a wonderful playground. We built multi-leveled tunnels and "secret" chambers out of straw bales; had wars with peashooters and slingshots. But most of all, we would put on shows in our very own "Big Top." So, imagine the following scene: way up at the top, along the ridgeline of the barn, ran a track originally used for hoisting hay. In the old days loose hay would be lifted up in a sling, by horses; then towed horizontally by rope to the best spot and dropped by trip-line into the filling haymow. Then it would be forked by hand (I have done this hot, sweaty work) into corners and remote spaces as the mow filled. Now, however, we would just back a wagon of bales into the barn, drop them one by one onto a conveyer, and spill them aloft to be stacked. But I digress again.

My wandering point is that way aloft, probably 40–50 feet above the barn floor, was a track from which hung the long, forty- or fifty-year-old ropes, that once lifted slings of hay. Holding a rope in one hand, with visions of Batman in our heads, we would climb to the top of a stack of bales and swing across the mow to another stack. No great danger there. We were rarely more than ten feet above the bales, which would catch us when, not if, we fell. However, when that proved to be insufficient excitement we took to swinging from haymow to haymow, (i.e. across the wooden barn floor below), sometimes simultaneously in opposite directions. "Look Ma, one hand!" You get the idea. I was then probably 12 or 13; brother John was 9 or 10. At this point Roger was still too young for a starring role — though we found other ways to put him at risk.

I am embarrassed to say that after rehearsing and perfecting our circus routine, after agreeing on the order of death-defying tricks, we would run to the house and get Mom to come out to watch the show AND WE WOULD CHARGE ADMISSION!!

The barn was a place to grow, to explore, to earn some money, to confront and overcome fears — and a place to play basketball.

* * *

Part 2: Basketball.

I have just read a news release about two basketball stories at San Diego State. The first trumpets the fact that for the past four years San Diego State basketball has outdrawn all basketball programs in California, including UCLA. The second announces construction of a new basketball training facility at SDSU. When I shared the news release with brother John, he responded, "Gee, I thought your current facilities were very impressive. There were no missing floorboards. The lighting exceeded 200 watts. You could run under the backboard without getting a nail in your side. I still miss our old hay mow basketball. If you could play in an environment where it was 30 degrees, you could play anywhere."

To provide some context for John's response it is necessary to journey back in time. It is hard to imagine the basketball mania of the mid-west, Ohio, Indiana, Kentucky, Illinois, in the 50s. The movie, *Hoosiers* set in 1954 rural Indiana captures it well: the local pride, the scrawny, not-all-that-tall athletes who played their hearts out, cheerleaders in below-the-knee, pleated skirts and letter sweaters, caravans of fans driving on back roads, past harvested cornfields dusted with snow.

We (I speak as a fan, not a player) were the Troy Luckey Trojans. Our coach was "Frenchy" Filiere, who doubled as a biology teacher. And we were good — often regional contenders for the Class "C" title. Our rural, consolidated high school of 300 was in Luckey Ohio, a village of perhaps a 1,500, five or six miles south of our house which was, in turn, about ten miles south of Toledo. Before I had my driver's license I could not go to most of our basketball games — perhaps only three or four a year, bumming pity rides from older kids. Instead, I would listen to the games huddled over our big old console radio that received as much static as signal. I suspect the radio broadcasts from those small gyms were only 25–50 watts.

Exciting as these high school games were, they were far away and remote, played by celebrities from a completely different social class. For us the real "home court" was not in Luckey, Ohio, but in our barn. The inner haymow, running the full length of the south wall of the barn was our basketball court. The front and back walls of the barn formed its ends. The North wall of the court, varying in height from 8 to 12 feet depending on the time of year, and how far we had drawn down our supply in caring for the livestock, was formed from stacked straw or hay bales. The "court" was open to the roof, higher above than any of us could throw a basketball. In retrospect I imagine the court was about 60 feet long, a regulation basketball court is 94 feet, and perhaps 20 feet wide less than half the regulation 50 feet.

Mom had someone build two oversized white backboards, about 5' x 8' from which our usually netted hoops stood forth, ten feet above the floor at each end. Around the perimeter of the court we had bare light bulbs, perhaps 150 to 200 watts each, typically two at each end, roughly to the right and left of where the foul line would be. To paraphrase *Blazing Saddles*: "We don't need no stinking foul line." The light was not good in that cavernous space, especially on cold winter nights and during the day some light would creep in through cracks in the barn wall, but once your eyes adjusted.... There were smells emanating from the livestock below — and welcome heat. Barns are full of birds, Sparrows, Starlings, Swallows and the occasional Barn Owl, and, of course, not dusted. Brother Roger reminds me of the powdered bird dung that filled the air as basketballs caromed off walls and beams — and that we inhaled carefree.

At the east end of the court, down by the floor was an opening from which one could drop bales of straw to the floor below; occasionally the basketball would escape through that portal and fall into the sloppy, wet manure below. No problem: someone, usually the youngest and least senior among us, would be dispatched to retrieve the ball. A few wipes with a handful of straw and it was fine. There has been a lot of talk recently about a shortage of microbes in this generation of kids' lives; no such problem on the farm.

I must confess that we had a bit of a home court advantage. We not only knew every angle and every shadow; we also knew where the dead boards were, i.e. the ones from which the basketball would only rebound halfway. On cold winter nights the basketball was less than spry.

Typically, we played three on three, though when cousins or neighborhood kids dropped by we could do a crowded five on five. For us basketball was not just a winter activity; it was year-round, weekends, after daily chores, etc... Sometimes we would just shoot alone, but most of the time it was a contest no matter how much we had to gerrymander it; e.g. three younger against two older; four of us civilians against two varsity guys. If there were only two of us we would often play "H-O-R-S-E." But the best times were with cousins, especially Uncle Ernie's two sons, Doug and John, and Uncle Herm's two sons, Larry and Merle. Doug and Larry were close to my age; John and Merle were closer in age to brother John. That was some serious basketball. Games would go on for three or four hours. We would bounce off walls hoping that a random nail was not protruding from the spot.

One of the pleasures of my San Diego State life was occasionally dropping by an SDSU basketball practice to watch "The Master," Steve Fisher, developing his young men. For a basketball wannabe like myself it was a pure delight. Occasionally, Coach Fisher would ask if I wanted to say a few words to the team. **But of course**. He would blow the whistle and we would immediately be surrounded by a forest of young men, so big that I had to consciously remind myself they were only 18 or 20 years old.

One afternoon, in trying to convey my love of their sport and my admiration for their talent/effort, I began my comments by asking, "How many of you know what a haymow is?" Silence. Nowadays, real basketball is not played so much in barns as on urban playgrounds. My brothers and I have fond memories of that barn: the work, the play, the camaraderie — just as Steve Fisher's young men will have fond memories of SDSU basketball: the work, the play, the camaraderie. Basketball is a great game — in part because it can be played almost anywhere: urban playground or Ohio barn. I know today's urban kids could wipe the floor with my rural basketball players of the 50s. But our microbes could take their microbes any day.

* * *

The Eat'em Bug (June 2018)

There were few things that could appall a widowed lady raising three young sons on her own: Treasured antiques smashed. Bird nests exploded with fire crackers. Neighborhood kids burned by more fire crackers. The garage painted by her "helpful" young son. End tables incinerated when her oldest son learned that you do not have to scrub off paint remover — just set it on fire and then brush off the ash. Like a Farmers Insurance agent, she had seen a lot.

Before I relate this family legend, let me set the scene. We are on a small farm in northwest Ohio to which our nurse mother retreated after our father died. She was looking for a wholesome place to raise her three sons with a bit of male influence supplied by her three farmer brothers. It is the early 50s. "Father Knows Best" has just debuted on the small TV screen. Elvis Presley is shocking parents who unsuccessfully urge Pat Boone on their sons and daughters as a more wholesome alternative. Eisenhower is home from the war and in the White House. There are no warning labels on ladders telling us that, "climbing may result in falls", or on irons proclaiming, "may be hot". On the home scene I am the oldest, at about 12; brother John is three years younger; "baby" Roger is bringing up the rear at about 3. There-in lies the first predicate of this tale: Roger is significantly younger than John and I. Like any good household of the 50s, there are rules. First among them, "Don't pick on your little brother." But there he is: a helpless, guileless, innocent, trusting temptation — perfect for experimentation.

John and I have previously learned that we are not allowed to physically harm Roger. We cannot induce electric shock, cannot feed him from our chemistry set, cannot abandon him alone down by the creek. But the rules of psychological terrorism are less clear. Mom, not suspecting the depths of our depravity, has unwittingly left us room to be inventive. Like the time John wired a toy microphone to our old radio and broke into a radio program announcing to Roger's young playmate that his father had just been killed in a car crash. But that is another story.

This story, our story, takes place on a winter evening, when boredom has done its work and our thoughts have turned toward Roger, quietly playing with blocks, wearing his booted pajamas. John and I begin talking with one another, knowing that Roger will overhear: "Have you heard about the Eat'em Bug? It's been seen here in Wood County. Police are on the alert, but there is not much they can do." Thirty minutes later: "I just heard a report on the radio that the Eat'em Bug got two small kids over in Pemberville. It seems to prefer the young ones." Roger, of course, overhears these conversations and cannot resist asking us what the Eat'em Bug is. We express surprise that he does not know and then proceed to fill him in. "The Eat'em bug is a round, glowing patch of light that devours any living thing in its path. It had been reported to be over in Indiana, but looks as if it has now come to Ohio." We continue: "It seems to prefer kids about your age and just took two kids over in Pemberville. Nothing left but their slippers. But I would't worry; Pemberville is over 10 miles away and there are lots of other little kids between the Eat'em Bug and you."

Mom is, of course, oblivious to all of this, quietly reading a book in her living room chair. As Roger's bedtime approaches John and I excuse ourselves, "Mom, we're heading up to our room to do some homework." That should have set off parental alarms but did not. John and I circle back and secret ourselves under Roger's bed, a large Sears and Roebuck flashlight in hand. Soon we hear Mom and Roger approach. We hold our breath as she reads a bedtime story to Roger. Then, this being the 50s, says a prayer with him... "*Now I lay me down to sleep, I pray the Lord my soul to keep. If I should die before I wake, I pray the Lord my soul to take.*" Yikes!, a perfect prelude to nightmares... and tucks him in. Quietly she withdraws, turning out the light.

The scene is set but not quite yet. John and I instinctively know that we have to allow time for Roger to settle in; to think a bit about the Eat'em Bug; perhaps to get a bit scared, alone in the dark room. After a proper interval, I slowly, silently reach my arm out from under the bed and aim the flashlight's beam at the window. Slowly I travel it across the wall and up to the ceiling. Now, in unison, John with two arms, myself with my one free arm, violently shake the bed from below. Roger lets out a scream and runs fumbling toward the door and his all-too-distant mother.

Now, the rest of this we had not quite thought through. We sibling torturers had not calculated how much time it would take to squirm out from under the bed. Mom, assuring Roger, his hand in hers, that it is nothing, is back with our "mark" before we can get out of the room. We are caught dead-to-rights with flashlight in hand. We hear I think for the first time, "I am appalled." John and I are banished to our room, struggling to suppress our smiles. Roger snuggles in with Mom for another story and a good night's sleep. Is it any wonder "Mom liked Roger best?"

P.S. When I checked the above with brother John asking how it comported with his memory of the event he sent this surely apocryphal response: Nicely done. You forgot to mention the after effects. Years later Mom took Roger out to *Holiday on Ice*. Everything was fine until the lights went out. The skaters were then illuminated by huge beams of light commuting from above. Roger almost fell down the stairs trying to escape.

P.P.S. But the response that ties it all together is this one from brother Roger: "I WILL SWEAR TO THE ACCURACY OF THE LIGHT BEAM OMINOUSLY APPROACHING ME. THAT MEMORY PERSISTS AFTER A MERE 64 YEARS."

* * *

Culture Shock (September 2021)

The year was 1953. I was 11 years old. Our move from New England to the mid-west was accompanied by a profound "culture shock," not unlike Dorothy waking up in Oz. Our clothes were wrong, gaberdine instead of jeans. There were smells like the spreading of manure we had not encountered before. Roosters crowing in the morning. Fireflies lighting the evening shadows. In short, I was ignorant of this strange new land. "There's a difference between hay and straw?" I asked. Cousins played games, e.g. Red Rover, I did not know. Firecrackers could be obtained on a kid's version of the black market. Soon there would be school busses to ride, with sex-ed classes offered by the juniors and seniors in the back rows, and a new school culture to be figured out as well.

But for now, it was summer. There was an unfamiliar world to explore. We fished for crawdads in the creek a half mile to our south using bread crusts and an open safety pin on a string. Braved the cavernous, dark and spooky barn. Walked the mile to Stony Ridge to buy BB's at Smithers' hardware store. (BB guns were a pleasant part of the culture shock of this strange new world). Lots to learn, lots to like, lots to be anxious about — the natural stuff of childhood.

We tend to associate "culture shock" with international travel, perhaps even regional travel within this country. But this experience of the new and unexpected, of strange customs and behaviors is not limited to travel; it is the very essence of childhood where every day brings its own culture shock as we courageously venture, willy-nilly into uncharted territory. Children are cultural warriors, learning why they can't tell Aunt Edith that her new hat looks silly, or why fart jokes in church are unappreciated, or even why the knife and spoon belong on the right. All of which is to say that, like every child, I was already a seasoned cultural warrior. But then the foreign strangeness of the rural Midwest took a dark and sinister turn.

Slowly at first, from deep underground where they had been biding their time, monsters began to emerge. Monsters with bulging red eyes, armor plate, and six spiny jagged legs. Monsters older than I. They climbed up the trunks of Grandpa's oak and silver maple trees. First by the hand-full, then by scores, finally by the hundreds. The trees were filled with empty suits of buff-toned armor.

What were these things?

I assure you we had nothing like this in Marblehead. Of course, like most culture shock, it could be tamed by putting a name to it: Cicada. I began to investigate. At first, I collected the exoskeletons from which they launched their invasion; empty husks, they clung to tree limbs and trunks. It turned out that their now-rigid legs made perfect clasps with which to surreptitiously attach them to the sleeves or perch them on the shoulders of unsuspecting female cousins. I waited patiently for the predictable scream. And we call the cicadas, pests!

Then a revelation in which one mystery of this strange culture merged with another. One evening, while collecting exoskeletons with which to torment cousins, I saw an adult cicada emerging from its exoskeleton.

Now it became clear: the bug-eyed monsters that filled the air with their two-inch-long bodies and their other-worldly sounds had come from these launching platforms. It was from these bases that they grew wings to spread out and terrorize the countryside. One more piece of the cultural puzzle fell into place.

What sparks this memory of an ancient cultural trauma? Just that I have once again encountered these monsters, this time in the strange and foreign land of Virginia. Now the culture shock is gone; only the wonder remains. If only I had a cousin to torment!

P.S. How, you might ask did I know the year was 1953? Simple, I subtracted 17 from 2021 to get 2004, take away another 17 (87), and another (70), then still another and you get 1953 — the year I was 11 and we had just ventured in to the strange and foreign land of Ohio.

* * *

Labor Day (September 2016)

I was a naturally lazy lad. I remember my Uncle Bob sitting with me at the kitchen table in Mom's house, in Ohio explaining that labor was good, that it was important, fulfilling. At the time I could understand labor only as a means to an end — not as a source of personal expression and affirmation, not as a way of moving the world and its history forward. Of course, not all labor is fulfilling. Much is repetitive and dulling — in fact, only a means to an end. But if you are fortunate enough to labor in the service of something larger than yourself, if you can work not just to eat but to build, not just for yourself but for others, then your labor and this Labor Day, are worth celebrating.

Son Matt signs his email: "laborare est orare" or "*to work is to pray.*" It provides the "text" for this Labor Day morning's reflection. The phrase Matt employs so appropriately stems from 6th century Benedict of Nursia who wrote in his "Rule of St. Benedict": "Ora et Labora", or "*pray and work.*" It was, I think a simple expression of what became the monastic life: work to sustain yourself; use that sustenance to praise god. Note that Matt's version is not "laborare *et* orare" but rather, (as it is now more frequently quoted), "Laborare *est* Orare," or "*to work is to pray.*" These are two very different bumper stickers. The first assumes no link between work and prayer; it is a simple conjunction: do this and do that. The latter says something far more complex and interesting: to do this *is* to do that.

Were I a theist, mine would be a "process theology" — i.e. that God is a work in progress and that we are agents of god's realization. How? By our labor, of course. St. Benedict was decidedly not a process theologian. One of his "levels of humility," not exactly a top 10 modern value, is to, "*accept oneself as a 'worthless workman.'*" What Matt's signature is saying is that our labor is not worthless, but rather a source of worth, potentially a source of ultimate worth.

There are many passages in Nikos Kazantzakis' *Report to Greco* in which he speaks to this thought. Here are two:

> "Blowing through heaven and earth, and in our hearts... is a gigantic breath — a great Cry — which we call God. Plant life wished to continue its motionless sleep next to stagnant waters, but the Cry leaped up within it and violently shook its roots: Away, let go of the earth, walk." It shouted this way for thousands of eons; and, lo! As a result of desire and struggle, life escaped the motionless tree and was liberated.... Animals appeared .... We're just fine here,: they said. "We have peace and security; we're not budging." But the terrible Cry hammered itself pitilessly into their loins, "Leave the mud, stand up, give birth to your betters....." And, lo! after thousands of eons man emerged. He has been fighting, again for thousands of eons, to draw himself, like a sword, out of his animalistic scabbard. He is also fighting — this is his new struggle — to draw himself out of his human scabbard. Man calls in despair, "Where can I go? I have reached the pinnacle, beyond is the abyss." And the Cry answers: "I am beyond. Stand up...." " "We mortals are the immortals' work battalion.

Our blood is red coral, and we build an island over the abyss. God is being built."

If you will allow that there can be "things sacred" for atheists like myself, that there can be a secular expression of prayer, that for us too "Laborare" can be "Orare," then you will understand why I take labor to be sacred. At its best labor moves beyond itself, touches the noble, the redeeming, the constructive. At its best, labor builds both the laborer and that upon which she labors. Like the sacred, labor is intoxicating. We "give ourselves" to it and (again, at its best) it gives us our selves right back. Our word "sacred" comes from the Middle English "sacre" from which we derive "consecrate." Most assuredly, not all labor is capable of consecration, but some is and to those of us without faith, it can be a type of prayer.

Labor is one of those few activities, along with loving Susan and raising our two sons, that have given me myself; I am most grateful for the gift. I like to think, but do not believe, that somewhere a smiling Uncle Bob is saying, "I told you so."

3. NOT ALL POLITICS ARE POLITIC

Years ago, as a young faculty member at the University of Maine I was one of a dozen colleagues who took out an "Impeach Nixon" ad in the Bangor Daily news. It was prompted by our Cambodian incursion, i.e. before Watergate. The university president sent a letter to me and my colleagues reminding us that we should not involve the university in stating our political opinions. I have subsequently had occasion to write such letters. As a university president you must take special care not to invoke the university in your opining. Hence it is with some pleasure that I herewith unburden myself.

Immigrants (August 9, 2015)

I am now sitting in the Philadelphia Airport awaiting a flight to Bangor, having spent yesterevening at the estate of the Serees (not their real name) of Princeton, NJ. The occasion was a black-tie optional fundraiser for Student Veterans of America. I was asked to make a few remarks.

The Serees' home had the tasteful trappings of wealth you might expect, but most of all it was graced by their crowning achievements: son Matthew and daughter Rachel. It was Matthew, 17, and Rachel's, 15, event; their parents never set foot on stage. It was Matthew and Rachel who welcomed us, Rachel by singing the national anthem. They entertained us with piano-cello duets: Matthew playing the piano; Rachel the cello (she first performed at Carnegie hall when she was 11). Together they selected passages to read aloud about heroism; some of their young friends joined in the readings. Both are strikingly beautiful/handsome — tall and lithe. Matthew in his tux; Rachel in a long, flowing, Indian-inspired red crepe gown with a wide golden hem. Both have broad, sensitive, smiling mouths, and wide, intelligent eyes, Rachel's black hair hung loose down her back. Each is poised and gracious. The dinner was outside in their beautiful, torch-lit back yard surrounded by evidence of their mother's expert gardening.

The Serees are first-generation immigrants from India; Rachel and Matthew were born here and behave as you might expect American young people to behave — only much better!!! And there-in lies a story. They would be the first to say that America has been good to them. One of the ways they expressed that good fortune was in a conversation with Matthew and Rachel approximately seven years ago. Believing that they had a responsibility to introduce their children to the world as it is and knowing that their cocoon distorts that world, they explained not only that they were unusually privileged, but that many others were not and that they had a responsibility to understand the circumstances of those who were less fortunate and to work to address their plight.

They announced that Matthew and Rachel would be responsible for their own foundation, not that of their parents, that they would choose the causes to be helped (they chose to support disadvantaged youth), and that they would take responsibility for hosting an annual fund-raising event. Last night's was their sixth. Previously they have addressed issues such as teenage pregnancy, gun violence, and poverty in nearby Camden, NJ.

There I was, sitting among perhaps 100, mostly Indian-American, guests: standing for a presentation of the colors; listening to the national anthem being sung; joining in a celebration of our veterans; watching two impressive young people, part of an impressive family; speaking heart-felt words about our need to recognize and support young veterans. Before we sat down to our delicious meal a Marine officer in dress uniform explained the military tradition of honoring MIA's and POW's with an empty table, set for them in continuing hope of their eventual return. As he spoke a white-clothed table stood solitary under an evening spotlight. It does not get much more American than that.

After the sumptuous feast of Indian food and some more performances, I had a chance for extended conversations with and Mr. and Mrs. Serees — the proud parents. We talked about values, about hard work, about raising children. They expect a lot from Matthew and Rachel; most importantly, they have taught them to expect a lot from themselves. Speaking of Matthew and Rachel, one of our very buttoned-down veterans said, "I wish I was that together at that age. Hell, I'm not that together now and I'm 37."

I could not help but wish that Donald Trump could have been there, not for the "pleasure" of his company, but in the hope that he might have appreciated the evening and the achievements of our hosts. I know that is somewhat unfair; Donald's diatribes are aimed at illegal immigrants and not Americans such as the Serees, who, I am quite confident, are fully legal. But the recent politicization of immigration, not a new phenomenon — think Italians, Irish, or my own Germans—is trending into a national xenophobia that is as ugly as it is short-sighted. Since who is "legal" and who is not is rarely apparent, many American citizens are wrongly tarred with this broad brush.

I do believe reasonable people can disagree about undocumented immigration. My own view is more welcoming. Southern California introduced me to many immigrants who were genuinely escaping oppression, who wanted little more than an opportunity to raise their families in peace, who were hard-working, family-oriented, education-valuing people. I could not help but see in them my German ancestors with open eyes of wonder and appreciation as they slid along the Erie canal on their way to mid-western farms. Of course, then the "welcome mat" was out for us.

My conservative brother John worries about illegal immigration — not in a xenophobic or small-minded way, but it concerns him nonetheless. Not presuming to speak for him, I think John believes these sojourners will potentially change this country he loves — and not in a good way. I agree that they will change our country, as have all other waves of immigrants, including us Germans, but I believe that change will be for the better.

Some conservatives, I do not know if John would share their beliefs, think that illegal immigrants are taking advantage of us. As I ate my cheap fruit salad at breakfast this morning, I thought that we were taking advantage of them. In any event, as one who has been educated in this nation's schools, driven on its highways, been sheltered by its veterans, it is hard for me to begrudge this later band of immigrants a bit of generosity.

John's intellect is at least equal to my own (I refer to him as "the smart one" of the Weber boys), but I think he might agree that neither of our beliefs is grounded in pure reason; each is prejudicial (pre-judged) in a way. I suspect John feels that these immigrants take more from than they give to our nation. I feel the opposite. Both views are not easily amenable to rational argument or demonstration.

Earlier this morning, after my fruit salad, I took a walk around the Cardinal-rich (the red birds, not the cross-dressing exhibitionists in pointy hats), Princeton campus. On the way out of town I drove past the Albert Einstein Museum — not a bad reminder of what immigrants can bring.

* * *

Democracy (June 2015)

The Greeks gave us many things: spectacular architecture, some early science, lots of impressive mathematics, a realistic appreciation of the human form, some quaint early philosophy and democracy. I find myself thinking about the latter this morning. My thoughts are prompted by an article in the NYT's Sunday Magazine of May 24. The article focuses on Yanis Varoufakis, Greece's Finance Minister.

As you know, Greece is in a very deep financial hole. Five years ago, they were almost a half-trillion in debt. It is hard to know what their current debt is. But on a 2012–13, Gross National Product of about $250B US dollars, a half trillion debt is a lot. For sake of comparison, Greece's GDP is smaller than that of Oregon; a little less than that of Louisiana—and it owes half a trillion dollars!!!

Heeding the call of self-interest, the European Union rode to the rescue with a $146B bailout, and then with another bailout in 2012. The price: austerity — reduced pensions, wages cut, government services severely cut back. All of which led, in turn, to 25% unemployment, homelessness, etc... It is a very sad situation with a collapsing economy (Greece's GDP has contracted 25%), and deep, widespread human suffering. It is, perhaps no wonder that after five years of "austerity" (with a German accent), the citizens of Greece voted in a left-leaning government (the direction of my own tilt) promising relief from "austerity," which is to say relief from the conditions to which they agreed when they accepted the loans.

The new government, led by Prime Minister Alexis Tsipras, has been trying to negotiate debt relief with, to date, little success. Extreme as the situation is, this is not an unusual phenomenon: debts are incurred; loans are extended; conditions are imposed; people resent the conditions because, of course they are designed to change the very behavior that engendered the debt in the first place. What interests me is the politics, the society, and the social contract. It is not surprising that someone would make promises he cannot keep: ("I will get us debt relief"), or that people would welcome and accept those false promises: ("I'll vote for that"). The wonder is what this sophistry says about Greek democracy.

Mr. Varoufakis proclaims, "I'm not going to humiliate myself, and I'm not going to become compromised in terms of my principles and in terms of logic." Evidently, his logic does not extend to keeping his promises or paying his debts. After all, Greece spent its way into this hole; indulged itself with expenditures it could not afford; placated itself with uncollected taxes. The story does not start with the bailout; it starts with the hole. And Greece, perhaps with the help of some foolish bankers, is responsible for that hole. So, too, it was Greece that sought assistance from the European Union; Greece that asked for the loan; Greece that accepted the loan with promises to repay and to adhere to its conditions which, incidentally, Greece proposed.

So, how does a serious, well-credentialed economist get himself to a place where he can expect Europe to write off $240B — and now miss its latest payment on the debt? By claiming his innocence. "I was against it all along" he argues. "We were the guys in Syntagma Square protesting...." He goes on, "... what we have here is a serious case of racism that all Greeks are the same, that whether or not they protested the bailout, they are still responsible for it." In effect, Varoufakis is arguing that these were not his debts and not his promises. With that Varoufakis has become untethered from the ancient Greek understanding of democracy.

The Oxford English Dictionary tells us that democracy is, "*a system of government in which all the people of a state or polity ... are involved in making decisions about its affairs, typically by voting to elect representatives to a parliament or similar assembly.*" Democracy is further defined as (a) "*government by the people; especially: rule of the majority* (b) *a government in which supreme power is vested in the people and exercised by them directly or indirectly through a system of representation usually involving periodically held free elections.*" The political scientist, Larry Diamond identifies four characteristics of democracy one of which is: "The active participation of the people, as citizens, in politics and civic life."

Democracy involves not only the right to participate in national decisions, but also the ownership of those decisions. The politicians who were inside passing laws while Varoufakis was outside protesting are "us," not "them." The people who dug the hole are "us" not "them." The people who made these covenants are "us" not "them." Protesting the bailout does not excuse you from it. Indeed, ownership or responsibility is one of the most powerful facets of democracy. One can claim innocence in a tyranny, but not in a democracy.

I grew up in a time when many, myself included, were protesting the Vietnam War. That did not excuse us from responsibility for the war. Indeed, I believe that the war cloyed so, precisely because we owned it; because we were part of the democracy that waged the war, in spite of our objections. Precisely because we were part of the democracy the war stuck to us like a tar baby. We could not walk away from it, claim it was someone else's fault. It is one thing to say, "They have it wrong." It is quite another to say, "We have it wrong." The former is naively free of responsibility; the latter accepts it.

My brother, John, is a conservative, perhaps as conservative as I am liberal. I think, however that he would share this understanding of democracy. I hated to be implicated in President Bush's invasion of Iraq as much as he now hates what he sees as President Obama's failings — not just because he sees them as wrong — but because he accepts that as a member of this democracy he is responsible for them and that his protests to the contrary, like mine against President Bush, do not excuse that responsibility but make it cling all the more.

In a democracy the fact that our vote was cast in a losing cause does not excuse us from responsibility for subsequent actions. The fact that we objected does not excuse us. The reason goes back to FDR's, "Let us never forget that government is ourselves and not an alien power over us." The song-writer Steve Earle offers a similar thought: "My objection to the death penalty is based on the idea that this is a democracy, and in a democracy the government is me, and if the government kills somebody then I'm killing somebody." Like it or not, for better or worse, to be a member of a democracy means not only to enjoy its freedoms, but to accept responsibility for its mistakes — Greeks taught us that.

* * *

Women (May 2016)

When I was young our country was in the midst of the civil rights movement, the sexual revolution and the Vietnam war. Those were turbulent times, but also times of promise. It looked as if a new generation was finding its voice, throwing off the shackles of the past, forging a new future. From my naïve viewpoint I presumed every generation would be more progressive (One is no longer allowed to say "liberal.") than its predecessor, as if prejudice and discrimination were on the run. How wrong was that!!!

It is clear, looking back, that much of that promise was false, much of the optimism misplaced. There is a lot I did not see coming: that we would be in an almost continuous state of war, that changing laws is not sufficient to change minds, that much of our self-confidence was empty bravado, the widening income gap, our failing, especially urban, schools, etc., and the selfish refusal to invest in our own society. I was happily confident that burning bras was igniting (pun intended) a new era for women; that soon they would be proportionally represented in board rooms, would be receiving equitable pay, would be assuming positions of political leadership.

So, you can imagine my disappointment to read a recent report on the "Best and Worst States for Woman's Equality." More about that in a moment, but first a global perspective:

-The U.S. now ranks 23rd on the World Economic Forum's list of the most gender-equal countries (down six spots since 2011). We lag behind such "emancipated" states as Burundi, Nicaragua and the Philippines.

>   -Although women comprise about 52 percent of all professional-level jobs, this past March, the Center for American Progress reported that women, "are only 14.6 percent of executive officers, 8.1 percent of top earners, and 4.6 percent of Fortune 500 CEOs."
>
>   -Two thirds of our minimum wage earners are women (even though women now represent the majority of college graduates).
>
>   -According to 2013's Global Gender Gap Report, the U.S. ranks №33 on the Health & Survival metric.
>
>   -According to the same source we rank №60 on the Political Empowerment metric.

What is holding us back in closing these gaps? Indeed, why are they worsening? Why do women still earn only "77 cents for every dollar a man makes," pushing down the U.S.'s global rank in wage equality to №67?

>   How do things look among the states?
>
>   -Hawaii ranks best in overall women's equality; Indiana, Texas, Idaho, Utah and Wyoming (50th) bring up the rear.
>
>   -The smallest pay gaps are in Arizona, California and Maryland; the largest in West Virginia, Louisiana and Wyoming.
>
>   -The smallest gaps in executive positions are in Alabama, Maine (We cannot "afford" to waste our women.), and Rhode Island; the largest in Idaho South Carolina and Utah.
>
>   -The educational attainment gap is smallest in Mississippi, Vermont and Louisiana; largest in Arizona, Idaho and Utah.
>
>   -The life expectancy at age 65 gap is smallest in Mississippi, Hawaii and North Dakota; largest in Montana, Idaho and Utah.

-Finally, the gap in political representation is smallest in New Hampshire, Hawaii and Washington; largest in Oklahoma, South Carolina and Wyoming.

Susan and I spent ten young years at the University of Maine (1969–79). We loved our time in Maine, but looked forward to the adventure of Connecticut and its access to NY City: the theater, restaurants, museums that Maine could not offer. However, we found a surprising thing about our time in Fairfield (1979–1984): Maine was more advanced, more progressive than Connecticut when it came to the status/roles of women. Why? The people of Connecticut were better educated, had higher incomes, access to more opportunities. It was a puzzlement.

So, like a moth drawn to the light, this philosopher developed a theory: Maine was too poor to treat its women as "pillar warmers"; they were needed as equal partners if ends were to meet. Connecticut at that time could still afford white gloves and canapés; Maine could not. To be sure, we humans often sadly get the world we choose/deserve. Many are inexplicably content with their daughters, wives, sisters earning less. I think, however, the issue is more nuanced than that. When her father died Susan's mother did not know how to write a check. Susan mastered that skill in high school. That makes it sound generational, but my mother, roughly Susan's mother's contemporary raised three sons alone after being a nurse, an airline stewardess and a Powers model. One would like to say that Title IX opened athletics to women, but Mom played on a state championship women's basketball team that played "half court" because of societal concern about "women's reproductive health." It might be argued that we have separate/unequal sports just so women will not embarrass men. Don't believe me? Try hitting a collegiate-level softball — or even seeing it pass for that matter.

A lot of this comes down not to generations — though we have clearly made progress on some dimensions of women's equality — and more to choice, both individual and societal. I suspect there is a certain culture, independence, autonomy, and freedom, in a state like Wyoming where women are paid less and are less likely to be in positions of political leadership that attracts people with, on average, fewer of those aspirations. While conversely, California…. But here, again, generalizations are dangerous.

We now have a remarkably qualified woman running for president: elected twice to the US Senate by the citizens of New York, Secretary of State from 2009 to 2011. Her would-be opponent, Donald Trump, who has never served this country in any capacity (but has served himself in every capacity), claims that were it not for the fact that she is a woman only five percent of the population would vote for her. Maybe this is not generational, maybe this is not regional, perhaps this is just good old-fashioned stupidity. So, why am I musing about these things about which I obviously know little? Some Trump supporters want to "shake it up" presumably by electing an untutored fool. I would suggest that perhaps the best way to "shake up" and perhaps also straighten out our broken country is by electing a woman.

* * *

Iraq War (October 2002)

The greatness of our country does not come simply from its natural resources, the industry of its people, its science and technology, or its military might. Underlying all that is a deep commitment to justice and fairness -- without which we would not be great, but simply large and powerful.

For over 80 years the United States has led the free world in a way that made its citizens proud and much of the world respectful. Occasionally our power has overwhelmed our sense of justice and fairness, but for the most part we have not abused that power and the position of privilege it has won us. Indeed, we have often entered conflicts not our own to defend less powerful states against aggression. That is precisely what we did when we stepped in to defend Kuwait against Iraq in 1990. Agree or disagree, oil or no oil, at least it was clear that Kuwait had been attacked and that we, together with our allies, responded in its defense.

When the United States first waged war against Iraq there were two checks whereby we could be sure that we were not abusing our power. First, in the words of the playground, "we didn't start it"; second, other states were prepared to join in the effort. Now we are proposing to "start it," to be the aggressor. That is to assume an awful responsibility not only for our youth, but for the often-noble traditions of this country. If our sons and daughters are to die in this cause, show us all, clearly and unambiguously why. Show us that other nations seek our help -- not by vote-trading, but honest requests from independent nations.

Our challenge is not Iraq, or even Osama bin Laden, it is living up to our ideals in spite of our perceived "injuries." As university presidents and chancellors, we have been entrusted with the growth and development of our nation's most precious asset, its youth. We teach them to temper their desires with concern for others and to make the case for their beliefs. We owe them nothing less.

We teach them the importance of reason and evidence. They deserve that evidence from us. Some battles are worth our youth. How is this one? Some battles are the price of freedom. How is this one? Some battles are nobly fought by honorable men and women. How can this one be? There is no urgency here. It is, and ought to be, very difficult to make a case for unilateral attack. Might did not make right when Saddam Hussein invaded Kuwait. Why does it now make right when we invade Iraq?

Why does this cruel dictator, among many, need to be replaced? And how is it our obligation to do so? Just because we can does not mean we should. Why are his weapons of mass destruction different from those of other rogue states that also threaten their neighbors? Show us that it is not about the oil. Show us that it is right, that it is just, that it is worthy of their young lives and of this proud nation.

Several generations of Americans have benefited not just from the military sacrifices of our fathers and mothers in WWII, but from the honor, integrity and selflessness with which they fought. Will future Americans enjoy similar respect because of this war? Or are we squandering not only the lives of these students, but our national honor and respect?

* * *

Political Views (September 2017)

My brother John is a proud conservative, a Trump supporter. A month or so ago he wrote a summary of his political philosophy and asked that I do the same. It is an interesting exercise. I recommend it. What follows is my response to John....

As per your request, a statement of my political views. I will not call it a philosophy since that word connotes more than a collection of opinions.

I am a liberal. I believe in the perfectibility of the human condition and in its progress over time. I do not believe in original sin, either human or political.

I believe our country is still a work in progress and that its present citizens are capable of making that progress just as well as previous generations.

I believe that the Constitution and our Declaration of Independence are works of genius that have served us well. I am not, however, a "strict constructionist." Times change, issues evolve; we must be prepared to address such matters as best we can — just as our predecessors were. Madison, Jefferson, Adams, *et. al.*, did not have the luxury of asking, "What would Madison, Jefferson, Adams do?"

I believe that we are capable of governing ourselves via the blueprint the Constitution provides. In doing so, we have won a civil war, freed the slaves, won the vote for women, beat back tyranny in two world wars, fought our way out of a depression, improved civil rights for minorities, (Southern democrats dragged their feet on that one, but LBJ got it done with Republican help.), cleaned up the environment, (Nixon had a hand in that.), though there is still much work to be done. I believe in government regulation as expressed in (among others) EPA, EEOC, FDA, HHS, OSHA,

USDA, FCC, etc... In short, I believe government is a force for good more than for ill.

I favor background checks for those purchasing weapons (I do not fear that our government will confiscate our guns in the middle of the night.) I do not believe Americans ought to have civilian access to military style weapons and ammunition such as "cop killer" bullets.

I believe that we have a moral obligation to care for those less fortunate in our society — not just an individual obligation, but also a civic one.

I believe that economic inequality is a major threat to our nation. I believe in the rectitude and efficacy of a minimum wage. I believe in a graduated income tax.

I believe in and trust the human intellect. I believe in the work of our scientific community and in its progress via falsification: evolution, vaccines, high-speed communications, computers, space flight, etc. I believe that global warming is a fact and that it is caused by human activity.

I believe that our greatest enemy is internal, not Russia or North Korea. That China is a worthy economic rival and not a military threat at this time. Withdrawing from the Trans Pacific Partnership is a HUGE gift to China.

I am in favor of free trade, but with the codicil that we take care of displaced workers.

I believe in and support the sadly flawed United Nations.

I believe that as human beings we have a critical interest in passing on our knowledge/culture/wisdom to future generations, and consequently that schools and universities are essential. Teachers deserve our support.

I am happy to pay my taxes in exchange for living in this country/state/community and benefiting from its services. I believe that we are underfunding our society; that our taxes are too low. Our unwillingness to invest in society and in one another is undermining our quality of life and our viability as a society.

I tend to be socially liberal — pro-gay, pro-women's rights, pro-environment, pro-choice, etc... I believe that immigrants are a strength of this country and that they contribute more to it then they take from it. I believe that black lives matter. I favor gay marriage.

On the other hand, I am fiscally moderate. I favor a balanced budget and would achieve it via higher taxes and reductions in defense expenditures. I would raise taxes to fully fund Social Security and Medicare.

I do not believe there is a serious issue of voter fraud or that denying the vote to 10,000 citizens to frustrate a single offender (when laws against voter fraud are already on the books) is reasonable or good for our democracy.

I believe gerrymandering is bad for our democracy whichever party does it.

I believe that wars must sometimes be fought, but that they should be declared wars, consequent to a vote of the Congress, which constitutional responsibility Congress has abdicated for most of my adult life. Moreover, those wars should be explicitly funded by Congress. If it is worth sending our youth into battle, it is worth the rest of us paying for it. Moreover, wars should be transparent, based on legitimate information, not like LBJ's Vietnam or Bush's Iraq.

I do not believe, "My country right or wrong." It is the opposite of patriotism.

I do not believe that money is speech ("Citizens United") or that corporations are people.

I believe that Congress should not exempt itself from the laws it passes.

The views expressed above are more generally supported by the Democratic Party, hence I am a life-long Democrat.

It is a source of embarrassment/amusement/satisfaction to me that many of my friends are Republicans.

*　*　*

July 4th (2014)

Susan and I are sitting on the second-floor deck of the garage apartment. We are here in part to get out of the way of the woman who is cleaning our house. It is a lovely Maine morning as we await the remnants of Hurricane Arthur, due this evening. The air is unusually heavy with humidity (better to carry the smell of close-by pine trees), but still comfortably cool. We are sipping tea — Susan's iced, mine just warmed in the apartment microwave. We are talking, and sipping, and smelling and most of all enjoying the view across the unruffled Bay.

The Wisteria I planted about five years ago has made its way (as I hoped it would) up the supporting posts and now twines among the balusters of our weathered railing. It is in perfect wedgwood bloom. Yesterday it would have been not quite full; tomorrow it will be ever so slightly past its prime. An occasional yellow swallowtail butterfly samples its nectar. [Digression: Wisteria hail from China and Japan. You can almost sense that in their beauty.

It is said that Japanese Wisteria twine clockwise and Chinese counter-clockwise. If so, ours hails from the Land of the Rising Sun.]

Susan's and my conversation, easy and comfortable, perhaps a sign of having recently celebrated our 49th wedding anniversary, ranges from our kids' impending visits, to the pleasing progress of our grandsons. We gossip about neighbors, approve of a present project of Frenchman Bay Conservancy, disapprove of our embarrassing Tea Party governor. Our conversation has no particular purpose or goal except the mutual pleasure it brings us. There are long quiet pauses, again made comfortable by time spent together. Sometimes it is nice to just **BE** and sip your tea.

And then, far out over the Bay we see it coming, heading straight for us, unmistakable — a Bald Eagle. It is still a quarter mile away, but no other bird has its broad shoulders and strong/deliberate wing beat. Our elevated perch has raised us enough that the Eagle is flying toward us at eye level. Now 300 yards, its white head plainly visible. Now 200 yards, the huge yellow beak can be seen. Now 100 yards. Still coming straight toward us. We are unconsciously holding our breath. At fifty yards it alters course ever so slightly (Does it see us?), flares its wings, drops its huge, feathered legs, and gracefully stalls onto the top of a thirty-foot Fir tree, an (admittedly long) stone's throw away.

There is a slight breeze from the south. Eagles tend to perch into the breeze, so its back is now to us. But its magnificent head is turned to the right, looking out on the Bay.

As it happens, I have the camera downstairs in my workshop. I fetch it and return upstairs hoping the Eagle has not flown away. It has not. Indeed, it stays for five or ten minutes until mobbed by crows and driven off. Why do crows mob Eagles, Ospreys, Owls, and large Hawks? Why do the larger birds not turn on their tormentors?

Cognoscenti of the Point, who of course include us, know that there's an Eagles' nest by the McKernan's house, perhaps 3/4 of a mile away. There are two chicks. This Eagle is probably one of that adult pair, though it is carrying no food back to the nest. Perhaps it is still searching? Perhaps it is taking a break and letting its spouse handle the kids for awhile. In any event, it has lingered and has made our Fourth.

Later, in the gathering storm, I will climb down "Susan's stairs" to our gravel beach and, following John Adams' instructions in a letter to Abigail, set off a token display of fireworks. Adams thought that our independence: *"...ought to be solemnized with Pomp and Parade, with Shews [Shows], Games, Sports, guns, Bells, Bonfires and Illuminations from one End of this Continent to the other from this Time forward forever more."*

"Illuminations" are my commemoration of choice. I like to think that my pitiful little rockets anchor the eastern end of Adam's continent. Finally, when Susan has gone to bed, I will indulge my favorite Fourth of July tradition: watching the musical "1776" which always makes me cry. Patriotism is a strange thing. A conservative friend has just shared with me a Facebook post in which he writes: "Happy Fourth of July. We are truly blessed to be part of the greatest Country on earth. We need to forget about all the liberals who are not proud to be Americans..."

I, of course, am one of those liberals he laments. An up-to-date ACLU card is tucked proudly in my wallet; I voted for, and continue to support, Obama, though I wish he would/could do more. I support immigration reform, gay rights, health care, a woman's right to choose, foreign aid, more investment in our schools, the whole nine yards. Indeed, I like higher taxes and marvel at people of means who say they love this country but do not want to pay to support it. True, as my friend rightly points out, I am occasionally embarrassed to be an American as when we launch a "preventive" attack against Iraq on trumped up charges. Or when we put our elections up for sale. Or when our dysfunctional Congress cannot conduct the nation's business. When we make it harder to vote. Or when we blithely pollute this beautiful land we claim to love.

But I am proud nonetheless to be part of a nation that has come so far, that cares about racial and gender equality, that respects religious diversity, that so generously sacrificed lives and treasure in World War II so Europe and Asia could survive. A nation that could send a man to the Moon, that could cure Polio and work to eradicate it everywhere. I am proud to be part of a nation that still attracts the best and brightest from around the world to its universities. I am proud of our veterans who fought in Vietnam, a war I avoided. And particularly proud of this generation of Iraq/Afghanistan veterans who have sacrificed so much for a nation that cannot even seem to provide them decent medical care let alone jobs.

I like to joke about being embarrassed that so many of my friends are Republicans. As it happens, much of my life has been spent with people of means who care about and support education. Whether for reasons of workforce development or human development, or just simple thanks- giving, they have been generous. Some are very conservative, supporters not only of education but of Republican politics. And yet we are good and mutually appreciative friends. Political disagreements enrich rather than diminish our conversations; they provide occasions for us each to grow and to broaden our perspectives. We often find ourselves acknowledging the cogency of one another's counter-arguments, even though they rarely change our minds.

Unfortunately, Adams was right when he predicted that "PARTY" might well prove to be our undoing: *"There is nothing which I dread so much as a division of the republic into two great parties, each arranged under its leader, and concerting measures in opposition to each other. This, in my humble apprehension, is to be dreaded as the greatest political evil under our Constitution."* So, we each celebrate this country and the Fourth in our own way. Long may our Eagle soar toward progress and improvement of the human condition for all.

* * *

Norway (August 2017)

Face it: we have transformed the United States into a second, if not third-world country. I can live with that; after all, someone has to play Avis to the world's Hertz. What I cannot stomach is that this transformation took place on our watch; we chose to be second-class. Newt and his ilk have had their way; they have "starved the Beast" –perhaps not recognizing that the "Beast" is us.

Now our bridges are unsafe, our roads are decaying, public transportation is a disgrace, schools are failing and we asked that it be so. Why? So, we could reduce the size of the federal government to the point that, to quote Grover Norquist, it was "small enough to drown in a bathtub." Except, of course, for defense; we can never have enough guns and war machines. Why reduce the size of our federal government? So, we can have more individual freedom — freedom to discriminate, freedom to adulterate our foods, freedom to once again plunge our economy into bankruptcy, freedom to pollute the environment, etc...

Sometimes it is explained that the federal government cannot spend our money as wisely as we do. In our superior wisdom we choose to purchase cigarettes, Botox, Doritos, Hummers, Mac-mansions, etc. All our elected representatives would do is take that money and blow it on bridges, roads, education, healthcare.... I am writing this rant from Trondheim, Norway — a pretty normal Norwegian town of 187,000 residents, third largest in Norway, nestled just 217 miles from the Arctic Circle, latitude @ 64 degrees, north. Norway is slightly larger than New Mexico with a population of 5.2M. The USA has a population of 316.67M.

The internet tells me that: If Norway were your home instead of The United States you would...

- be 50.68% less likely to be unemployed
- have 26.99% more free time
- use 92.74% more electricity
- be 89.26% less likely to be in prison
- experience 44.44% less of a class divide
- be 76.32% less likely to be murdered
- be 59.81% less likely to die in infancy
- live 2.04 years longer
- consume 16.07% less oil
- make 4.92% more money
- be 83.33% less likely to have HIV/AIDS
- spend 1.8% more money on health care
- have 9.91% fewer babies

We have the "freedom" to die in infancy, to waste away in prison, to be unemployed, to be murdered and to live shorter lives. Not being rugged individualists, Norwegians lack those freedoms. (For the record, it should be noted that Norwegians are far more rugged and self-sufficient than we.) Part of what is galling me about our society's short-sighted stinginess with itself is that people who claim to love our country are the very same ones who want most to "starve the Beast." How can one claim to love a country and yet refuse to support it? Perhaps they think that our country is its economy and not its people. And, of course, historically they do a terrible job with our economy; think depression and the recent great recession. Norwegians love their country and are not afraid to express that love by supporting it with their taxes. The difference between our two nations is well-expressed in our differing tax rates. It is hard to compare, but the "Nation Master" internet site suggests that the average tax rate in Norway is 51.27% while ours, at 15.91%, is approximately a third of that.

From another internet site: "In Norway the average gross annual wage was ...$63,336 and the take-home pay $45,095. .... In the USA in 2014, the gross annual wage was $50,075 and the take-home pay $37,637. The tax wedge, which is the difference between the total labor costs to the employer and the net take-home pay for the employee also was higher: 37.0% in Norway compared to 31.5% in the USA. In short, employees earn more, take home more, and cost their employers more in Norway than in the USA." All this means that Norway can afford to take care of its citizens, who in turn take care of her. We do not care for our country and therefore it cannot care for us. In Norway roads are well-paved, trains run on time — (not our "give-or-take twenty minutes," but rather give-or-take twenty seconds). Health care is provided. A computerized system monitors the frequency of visits to the doctor — you make a small co-payment and are allowed one visit a month with additional appointments being made at your expense.

There is a centralized system of pharmacies — all linked to a national computer system. Our Norwegian host can go to any pharmacy in the country, inquire if there are any refills remaining on his prescription and if there are, have his prescription filled. And, incredibly, there are no death panels. As noted above Norwegian longevity is two years greater than our own. Public university education is free in Norway. Norway has a budget of $286B, about a tenth of our $2.45T. It has a budget surplus of 14% of GDP, compared to our deficit of -6.8% GDP. Its GDP per capita is twice ours. All-in-all Norway seems to be a place/society that works: it is literate, humane, clean, efficient and happy. "Happy?" you ask? Yes, happy. There is an International Index of Happiness established in 2011 by the United Nations. We rugged individualists in the US rank 14th; the socialistic Norwegians rank 1st.

From Wikipedia: The 2017 report features the happiness score averaged over the years 2014–2016. For that timespan, Norway is the overall happiest country in the world, even though oil prices have dropped. Close behind are Denmark, Iceland and Switzerland in a tight pack. Is it possible that John Wayne led us into a wilderness? Part of Norway's happiness derives from its socialist tradition. When picking cloudberries in the remote mountains of Norway, our host, Inger, remarked that picking cloudberries was a perfect metaphor for social democracy in Norway. The cloudberries ripen slowly, over a period of several weeks. No one gets them all. No matter how rapacious a picker may be, there will be some left over to ripen for tomorrow's gatherer.

In another conversation Inger noted that Norwegians do not aspire to be different from one another. They are happy to be similar — and similarly happy. Houses, cars, wardrobes do not need to be bigger than those of their neighbors.

One of the many blessings of travel is that it provides a vantage point from which to see ourselves. When abroad one learns not only about other cultures, but about one's own. For better or worse, I am an American. Occupying a position of comfort and privilege, I have no wish to emigrate to Norway. But I am not so blind that I cannot see the advantages of their system and the short-comings of our own. If I were asked to re-invent the world it would look much more like Norway than like the barely recognizable United States.

* * *

Save Our Bay (February)

Poverty sucks! It literally diminishes our ability to be ourselves, to do the right thing. It compromises opportunities for education; for a healthy diet; for medical care; for employment; even for longevity. This should come as no surprise to us Mainers. At $55,602 our beloved State of Maine ranks 36th in per capita income. One of the consequences of our relative poverty is that we are more easily taken advantage of, more easily exploited.

Over 40 years ago, when I was an assistant professor of philosophy at the University of Maine, a student of mine asked if I would join a Master's committee to examine his thesis in Agricultural Economics. What harm could a philosopher do? As is so often the case in life, my intent to be helpful to someone else turned into an educational opportunity for myself. The student had written a full-of-insights thesis comparing Maine's economy with that of a third-world nation. Ours is largely an exploitive economy; an economy that extracts raw resources. We provide very little, job-producing "value added." Instead, that potential is shipped elsewhere while we are left with depleted forests and seas. The latest figures show that Maine ranks 49th among the states in value-added per worker, trailing the U.S. average by 24%.

Why would we let this happen? Because we are poor and desperate for any jobs we can get. Poverty forces us to take the low-percentage, bird-in-hand rather than bide our time for better opportunities. While wealthier states can afford to resist the temptation of cheap exploitive jobs, we are consistently suckered into them. Why despoil the forests of Massachusetts or Connecticut if we can trash Maine instead?

It is not just that we allow ourselves to be exploited by other states; foreign countries are getting in on the trashing of Maine. A case in point: Norway ranks third internationally with a per capita income of $82,500, 48% higher than Maine's. Its wealth lets it take better care of its citizens, free medical care, free higher education, paid parental leave, etc., which, in a "virtuous circle," produces more wealth. Norway's wealth also allows its citizens to take better care of their environment, and hence reap long-term benefits.

This explains how it is that a Norwegian business seeks to export its pollution to Maine in the form of an ocean-based, industrial-scale fish farm at the heart of our Frenchman Bay. Norway regulates fish farms far more rigorously than we do. Perhaps that is because it values its beautiful coastline more than we value ours. A more likely explanation is our poverty and the lack of regulation it spawns. This Norwegian company proposes to exploit our clean, clear waters and Maine's more lenient regulations. In Norway a fish farm is allowed to produce up to 3–5,000 pounds of fish per year; in Maine we have no such limitation. The 100-acre, floating factory, complete with a network of floating docks and two large barges moored near its pens, that these Norwegian investors propose will produce up to 66,000,000 pounds of fish per year. Is that a lot? Yes. It would be the equivalent of 13,200 of the maximum-sized fish farms allowed by Norwegian regulations. No wonder these Norwegian investors want to take advantage of us.

All those years ago, when my student argued for a "value-added" economy I thought to myself: Maine does have a value-added economy. It is tourism, where most of the jobs stay in state, where people come here, rather than sucking resources out. Why do they come? Primarily to enjoy our clean, beautiful environment. Over two million people come to visit Acadia National Park (on whose doorstep these Norwegian investors propose to anchor this atrocity) every year. This Norwegian project not only exploits our poverty, it damages our most valuable resources, both economically and aesthetically.

Some pleasures are open to us all regardless of income: for example, enjoying the view of Frenchman Bay from the top of Cadillac Mountain. Close your eyes; imagine that view you know so well: beautiful islands floating in a pristine Bay. Now imagine looking out from the top of Cadillac to see 100 acres of fish pens. To put that in perspective Bald Porcupine Island which sits so beautifully in Frenchman Bay is 32 acres; Burnt Porcupine Island is 40 acres; Sheep Porcupine is 22. Add them up: together they are less than the 100 acres this Norwegian fish farm envisions claiming for itself.

I began this essay with the cliché, "Poverty sucks." I did not, however, say what it sucks. Poverty sucks human and natural potential. It condemns us to be less than we can be; to compromise our future; to be timid in our defense of our self and of Maine; to grasp at the always false promises of hundreds of new jobs, while abandoning the actual hundreds of lobstermen, clammers, wormers, scallopers, etc, who depend on Frenchman Bay for their subsistence — not to mention the thousands of hoteliers, restaurateurs, guides who depend on Acadia National Park. Now our poverty even threatens to suck away that beautiful view of an unsullied Frenchman Bay.

Poverty wears various faces. There is a proud poverty that works hard and waits for a break. There is an ugly poverty that tries to get mine at the expense of others. But then there is a stupid poverty that sells itself and its future to the lowest bidder. We might be poor, but we do not have to be stupid.

* * *

Memories (June 2021)

"Hi, Grandpa. What ya doin'?"

"Just sitting here on the deck looking out at the Bay."

"What ya lookin at?"

"Memories."

"Grandpa, you can't see memories."

"I can, Punkin. I look out and see the Bay the way it used to be."

"Hasn't the Bay always been this way?"

"No, when I was your age it was a different place altogether. I would sit here with my grandfather in Adirondack chairs he built and just soak up the Bay." The air was so clear you could almost taste it, none of the diesel smell we have now. Back in the 2020's you could see the bald top of Cadillac across the Bay, holding up the sky over Acadia National Park."

"Where, Grandpa?"

"There to the south, that hazy silhouette. In the early morning you could hear lobstermen talking to each other on their two-way radios. The Bay was full of lobster buoys, each one marking the end of a thick line that your eyes could follow deep into the clear water. At the end was a lobster trap, likely as not with a lobster in it, maybe two or three. My grandfather and I could look out and count 70 or 80 buoys all different colors, catching the early morning sun over a calm Bay. What do you see now?"

"I count ... eleven."

"And birds! Back then the Bay had about 20 pairs of nesting eagles; osprey hunted, Eider ducks spent their winters with us. When I was young it was unusual not to see at least one eagle every day. When was the last time you saw an eagle or heard it scream, Punkin?"

"I'm not sure I've ever seen one, Grandpa."

"They've mostly passed us by; moved up the coast to the other side of Gouldsboro. I used to sit out here at night with my grandfather and marvel at the Milky Way. You can't see it anymore. The diesel fumes and the light pollution have obscured it. Hell, you can't even see the Big Dipper. It used to pour its blessings onto our cabin; used to feel like you could reach out and touch it."

"What's the Big Dipper, grandpa?"

"It's a group of seven bright stars shaped like a dipper."

"It's gone?"

"No, even we can't extinguish the stars. They're there, it's just that we can no longer see them. I remember the quiet of those nights, the loudest quiet I ever heard. It shut me up, I'll tell you that. I would listen, until it got so cold that I had to go inside and get ready for bed. In the summer over two million people used to come from across the country — no, from around the world — to see this Bay. Believe it or not, there were traffic jams in Ellsworth."

"Was that a good thing, Grandpa?"

"Well, it was a bit of an inconvenience in the summer, but it meant a lot of good jobs in hotels and restaurants and shops throughout the area. Not many people around here who wouldn't like to see those traffic jams again."

"Why did it change?"

"Because my generation cared more about its own short-term gains than about you and your children. We cared more about money than about the land. We were short-sighted and greedy. You've been studying Native Americans in school: did they teach you that the Haudenosaunee felt responsible for preserving the sustainability of their world for seven generations?"

"Seven generations. What would that mean, Grandpa?"

"Let's count starting with my grandfather, the one I used to sit with on this very spot and watch the Bay: he would be your great, great grandfather; then my father, your great grandfather; then me; then your dad; then you; then your children and finally your grandchildren."

"That's a lot!"

"Yes, it is. We have failed the test of the Haudenosaunee; we weren't able to preserve this once-beautiful Bay for you and your children. We owe you and all your classmates at Sullivan's Mountain View School an apology. We took that old Bay away from you. Sold it, really, for a handful of magic beans."

"Magic Beans? Like the story."

"Yes, instead of a cow, we traded our air, and water, and the natural beauty of this Bay for a pocket full of empty promises. And it's not as if we didn't know. We used to have urchins in the Bay, until we over-fished them. When they left the starfish left as well. There used to be schools of mackerel swimming within a stone's-throw of this shore, but we poisoned the water and fished them to extinction. Same with the scallops. They went the way of the ocean cod and with them another part of the life I had hoped to pass on to you".

"Grandpa, what can we do to get it back?"

"I wish there were a way, Punkin, but once it's gone none of us can bring it back. You remember from Sunday School the story of the Garden of Eden? What they leave out is that you never recognize Paradise until it's gone."

* * *

A Guest Essay By My Son, Matt (August, 2021)

Dear America-

Please knock it off about Afghanistan. Say thanks to the women and men who served. Acknowledge the sadness of the situation and do not belittle yourself and your country in recriminations.

Twenty years ago, America struck a blow against Al-Qaeda and denied a safe base of operations to the Taliban. Then we stuck around and tried to help. During these past 20 years, we earnestly attempted to advance the nation insofar as we could figure out how to do so and now we have moved on. It is not an unwise decision so much as it is a sad decision. Please, America, be brave enough to acknowledge the sadness rather than projecting blame. Your infighting is disrespectful to all who have served from our nation, all who partnered with us in our assistance across the world, and all who suffer now on the ground.

I worked in Afghanistan for seven years. I privatized a poultry farm, promoted agricultural lending, and ran a large agricultural assistance program in the provinces of Kandahar, Helmand, Uruzgan, and Zabul. Through the generosity of the American taxpayer and under the protection of the greatest military on earth, I helped teach people in Afghanistan new agricultural techniques. I played a part in advancing the infrastructure for veterinary care, agricultural credit, and sound agricultural policy. I worked shoulder to shoulder with people from 42 other countries to improve a place whose previous leadership promoted regressive social policies and harbored one of the greatest single enemies of the American people in the past century.

What we need to do now is to say how grateful we are to the women and men who stepped into harm's way, left their lives and comforts behind them, their communities and their loved ones, and ventured to a strange land with the ambition of limiting bloodshed and doing some good for a country in need.

"Some" good is all I was able to do in my last 20 years. What about you? I had some career highs but my partner and I also broke up. War-zones are not good for relationships. One of my projects was cancelled when USAID, the US governmental agency that oversaw the bulk of our civilian engagement programs in Afghanistan, wanted to pursue a different strategy. Letting go 300 staff is a feeling of failure I would not wish on anyone. None of that diminishes the following truth in my life nor should it in yours: The sacrifices of the American people and the ambition of America to engage a far-off land and to improve that land as we could imagine improvement, is at the heart of what is admirable, and honorable, about America. If we must fail, let us fail in the attempt to aid and advance a people, rather than failing to live our values or to engage with the world boldly.

The anger you are feeling is the foreground of sadness. It is sad that a nation on the other side of the world where we spilled blood and worked alongside 42 contributing nations to build a better country was not ultimately a place we well understood how to help, where we could well agree on how to help, or where all of our efforts were fabulous successes. The reasons for this are not malevolent. Across our great country we often can't comprehend people of different political affiliations and yet the optimism that is definitional to American culture allowed us to hope for a ready empathy with people whose traditions are not our own. America, the land of innovation, expected to achieve a consonant world view with Afghanistan, a land with one foot still planted firmly in a time separate from the trappings of modernity and modernity's attendant beliefs in women's rights, inclusion, diversity, and non-violence.

More than 20 million Afghans out of a population of 35 million were born in these last 20 years and exposed to values that we cherish and believe are essential to the modern world. We cannot go back and redo our participation in Afghanistan now, but we can be proud of what we have done.

We live in a world where threats loom and that is scary but we are a people capable of combating those threats, of protecting our values, and even of calling-it-a-day when our outcomes have been imperfect and it serves us to do so. Say thanks to those near you who have served and be proud of your country for its attempts as well as its outcomes.

4. CHASING SOPHIA

People sometimes wrongly associate "philosophy" with wisdom. In fact, if we are wise at all it is in knowing the limits of our knowledge. "Philo-sophia" means the love of wisdom; not its possession.

Philosophic Essay (October 2015)

Think about the principles of being that underlie our universe — the ultimate values that support and sustain us. Big assignment, but give it a try. Take a moment and think about what matters most. Upon what rocks is reality based? You might offer atoms, or quarks; perhaps space and time, or mathematics. Maybe God?

We don't ask such questions much now, but there was a not-so-remote time in human history when this question captured our attention. It was only 115 generations ago that Plato wrestled with this quandary. His predecessors had seen ultimate principles in things such as Earth, Air, Fire and Water. But as Plato asked himself what was most fundamental he identified Truth as an ultimate principle. I bet you did not list that one. Equally strange to our metaphysic, he chose Goodness as the second (you probably didn't get that one either; I certainly would not have). But most strange and wonderful of all was Plato's third transcendental principle: Beauty. Think of that: a world built on Goodness, Truth and Beauty! Seems a bit far-fetched, even for Star Trek.

Beyond that, Plato saw each as an expression of the other and the three together as an expression of THE ONE. This is arguably the template from which early Christian Church Fathers like Ignatius of Antioch, Justin Martyr and ultimately Tertullian fashioned their doctrine of the Trinity. But that is another essay for another writer. Here I am concerned with the wonderful thought of a world, the ultimate principles of which are Goodness, Truth and Beauty. Extraordinary!

One of these transcendental pillars is, I think, especially noteworthy. When hearing that Plato listed Truth as an ultimate principle we can nod and say, "OK. That wouldn't have been my call, but...." And so, too, with Truth; one can imagine how a rational person might place truth in his/her "trinity." But Beauty. That one astonishes me. Not because it is wrong or implausible, but because it is so foreign to our contemporary thinking. Truth and goodness, maybe, but beauty??? Surely, none of us would have listed that. And yet, I think this may have been one of Plato's greatest insights.

What provokes this essay? I am in San Diego. When here, beyond the usual meetings with friends, the football or basketball games, I make a pilgrimage to the Lodge at Torrey Pines. This time I have done it twice in five days. Why? Because it is beautiful. Not for the food, which is good, not for the excellent service, but for the beauty. The rolling golf course (the roughs are now brown from the drought), the sea beyond, the Torrey Pines themselves simultaneously contorted and graceful, the Greene and Greene architecture. I come just to BE in the presence of beauty. It quiets me and, though I do not feel broken, it mends me nonetheless.

Can't afford the Lodge? You can BE in the presence of beauty by the ocean, watching a sunset, following the flight of birds, enjoying the graceful nod of flowers, driving in the mountains, etc... Beauty may be precious, but it is not rare — nor must it be expensive. If you are willing/able to look you can find it almost anywhere. Monday morning, I met an SDSU faculty friend for tea at a new Starbucks on campus, built where an old, outmoded lecture hall once stood. We picked up our beverages and walked out onto an open plaza with casual chairs and conversational areas under a high canopy. As a warm breeze ruffled our napkins we could see out to the northwest, perhaps 20 miles, all the way to La Jolla and the coast. It was beautiful, and it was free — and best of all, the students knew and appreciated that.

[Digression: which reminds me of one of my favorite memories of SUNY Oswego. When Susan and I would venture out for an evening walk on campus we would often make our way almost a mile along the shore to a bluff overlooking the lake. There, on clear/warm spring or fall evenings, students would gather to enjoy the lake and to watch the sun set. One "gift" of Toronto to our west, northwest is that it blows pollution into the evening sky turning it a brilliant red. In our eagerness for stupid lists, like the world's best beaches, this view is often included among the world's ten best sunsets. In any event, students will stand, or sit on the ground, or on the occasional bench, speaking in hushed tones, watching the sun set. When the rising horizon finally eclipses the sun, they will spontaneously stand and applaud — an expression of our innate appreciation of beauty and, perhaps, of hope for our world.]

If you can contrive to place yourself in the midst of beauty and allow yourself to really be there, you will find that it quiets, restores, soothes and heals your spirit. And this was the wisdom of Plato; he recognized that; saw that if you can fill your life with goodness and truth and beauty it will be a fuller, richer life. Beyond that, Plato understood Beauty to be more real than the ordinary stuff of our lives; that it somehow expresses THE GENUINE.

Some free-range beauty for your morning:

P.S. As Plato taught us: *"The contemplation of beauty causes the soul to grow wings."*

P.P.S. As you can see, the preceding essay was written in 2015, almost eight years ago. I am moved to add this note because I just found a similar thought in Barry Lopez's masterful book of essays entitled *Horizon*, (Vintage Books, 2019). In it he relates the Navajo concept of *ho 'zho'*: "a complex idea, it's often loosely translated into English as 'beauty,' but the word refers as well to a state of harmony that pervades the world, and to a general state that in English means 'to be in good health'" (143). A person not of good health is deemed to have deteriorated. She/he needs to be restored to her/his original state of equilibrium. "Restoring a person to a state of 'beauty' requires that the singer 'make it incumbent upon the universe' to recreate in the *patient* those conditions in the natural world that signify—for Navajo people— coherence and harmony. The singer's intention, roughly put, is to make the one sung over 'beautiful' again" (Lopez, p. 144).

* * *

Reflections on 75 (March 2017)

I recently received a thought/memory-provoking Christmas gift — a much-coveted "Cranbrook," sweatshirt, the prep school I attended, (Note, I did not say "from which I graduated."), in Bloomfield Hills, Michigan. I have looked for one in the campus store whenever I have been back to visit that beautiful campus, but with no luck. I live in a world of free sweatshirts. Why would I covet this one? Because it has Cranbrook's motto emblazoned on its chest: "Aim High."

I was actually enrolled in this place of learning due to the insight of my math and Latin teacher, Miss Rolfes, who somehow divined that my mediocre grades were due to the fact that I was not being properly "challenged"- a charitable diagnosis. So off went this highly impressionable/naive/socially inept young man to play with the sons (it was an all-male school at the time), of "Big Three" auto executives. What could possibly go wrong? There I was being indoctrinated into "Aim High" at a time when "aim" itself had not occurred to me, let alone a direction.

Many of my classmates intuitively understood that admonition to mean medicine or law or corporate leadership. Having missed the introductory lecture, I took it to mean philosophy. Why? Truth be told, simply because I enjoyed it and perhaps I had not read the clause in the fine print about poverty. These were, of course, the musings of youth; the presumption that "Aim High" referred to career and not to self.

What does "Aim High" look like now as I celebrate 75 trips around our sun. What would I take high to mean today after I have, as Agnes Gooch says, "lived?" There is Plato's classic sense of high as fully realizing the form or type. Hence "high" would lead us toward being most fully human. This is, of course, a crock, the ethic of the Penobscot Kennel Club and, more ominously, of Nazi Germany.

It was never quite clear to me what it meant to be human, let alone to be fully so. We each decide for ourselves what it means to be human and invent ourselves as we go along. We do not come with operating instructions, blue prints or directions. I still remember being in the locker room with the big kids after a soccer game when one of them asked another what he was doing that evening. "I have a date," he responded, "with Susie Pickering." His interrogator turned to me and said knowingly, "She is really good." Now, I ask you, what functionality did he have in mind?

Plato and his pupil Aristotle took being "fully human" to mean being guided by reason, convenient if you happen to be a philosopher, less so if you are a married man. In the Middle Ages aiming high meant reaching for union with God through devotion and selflessness. I could never quite get into that one. I did, however, like the Renaissance notion of full actualization of one's talents/abilities -- exemplified in Italy's Giovanni Pico della Mirandola, (1463–1494) who was a linguist, author of 900 theses that he offered any philosopher/cleric to come to Rome to debate, all expenses paid, and who, so it is said, could with his feet together leap over the head of any man.

After the Renaissance philosophers more or less got caught up in their own arguments and generally gave little thought to how best to be human. Topics like epistemology and linguistics moved to center stage. Sigh. But then "my guys," the existentialists, entered from stage left — led by Soren Kierkegaard and Friedrich Nietzsche. Theirs was a tradition focused on how to best be human, united by a belief that there is no pre-existent human essence and that we each have to build it for ourselves by way of our choices/actions. Of these, my favorite was/is Albert Camus the Algerian / French / journalist / resistance fighter. You might know him via *The Stranger* or *The Plague*, but you might have also been introduced to him through his *Myth of Sisyphus* which begins with the provocative claim that "The only serious question in life is whether to kill yourself or not."

What Camus is really asking is, "if you know the truth — that there is no purpose to human existence, that there is no center in which to anchor right or wrong, that our sun will flicker out in a few billion more years and that human life is full of heartache and disappointment — if you knew that 'going in' why would you chose to continue?" The important thing to understand about Camus is that his *Sisyphus* is dedicated to the proposition that you ought to resist suicide. We ought to have no illusions about the abyss across which we skate every day, and yet we ought to lace up.

Why? How? Not out of any illusion, not from any false hope, but out of, for lack of a better word, self-respect. It is possible to acknowledge the abyss and not be defeated by it, possible to know the truth and persevere nonetheless. For Camus, the real meaning of "Aim High" is not to reach toward an imaginary heaven, not to hope for divine approval, but to affirm yourself in their absence. In one of my favorite passages from *Resistance, Rebellion and Death,* Camus wrote to a German friend who shared his atheism:

> *You never believed in the meaning of this world, and you therefore deduced the idea that everything was equivalent and that evil could be defined according to one's wishes. You supposed that in the absence of any human or divine code the only values were those of the animal world — in other words, violence and cunning. Hence you concluded that man was negligible and that his soul could be killed, that in the maddest of histories the only pursuit for the individual was the adventure of power and his own morality, the realism of conquests. And, to tell the truth, I, believing I thought as you did, saw no valid argument to answer you except a fierce love of justice which, after all, seemed to me as unreasonable as the most sudden passion.*
>
> *Where lay the difference? Simply that you readily accepted despair and I never yielded to it. Simply that you saw the injustice of our condition to the point of being willing to add to it, whereas it seemed to me that man must exalt justice in order to fight against eternal injustice, create happiness in order to protest against the universe of unhappiness....*

Now, closer to the end of my journey than to its beginning, when I think about "Aim High" I do not think so much about career or about my philosophic tutors as about being a whole person; being a good husband, father, friend. Finding a little filament of life's struggle that I can tug on, that I can lift to a higher place or condition — something larger than myself to which I can devote my energies. As with so much else, the challenge is not external, but internal; not advancing along a career path or mastering arcane texts, but rather learning to live a fuller, more open life.

How? First through travel, through opening yourself up to people who are different from you, listening to their songs and eating their food. By finding someone with whom to share life's many pleasures/mysteries/challenges. By listening and asking questions. And by surrounding yourself with beauty, both natural and man-made. This does not require travel or wealth, but rather an openness to the blue of the sky, the green of a leaf fluttering against it, the song of a nearby bird. Just take off the glasses of self and look around. Also look inward. Find that voice that is uniquely your own, trust those deep instincts and your own native wisdom. Practice gratitude. Even in the worst of human life, there is cause for giving thanks. Keep learning. That is easy when you are young and learning is a way of life, when you are in school, when you are beginning a career, etc..., it is harder (but just as important) as you grow older. Read real books, not fluff. Stay engaged in the news. Care about your country, but not so much that you cannot see its faults and endeavor to improve it.

Finally, I would urge humility: the recognition that you may be wrong, that others may be right, that the world is complex with few if any simple truths. You and I do not have a privileged purchase on truth. Perhaps my treasured sweat shirt should more modestly read not "Aim High," but rather, "Aim Inward" — trusting Joseph Campbell's wise advice: *"The privilege of a life time is being who you are."*

* * *

Hallelujah

In the pages of philosophy, it is hard to find a stranger, more troubled soul than that of Soren Kierkegaard. Brilliant, inward, awkward, lyrical — misfit in time and place. He lived a life of financial comfort and of human distress. Kierkegaard was a Christian, but in a way most of us can hardly imagine. He took it seriously. His harsh, unforgiving Nordic god was a daily presence telling him, for instance, to leave Regina, his fourteen-year-old love, to launch quixotic jousts with the tabloids of his day, to be outwardly gregarious while inwardly solitary. There was not a day in which he was happy, or whole, or at peace in his twisted internal world. And yet, there is a passage in Kierkegaard's, *Point of View for My Work as an Author*, that was always inspired me, a passage in which he gives thanks for his painful, tormented life. Speaking of himself, he writes: *"... the author who historically died of a mortal disease, but poetically died of longing for eternity in order to do nothing else than uninterruptedly thank God."*

I love Kierkegaard, but I do not share his god. Unlike Kierkegaard I have lived a life of comfort — both internal and external. Unlike Kierkegaard, I like being me. Like Kierkegaard I feel the need to give thanks. But to whom? Or what? That is the atheist's dilemma. It is not divine comfort for which we long, or moral guidance; it is an ear to which we can raise a "Hallelujah." Just as a falling tree sounds in the unhearing forest, so too I must make my sound. Unlike Kierkegaard, I know that my thanks go unheard, but they must not go unsaid:

> *Hallelujah to the sun as it's peach-blue rays slide down the side of Cadillac and spill across our still-silent Bay.*
>
> *Hallelujah to the loon who waits for its warming rays.*
>
> *Hallelujah to the breeze as it quickens, to the cloud as it thickens.*
>
> *Hallelujah to crocus, the lily, the rose; to the redbud, the dogwood and wisteria.*
>
> *Hallelujah to the blue jay, to the junco, the phoebe and flicker.*

Hallelujah to the waves as they lap our shore, to the tide waxing and waning, to sea weed waving, to crabs skittering, to gulls bickering, to tide pools warming in the sun.

Hallelujah to the scent of pine needles in the rain, and seaweed on the rocks.

Hallelujah to work, to colleagues and friends, to fireside conversations.

Hallelujah to teachers, to craftsmen, to reachers.

Hallelujah to wine and good books.

Hallelujah to women, their insight and care; and a special Hallelujah to she who's been there to share in the journey. For all I shout Hallelujah in the silent forest. Though the call goes unheard, it would be ungrateful not to sound it.

* * *

Under the Surface (Spring 2015)

There is a rhythm to our Bay. Tides rise and fall, seasons come and go, the salt water flows from green to dark grey to sky blue. One of the rhythms, most apparent to sailors, is that of the winds. Typically, they are calm in the early morning; pick up with the rising/warming sun; become gusty in the heat of the afternoon and then settle down again in the evening as the sun fades and temperatures retreat. So, it is that I am usually greeted by a calm, sometimes glassy Bay in the early morning.

This morning, with the sun not yet up above the eastern trees, is typical. The Bay is so calm that brightening Cadillac Mountain is reflected on its pale blue surface. Small birds, like Pie-billed Grebes, or Guillemots are readily seen now but will be invisible when the surface is rippled in an hour or so. The Bay is so quiet that it seems almost asleep. No ripples, let alone waves reach our shore. Instead the Bay is calm, its breath gently rising and falling.

Having done my early morning Tai Chi, I am at breakfast looking out on our bird feeders. Still too early for the hummingbirds, but not for the Pine Siskin, Juncos, Purple Finches and Gold Finches, and the Bay beyond. Suddenly, abruptly the placid surface explodes about 200 yards off shore. Water is spraying in the air, large water-shrouded, forms are curving up into the air and back down again. What are they? I do not know — though this is not the first time I have witnessed such eruptions.

Could they be male seals battling for mates? Possible, but it is too late in the season for that — unless, of course, they are just adolescents pretending. Could it be a contest between porpoise and seal? Perhaps. The rounded shapes might fit either. Could it be predators having rounded up a small school of fish and having breakfast? I do not know. It is hard to focus the binoculars on them because they are above the surface so briefly: up for a second or two; down for 30; up again in another place. The battle, or feast, continues for about five minutes; and then, quiet. The surface returns to polished mirror. The ripples caused by the explosion roll out toward flatness. It is soon as if nothing had happened.

But, of course, something did happen, something that reminds us of how false the quiet is; that beneath the mirror, life and death struggles are going on. The world is not what it appears to be. With this surprisingly insistent early morning thought I am reminded of how surfaces lie. It has been cold and gray the last few days. My flats of Nicotiana and Snap Dragons, Salvia, and Petunia seem to have been in hibernation; no growth is apparent. But when I pop them out of their containers for planting I see that they have been busily at work growing roots. Up the road the Peterson, house sits quietly, undistinguishable from fifty similar houses scattered around the Point. But our weekly paper, the Ellsworth American, tells me that police were summoned for a "domestic dispute"; charges of abuse are to be filed. Once again, the surface lies.

If you want to understand our Bay you have to look beneath the surface to the drama unfolding there. If you want to understand our garden you have to look past the carefully arranged mulch to the roots, worms, and microbes laboring there. If you want to understand families.... I first came to recognize the duplicity of surfaces when I learned that our word "understand" is actually made up of two words: "under" and "stand"; to understand is to recognize what "stands under." Without that one lives only on the surface. A richer world lies beneath. If we look only at the surface we are likely to miss much that life has to offer.

As a junior faculty member our department chair asked me to attend monthly meetings of the faculty of the College of Arts and Sciences and to sit with him. Afterward, perhaps over a cup of coffee in his office he would patiently explain what was happening "beneath the surface." What the Chair of Political Science was actually trying to accomplish; why the chemists were resisting? We are surrounded by surfaces everywhere, but if we will look carefully, be patient, be inquisitive, the surfaces will dissolve and open onto worlds of wonder. This was the insight of the pre-Socratic philosopher, Heraclitus: the bow seems quiet and still, but beneath its curves hide forces in tension. And so it is, even on a quiet spring day in Maine.

* * *

Veterans (January 10, 2015)

I am here in San Antonio at the Student Veterans of America national conference with over 1200 student Veterans from campuses around our country. It is my fourth SVA conference and clearly the best one yet. HO-RAH!!!

Yesterday afternoon we heard from VA Secretary, Robert McDonald, former CEO of Proctor and Gamble — and a West Point grad, who is in the process on overcoming the inertia of one of the world's largest organizations. He spoke for 20 minutes about the change agenda of the VA and then took questions/comments for another 40 minutes from his constituents. Very impressive.

Last night Vice President Biden and his wife, Dr. Jill Biden, spoke. She was great; he was transcendent. Say what you will, that man can give a speech. I do not doubt that there are Republicans who could have given his remarks (about how important it is that veterans get their degrees so they can continue to serve our nation in positions of responsibility and influence), but as a life-long Democrat, he made me very proud. I have now added a Vice President of the United States "Commander's coin" to my collection — something is going to have to leave the display case.

This morning, perhaps best of all, we were addressed by Kyle Carpenter, one of two living Metal of Honor recipients — a wonderful young man, now a student at the University of South Carolina and an SVA member — who passed his Congressional Metal around the audience because he believed that each of those Veterans deserved it as much as he. He had jumped on a live grenade to save his buddies, was declared dead, endured painful years of rehab, etc... You get the idea: a great conference full of awesome, inspiring people.

I am now sitting in a huge ballroom, listening to a panel discuss Campus Climate. Since I know a bit about that I find my mind wandering. How did I get here? How did life bring me to this place, so different from where I started out?

It would be wrong to call myself a draft-dodger; I did not have that courage. Instead, I sought and obtained academic deferments to continue my studies, and continue, and continue. Fortunately, our nation recognized its need for well-educated philosophers. I hope you can intuit the blush on my face. I was, of course, and still am, opposed to the Vietnam war. I attended anti-war demonstrations as far back as Notre Dame. I was among the leaders of some demonstrations at the University of Maine. I was one of twelve who paid for an "Impeach Nixon" ad in the Bangor Daily News — well before the Cambodia invasion. Strangely, Nixon was not deterred.

Truth be told, there were not many Veterans at the University of Maine in those days — or at least not visibly present. Same was true for Fairfield, St. Cloud State and SUNY Oswego. It was not until San Diego that I actually began to interact with military, active and veteran. Susan and I were invited to aircraft carriers, I got to dive on a submarine, fired rounds at Camp Pendleton, flew in a C-17 Globemaster, visited Special Forces installations around the country, etc... Susan and I would stand on our balcony when we lived in Coronado and watch war ships return from deployment, their decks outlined with sailors dressed in Navy whites. But that was largely the "romance" of it all and, I am confident, not why I am here.

Not surprisingly, I met lots of Veterans at SDSU, among our alumni, and in the community at large. San Diego is, after all, a military town. Through those interactions I regularly met people (often quite young) of character and integrity. But, of course, Veterans and active military have no monopoly on that. I find myself once again turning to Kierkegaard to explain my appreciation of these veterans. I know some of you have heard me speak about this "melancholy Dane" before, but indulge me this context.

Kierkegaard saw the lowest level of human development as what he called the "aesthetic." These are people with no capacity to make a genuine choice, to select some one thing and forsake others. They are in effect adrift in life. They lack Lady Macbeth's "sticking point." K's symbol of the aesthetic is the unmarried man, whom he sees as unengaged in time precisely because he cannot choose and hence cannot develop a history. The Aesthetic man puts himself first, subsumes his whims to nothing beyond himself. No matter his age, he remains a child. K. Captures this stage of human development in Volume I of his two volume *Either/Or*. This first volume is literally named "Either," which K. intends to indicate the inability to choose. But beyond the aesthetic, in Volume II, lies the higher path of the "Ethical." This volume is titled "Or" to underline the ethical person's capacity for choice. She is capable of subsuming herself to higher principles/causes. K. calls these "universals" by which he means that one is willing to bind oneself to the rules (e.g. marriage), to something beyond herself. In his phrase, K's ethical person is capable of subsuming herself to the universal.

Kierkegaard's example of this stage on life's way (the title of another of his books), is the Married Man (we would now add, woman). The married man is capable of commitment, capable of subsuming himself to principle, capable of forgoing his individual pleasures for the universal principle of marriage. He can make and keep a promise. And because of that capacity to harness oneself to a principle/cause/universal, the ethical person is capable of choice and hence enters history.

In retrospect, as I sit among these Veterans, it is that capacity to take an oath, an oath with consequences for one's personal behavior, an oath that will sometimes be uncomfortable, that I admire. All these Veterans were volunteers, all raised their hands in time of war with near certainty that they would be placed in harm's way. I admire the integrity that enables such sacrifice. I like spending time with people who can take an oath.

To take an oath requires caring about something beyond yourself, requires integrity (without which one has no self), and requires self-sacrifice. Most of these Veterans were very young when they took that oath; doubtless some had no idea what it entailed, what it would require of them. But they stuck with it. They endured the boot camp of life. They subsumed themselves to a "universal." They obeyed the rules. And they came out the other side with a sense of integrity that is too often missing in our fellow human beings — especially those of their young age. The oath they swore took many to very nasty places, demanded of them nasty actions that most would have preferred not to do or see. But they literally put us above themselves, exposed themselves to danger and mayhem in our behalf.

To be sure, the military are not the only such people. I had the privilege of working with many people of integrity and self-sacrifice who fit K's standard of subsuming themselves to a universal. But now I sit here among these veterans and marvel at what these young people have been through in our name, at what they have sacrificed, at their capacity to take an oath. It pleases me to be with them.

* * *

An "Ingrown" Lecture (March 2002)

Today is my sixtieth birthday. The aloe plants by the pool are about to bloom; even now, at 6:00 a.m., the hummingbird feeders are busy; the scent of jasmine fills the air. And I am suffering from an ingrown lecture...

The lecture is not mine, but one which I have always loved. It is Nietzsche's story of Zarathustra who in the early morning came down from his mountaintop proclaiming the overman -- which is to say, proclaiming the rich possibilities of the human condition. Celebrating humankind's insatiable drive to grow and develop and create. "*Man is a rope between beast and overman.*" It is the forever-wondrous cry of youth: out with the old; make way for your betters. However, as he wanders in the valley Zarathustra begins to sober. He meets there what he calls, "the rabble"; hopeless, spiritless, down trodden beings incapable of growth or creativity, unable or unwilling to move the human drama forward. It is not unlike Susan's sadness when she would come home from teaching at Elkhart High School where fifteen-year olds would be putting in time, waiting until they turned sixteen and could legally drop out to perpetuate the cycle of poverty. Alas, the rabble soured Zarathustra's delight in the morning and poisoned his well of creativity. The existence of the rabble caused him to question the possibility of the overman.

But, wait, there is always hope. If the present is too discouraging, we can find our courage again in the hope of a better future. If there is no joy for us here and now, perhaps we can rekindle it with images of a better future. Maybe this new grant and new curriculum will hold these students in class; perhaps their children will not drop out. And so, with a little help from the narcotic of hope, transporting us beyond and above the rabble to a better, more perfect place, life remains livable, the dream of the overman continues — if only as a dream.

And then Zarathustra encounters his greatest challenge, the snake that crawls down his throat and chokes off even the hope of future greatness. It is his recognition of the "Eternal Return," the sure and certain knowledge that a finite world, set adrift in infinite time, is condemned to forever repeat itself. All progress is an illusion. The optimism of youth will always be accompanied by arrogance and ignorance, there will always be a system office, the budget will never be big enough, sports fans will always believe their teams are inadequately supported, the library will never have enough books. Despair. Nausea. All is lost.

And then the most wonderful thing happens. Rather than being defeated by the hopelessness of the Eternal Return, Zarathustra embraces it instead. Beyond all logic, in an act of heroic folly he accepts life: accepts the rabble, the system office, the limited budgets, the arrogance of youth, the sports fans -- accepts it all and concludes with a wonderfully life-affirming: "*Was that life? Well then, once more.*" Which is to say, if you will pardon this poor philosopher's gloss on Nietzsche's great text, he becomes a higher man, not by fantasizing about a distant paradise, but by hugging to himself this world with all its joy and sadness, its greatness and its imperfection. Only then can life -- this wonderful, fleeting gift — be savored in all its fullness and richness.

And so, as I head out on my sixty-first circuit, I want you all to know that I feel inexplicably fortunate to have been able to walk this valley with Susan, to have two fine sons, to be an educator, and to have found such good, bright, funny, and inspiring family and friends along the way. I would do it all again, every minute, every step and misstep, every success and failure, just to be with you again.

* * *

Home (April 2016)

It feels good to be home. But why? We all know the feeling of familiarity and comfort that welcomes us home. But the deep pleasure of homecoming is more than that. Not just escaping the hassle of being on the road: wrestling with luggage, reservations, maps and directions; more than the cliché of "sleeping in your own bed." I think the pleasure of coming home is about returning to a place that you have invented; a space that reflects yourself, even projects yourself.

Sartre believed that we are not pre-programmed with a given nature but that we have to invent ourselves though our actions. That is the basic meaning of his philosophic bumper sticker: *"Existence precedes Essence."* We are all literally "works in progress." That self-invention is not only a product of the actions we choose, but also of the things with which we surround ourselves. The clothes we wear, the cars we drive, the music we listen to, the art on our walls, the photos on the shelves — — — all reflect the self we are constructing.

Visit any freshman dorm and you will see this phenomenon at work in the posters chosen for the walls, the bed-linens/carpets, etc... When I was in graduate school I used to drink scotch. What kind? "Teacher's," of course. Your home and mine are stories we have created through time: mementos from travels, pictures that speak to, and of, us, the books on display, that banjo clock Susan gave me for my 50th birthday, the orientals from that shop in Turkey, the Japanese doll from Kazuo Inamori, the initialed box I built for Susan... Part of the pleasure of homecoming is coming back to the self you have worked so hard to create and express.

Indeed, it is a pleasure to read the history written on my walls. The friendships reflected in gifts given and proudly displayed; the house itself, built by a friend, the gardens tended over the seasons... Each tells a story: my story. One that I am still writing. It is a pleasure to return to that story, to review it, to contemplate how to extend it. To be sure, that story is not manifest to all. Indeed, now that Susan is gone I am the only one who knows it. When I am gone these things will just be things — some of which will be discarded without any idea of the significance they held for me: of their stories, of the "me" they expressed.

And so it should be. Sartre argued that because a human life is the record of its actions/choices, it cannot be known until it is complete, i.e. until one has died. When life is finished it may be known, summed, but not before. Conversely, while death fixes the person it frees the things. Meaning drops from their shoulders; they cease to be part of a life and become instead part of a garage sale. This sounds more morose than I intend it to be. We are all story tellers. We ourselves are our greatest story; our homes are part of that invention. This little house in which I am writing is snug and full of stories; I am one of those stories.

* * *

Love: A Triptych (February 2015)

Essay One: Innocence

Love is a relationship. We all know that. But what kind of relationship? What does it mean when we say we are, "in a relationship?" Indeed, when/how are we ever not in a relationship? We are always older than or younger than, to the left of, to the right of, taller than, shorter than, etc... What these and so many other relationships have in common is that neither pole of the relationship, neither party to it, is changed by it. Indeed, the stone "to the right of" is the very same stone when moved "to the left of." I am just as tall when I am "taller than" as I am when I am "shorter than."

If love is such...then it's not much. Somehow, when we respond to an inquiry by saying, "I am in a relationship," we intend something more than the non-transformative relationships cited above. But what? For starters, we mean to say, "I am not the person you take me to be. I am not free to be in a relationship because I am already in one." Unlike the non-transformational relationship of taller than, in which I can simultaneously be taller than this person and shorter than that one, when we say we are in a relationship we intend something singular, something exclusive.

Love is also temporal in the sense that it must take place in and over time. It is an ongoing relationship, one that lasts, perhaps not forever, but love is not a passing fling. Here, again, to say, "I am in a relationship," speaks not just to the moment, but to prior moments and to intended subsequent ones.

When Susan and I were first married, at Notre Dame and then at the University of Maine, it was a time of young couples making their own entertainment with cocktail parties — though if memory serves there were few cocktails, and certainly no cocktail dresses. We were more of a bottled beer and boxed wine crowed.

Inevitably, as the party would progress Susan and I would become separated. I could always tell where Susan was by her laugh. When friends asked Susan where I was she would answer, "Do you have a fireplace? If so, Steve is leaning against the mantel." And so I was, pre-beard, smoking my pipe, trying to look wise — and, perhaps, a smidgen above it all. While there, I would rehearse my name (just in case anyone ventured to introduce themselves) and think of philosophic bon-mots that I could fall back on if needed. My favorite was this one from Kierkegaard (that I can still recite from memory): *"The self is a relation which relates itself to its own self. Man is a synthesis of the infinite and the finite, of the temporal and the eternal, of freedom and necessity, in short, it is a synthesis. A synthesis is a relation between two factors. So regarded, man is not yet a self."* (from, *Sickness Unto Death*)

Is it any wonder that more people were gathered around Susan than around me!!! The point of my digression is to provide credit for a plagiarized thought. Substitute "Love" for Kierkegaard's "the self" and you get: *"Love is a relation which relates itself to its own self.... in short, love is a synthesis. A synthesis is a relation between two factors. So, regarded, the relationship is not yet love."* Love is the willing, even joyful suspension of oneself, the loosing of oneself in another. That is love; the rest is "taller than." To be "in love" is to be outside yourself. Love is not to be one person related to another, but to be transformed into a relationship that relates itself to itself. The relationship transforms the related. Not separate poles, but merging into a relationship. To be in love is to lose your self-consciousness, to (in a very fundamental way) become a child again. How? By regaining one's innocence. By escaping the prison of self-consciousness.

Essay Two: Armor

But, of course, love is not as simple as "loss of self," merging into a relationship without poles. Love would be meaningless were there no poles to be erased.

Before one can be in a relationship of love one must first be a person, an integral self. That is what is wrong with "puppy love." It does not lack in intensity. It lacks a grounding pole. The puppy lover is not yet a self and hence lacks the gravitas, the centeredness, the integrity to enter into a relationship. You cannot lose, cannot give up, cannot surrender, what you do not yet have. To be in love you must first be a whole, self-aware person. Which is to say, the lover must not be an innocent. What do I mean by that? To be innocent is, literally, to be not experienced or worldly, to be naïve. To be an adult is to no longer be naïve. It is to know the ways of the world. To know that there are good and bad people out there. The innocent is, a simple, guileless, inexperienced or unsophisticated person. The adult is a person of experience. He or she must live in the world, must know him or herself. And so, to be an adult is to erect defenses, to don one's armor.

A child is innocent in two ways: first, in the 15th century sense of being harmless, i.e. non-threatening; second in the 17th century sense of being as yet unharmed by the world, i.e. free of sin or guilt. If one is to enter into a relationship of love one must not be an innocent; one must, like "Auntie Mame's," Agnes Gooch, have lived. And by "lived" we mean not existed — the way a rock might — but to have been a self-aware participant in the world. I am tempted to say, "In the real world," — a world capable of threat. Another way to think of this is that the self must have developed a shell with which to withstand the onslaughts of the external world. To be a whole, self-aware person in the world is to wear a suit of armor. I do not mean that to sound paranoid, but rather to reflect the reality that with the loss of innocence comes an exposure. Is it any wonder that Genesis expresses this loss of innocence as an awareness of nakedness??? The reason that child-molestation is so repugnant is that, like exploitation of the insane, children are "shell-less," unsuspecting, defenseless.

Kierkegaard's problem, see essay one, was that our self-consciousness puts us at a distance from our self and thereby, more importantly for him, from God. Our problem is that loss of innocence, the growth of a "shell" separates us from ourselves — and from others, hence from love. So, herein lies the challenge of love. Both to be an adult and to suspend one's defenses. No defenses and love is not a significant relationship; with defenses it is an impossible one. To lose one's innocence is to become self-conscious, to enter the world and to don one's suit of amour. To fall in love is literally to be "disarmed," not in a Venus de Milo sort of way, but in one's exposed nakedness — which has nothing to do with nudity. Therein lies the courage of love.

Essay Three: Innocence Revisited

Now we come to the hard, have-your-cake-and-eat-it-too, part of love. To be in a relationship of love one must be a self, a whole, integral person. To be in love one must lose one's self, literally cede it to the other — but, of course she/he has had to cede her/his self as well. So, to whom it is that you lose yourself? Therein lies the paradox of love.

In another, religious, context Kierkegaard would say that you must lose yourself in order to gain it again. One is reminded of Matthew 18:3: '*Verily I say unto you, except ye ... become as little children, ye shall not enter the kingdom of heaven.*" Which is to say, unless you become innocent…. The very arms by which we, as adults, defend ourselves from the world separate us from K's god — and from one another. Which brings us back to where we started. Well, perhaps not quite. Each partner loses him/herself to the relationship, because, as noted above, if the relationship is still a synthesis, still a duality, then it is not love.

When I was young and horny, and just dipping my toe into the mystery that is woman (turns out that was the wrong appendage!), I plotted for just the right moment, the right circumstances. Like a bowerbird, I carefully arranged lighting, dripping candle in straw-coved chianti bottle; chose the right music, mostly Sinatra; presented a fancy-sounding, but not fancy-costing, foreign wine; plumped the pillows. AND…. Nothing! This was, of course, magical thinking. Trying to cast a spell with lights, sounds etc…

It was only later that I came to understand that the object of my machinations was herself an adult; that she was not innocent; that she was armed. She could see through my charade from the moment I opened the door. Gradually, I came to understand that she needed to "allow" this fiction to become real — needed to engage in, what Kierkegaard would have called, a willing suspension of dis-belief, a return to innocence. In terms of our earlier essays, she would have to set aside her armor. Any love, not just romantic love, is a willing but not willed suspension of disbelief; it involves becoming childlike, innocent, setting aside the armor of adulthood. Literally being disarmed. "Unless ye become as a child…"

How does that happen? How do we intuit with whom we can be defenseless? I do not know, but one thing is clear — it is not a rational process, not the conclusion of a syllogism. And at the same time, it is not, as I said above, willed — not voluntary. Of course, one can will an evening's pleasure, armament in place, but one cannot will love.

The French philosopher Blaise Pascal wrote a famous proof for the existence of God: Either God exists, or not. If you believe God exists and are wrong, you lose nothing; if you believe God exists and are right, you gain all. Conversely, if you believe God does not exist and are right you gain nothing; if you are wrong, you lose all. Clearly, the smart thing to do is to believe. BUT, you cannot choose to believe, cannot reason yourself to belief in God any more than a ten-year-old can choose to believe in Santa Claus because it might be the smart thing to do.

And so, it is with love: it is not voluntary. It can be learned; arranged marriages can work. But the love, if it ever arrives cannot be turned on like a switch. Rather, it is a process of turning off the switch of adulthood and recapturing our childhood innocence. Only when we can let down our defenses, only when we can lose ourselves in a relationship, are we strangely one again, not only with ourselves but with another. Therein lies the wonder of love.

Let's go back to Kierkegaard who tells us: *"The self is in sound health and free from despair only when, precisely by having been in despair. It is grounded transparently in God."* Our plagiarized version now reads: "The self is in sound health and free from duplicity only when, precisely by having been duplicitous, it is grounded transparently in love."

All of which is to say: we start life as innocent wholes; we are simply who/what we are. As we mature and become self-conscious we become separated from ourselves, and from one another. We are no longer innocent; armor is deployed. Were it not for this transition into adulthood, love would not be miraculous because there would be no gap to be bridged. But having become adults, having lost our innocence, NOW love is a wonder. I hope your life and the emptiness that comes of self-awareness is filled by the wonder of love. Happy Valentine's Day.

* * *

Philosophia (September 2013)

I write to share a poem. It was written by Charles Virtue. I did not know him well — in fact, I barely knew him at all. When we met I was a brand-new Ph.D. just joining the Philosophy Department at the University of Maine. He was recently retired. I only met him once or twice. First when the Chair of the Department brought me to meet him — new blood to meet the old. Charles was rather frail by then — old, gray with a wispy goatee.

I would like to write that he was an "elder," but that would suggest a respect that was not there. Affection, yes; respect, no. At least that is the way this junior philosopher with his newly minted decoder ring interpreted the body language and unspoken words of his senior colleagues. My take was that Bob, our Chair, felt Charles should be kept in the fold, felt that he would appreciate the visit, felt it was the right thing to do. I went along, eager to please, but with the discomfort that accompanies youthful visits to the aged. I am perhaps older now than Charles was then.

I do not remember the visit much, only Charles carefully descending the stairs to greet us. I vaguely remember meeting him once again at a social gathering of philosophers, which is not the oxymoron you might imagine it to be. By then we knew that Charles was dying. Truth be told, I was not saddened by the news, after all, I hardly knew him and was too young to manufacture artificial grief. Shortly after his death a poem Charles wrote as he was dying was given to Bob who in turn shared it with the rest of the department. It is a poem about philosophy. And, of course, as a new faculty member I was full of philosophy. It was to be or so I thought my professional life.

For reasons I cannot explain that poem impressed me mightily and has stuck with me throughout my life. Not that I recite it daily, or that I could recite it even now. Rather, that lines from the poem jump into my almost subconscious memory from time to time, elicited by thoughts or events. It is not a great poem any more than Charles was a great philosopher. Its thoughts are not new. I did not value it as the dying statement of an old friend. Instead it moved me as a love poem about a new friend: philosophy.

Now something else that, like so much of life, is improbable. Susan and I were close friends (the sort of friends who vacation together), with a young dentist and his wife. She was/is a talented artist and one of Charles' not-too-distant-relatives. I have forgotten whether Susan did this as a birthday surprise for me or whether we agreed upon it together, but we asked Fran if she would render the poem in a suitable calligraphy making it look something like a medieval manuscript. Fran did a wonderful job. The framed poem hung in my office throughout my career until I retired and grew into Charles, which is to say old and more remembered than known.

One more word about the poem: it is as I said a love poem. That ought not to surprise since most of those who may read this will remember that "philosophy" comes from the Greek "philo-sophia" meaning the love of wisdom. For reasons I have never understood most people, if they think of philosophy at all, put the emphasis on "wisdom," on Sophia -- the way young men think love is about its object. But philosophy is philo. It is the pursuit of Sophia, not her possession. The never-satisfied longing for an elusive wisp that when approached vanishes into deeper levels of mystery.

Charles' poem is about the pursuit to which that dying man had devoted his life. One further preface before we turn to the poem itself. Charles is not writing about his trade, about philosophy departments in universities, about journals or classrooms, about tenure or promotion to "full professor," as if there was such a thing as a "partial professor." No. Charles is writing about a quest that any of us can undertake, that many do undertake. A quest that does not require a Ph.D. It is the most human of all endeavors: the effort to understand.

Charles' poem:

> *Friend,*
> *What can I say?*
> *Only this:*
> *in the end*
> *seeking and finding are one.*
> *in the end*
> *the final questions have no answers*
> *the ultimate problems have no solutions*
> *and yet these and these only*
> *are worth a man's heart's blood.*
> *In the meantime*
> *working, playing, walking, leaping, staggering on*
> *by well-worn paths, traversing dusty foothills;*
> *searching, grasping, slipping, sliding,*
> *climbing and doubling back,*
> *breaking through*
> *or out*
> *or down.*
> *Courage, man –*
> *sing, sister,*
> *laugh and weep.*
> *Endure,*
> *Philosophy*
> *that dear delight*
> *most stately when most homely*
> *strongest when most fragile*
> *written on wind and wave*
> *soaring eagle and scuttling crab*
> *The Bomb*
> *and the Lamb of God.*
> *The end of all our seeking*
> *The strength of all our knowing*

*The light of all our striving
Is the seeking
Itself.
Meanwhile, there is work to do.
Peace.*

Your friend,
Charles Virtue

Here's to Charles, to unanswered questions, and to "the seeking."

* * *

The Mystery that is Woman (November 2012)

Philosophers are, as you know, attracted by mystery. For Plato it was "the Good, the True, and the Beautiful," for Plotinus "the One," for St. Anselm, "that than which Nothing Greater Can Be Conceived." For me it is women — the Other.

This gap, this otherness between the sexes is present from the very dawning of our lives. The baby struggles for a first word, "DaDa" or "MaMa," and is corrected if the gender is not right. Our language itself is gender-based — not in the sense of German, French or Spanish — but in the sense of "he said" vs "she said."

When I was an undergraduate I took an introductory Psychology course in which we were told of an experiment: subjects were shown a spectrum of light and asked to delineate (i.e. draw a line) between various colors. A simple exercise, the same spectrum of light, and yet women drew twice as many lines as men. Why? Because they see twice as many colors. Imagine that; just as the colorblind see a different world from those whose retinas record colors, so too, women see and live in, a different world. This explains why Susan knows, and I do not, when the colors of my clothes clash.

But, this is just a linguistic and cognitive difference. It is clear that there is more involved as I watch our grandsons spar with their Star Wars light sabers. We are raised differently. And it is not just guns vs dolls, it is a difference in the way we learn to regard the world, understand our place in the world, the way in which we regard ourselves and our relations with others. The result of all these biologic and environmental differences is two distinctly different ways of being in the world. And there is the mystery, the fascination. How can she not know that that bowl will not fit into that box? How can he not know that shirt is green and not blue? But more importantly, how can he not see that person's distress? Why is she so deferential? Forgive the cliché. What interests me here is that there are these two different, sometimes distinct, ways of being in the world. More apropos, that there is a way of being in the world different from my own.

Occasionally, when I thought we were enjoying a Sunday dinner in the dining room with our two teenage sons, Susan would suddenly stand up, take her plate and leave to eat alone in the kitchen. I would inevitably go out and inquire, "What's wrong?" only to be told that the room was "so full of testosterone" that she could not take it anymore. Different worlds. Who knew? You would think I would know. I was raised by a widowed mother, had the benefit of some great female teachers, and spent most of my professional life with women. Indeed, Susan believes that what administrative success I had was due to being surrounded by competent women.

It would be easy in an essay of this sort, to descend into cliché, which I do not want to do. So, I will try not to speak so much of women's sensitivity and intuition — though I have witnessed each, or of men's competitiveness and obtuseness — though I have witnessed each. What interests me is the otherness, the mystery of another, different kind of, human being with whom you can communicate, but not quite; with whom you can share experiences, but not quite; with whom you can merge, but not quite — still asking, "Was it good for you?"

There are many things that enrich and complexify human experience, the "two-sexesness" of our condition is one of them. When I was growing up I spent a summer working on a farm in northern Ohio. The farmer raised champion black angus that we would show around the state at county fairs. One of the things that you might not realize is that the hoofs of such critters have to be trimmed regularly. As we were hard at this task I asked him if it hurt the cattle. He rightly answered, "How could I know?" That irreducible otherness is not a surprise in the animal kingdom, but within our own? Perhaps that is why Aristotle thought women were another species — and he was married!

Imagine a flat, two-dimensional world seen through only one eye. Consider how impoverished that would be versus a three-dimensional world created by two eyes seeing from ever-so-slightly different perspectives. The beauty of our difference is that it enriches each of our worlds and shows us each that we do not have a "true" perspective. Part of the value of female colleagues, if you are a male, is the different perspectives they offer, the "ah ha" moments when they point out that perhaps that action, whatever it might be, was not intended as an insult to your "manhood."

* * *

Goodness, Truth and Beauty (September 2012)

Plato was wrong: goodness, truth and beauty are not eternal — any more than we are. But unlike us they can persist — if we continue to invest them with life and energy. We do not ride on goodness, truth and beauty; they ride on us and on our will to keep them alive. Our human challenge is to seek out truth and to nourish it; to discover beauty and to cherish it; to recognize goodness and contribute to it.

Part of Plato's mistake was in that word "recognize." He believed that goodness, truth and beauty were eternal forms. In a previous life we had known these eternal forms in their purity; the challenge here on earth was to recall or "re-cognize" them. That is a comfortable and perhaps comforting thought, but a strangely childish one. It renders us without responsibility. For Plato goodness, truth and beauty will persist no matter what we do or fail to do.

I prefer the more modern, admittedly egocentric, thought that goodness, truth and beauty hang by a thread, in danger of forever slipping away — and that once lost, they will be forever beyond human recall. This means that we must each fight for truth and not acquiesce to the cacophony of falsity the surrounds us; that we must each seek out beauty and sustain it whether it be in the natural world, or the world of artists; that goodness must first and foremost be our own. It is in that spirit that I offer the following

For goodness: Chuck and Belinda Lawrence of Blue Hill Maine are funding a track for the local high school and community. They run a small general store and will be donating $100,000 a year for five years.

For truth: This morning a Coopers Hawk took a Blue Jay at our feeder.

It was no contest; the jay could not compete with the hawk's talons and ripping beak. Nonetheless the battle lasted a full nine minutes. Afterward, when the hawk flew away with its prize, goldfinches and chickadees returned to the feeder within five minutes. Life goes on.

And for beauty: these six loons emerging from the morning fog.

My point is not that GT&B reside only in Maine but rather that they reside wherever and whenever we care enough to seek them out.

Plato imagined that the challenge was to "recall" their perfection. It is instead to find and discover them daily. If Plato were right these eternal forms could live on without us. In fact, they live on only when we discover them. If Plato were right we could somehow find an example of perfect beauty, or truth or goodness, and enshrine it for future generations to see and appreciate. Were that possible, of course, we would still need to remind our successors that these artifacts represented something beyond themselves. Soon the "thread" would be broken and the object would be just one more thing.

The recurring act of human creativity and will that illuminate the good, the true and the beautiful is more about us than about anything "out there" — be it tangible or not. And so I offer the above. They have no particular value except that they are my discoveries for this particular day in Maine. Surely your world has similar treasures. They are certainly not eternal. On the contrary they are fragile and fleeting — which makes us love them all the more.

* * *

Tidal Falls (June 2017)

Time tumbles by like the tide spilling out of Taunton Bay and coursing across the rocks at Tidal Falls[1] — a constant stream of movement on which we are carried to and fro. But there are special places where we can momentarily step out of time's stream, where we can mark its passage, and our own.

Tidal Falls in Hancock, Maine is such a place for me and perhaps for you. A place of natural beauty where, like the Falls itself, memory allows us to reverse the stream of time and to reflect on its occasions: holding hands as high school sweethearts, watching toddlers explore its tidal pools, teaching sons to skip stones across its rolling current, enjoying Monday Night Music as daughters scamper across its rolling lawn, pointing out eagles, and picnicking with friends.

And now more recently, the stream accompanies our teaching grandchildren about tides, helping them distinguish Seals from River Otters, Eiders from Buffleheads. Sitting together in the evening, as we did so many years ago, holding hands, watching the sky as it morphs from blue to yellow to pink to grey. Perhaps driving down the hill on a solitary winter's evening, seeking a place to be alone and contemplative. The stream of time flows on, continuing to spill across Tidal Falls; its powerful current bubbles with surprises. What a joy it is that there is a spot where we can step outside the stream of time to appreciate its movement — a yardstick of our lives on which we can mark and savor life's moments. Such a special spot, such a preserve, both of nature and of self, must be cherished, conserved and shared — a treasure of tranquility, an invitation to reflection and appreciation.

Before Immanuel Kant there were two competing schools of western philosophy. Rationalists like Descartes and Spinoza relied on pure, deductive reasoning. They did not trust the senses but sought instead the 2+2=4 certainty of pure reason. Empiricists, like Hume and Locke, on the other hand relied on their senses to inform them about the world.

Rationalists had certain knowledge, but not necessarily about the "real world" (e.g. I know that IF there are five balls and you remove two of them, three will remain). But rationalism could not deduce whether there were "in fact" five balls; only our senses could tell us that. But what our senses told us might be wrong; perhaps we were dreaming or hallucinating.

---

[1] Tidal Falls is a reversing falls, flowing in each direction propelled by Maine's 11–13 foot tides. The incoming tide rushes from our right to left as it fills the recently-emptied Taunton Bay. Later the now-filled Taunton Bay sends its waters rushing out from our left to right as it empties into the retreating tide of Frenchman Bay.

Empirical knowledge could be misleading and undependable. We have seen the sun rise every morning in the east, but there is no certainty that it will do so tomorrow. Senses can tell us about the external world, but the knowledge they yield is at best probable.

What to do? Immanuel Kant stepped in with a genuinely revolutionary idea. Certainty, he argued, lies not in the unknowable world "out there," but in our minds which structure that world through the categories of space and time. We can know that the next stone we see will be three-dimensional even if it is on the far side of the moon — because we can only see three-dimensionally. We know that tomorrow will not precede today because the time we impose on our perceptions is linear. We can have some certainty about the external world because that world is, in fact, a product of our minds which actively structure/compose it. It follows that we can never know the "thing in itself" because we can never step outside our active minds. Space and time will always be with us because we are their source; we "secrete" them. But, we all know that is not quite true....

There are moments and places where our structuring minds seem to step aside, seem to pause in their composing. We all know such moments. Working in the garden, painting a watercolor, reading a good book we can lose track of time. These are blissful non-moments, non-experiences. Do they put us in touch with a pure reality beyond our structuring? I do not know, nor, I would argue, could I. But you and I both know the bliss of such moments.

For me, Tidal Falls provides such a "release." I am drawn into its dark rolling liquid hills and white bubbling haystacks. Water rushes by in a way that eludes my humble geometry and stops my internal clock. I am hypnotized and bidden beyond myself. Such portals may be found if you seek them out, wormholes snaking through space and time and beyond our cocoon of self.

* * *

Life (October 2014)

I don't understand life — the hummingbird at our feeder, the urchins in our Bay, the pine pumping sap fifty feet high to support a bald eagle — it is all a full-of-wonders mystery to me. And yet, as Susan struggles for breath, I find myself reflecting more and more on life: what it is, and what it might be to lose it. Not being a biologist or a physician, my thoughts are unencumbered by knowledge, just the reflections of an old man.

The first image that comes to mind is Michelangelo's "Creation of Adam" on the ceiling of the Sistine Chapel — a magnificent conception of a deity passing the spark of life to mankind. Of course, there would have to **BE** a deity for such a concept to be of much worth and.... Still, I like the animating sense of linkage, of touching. It would seem to suggest that death might be a similar moment of withdrawing the spark. "God in His infinite wisdom" and all that.

My own conjecture is different. It is set long ago, perhaps around volcanic vents deep in the ocean. Complex molecules such as amino acids mingling and co-mingling, twisting back and forth on themselves until they began to produce an internal cohesion. More mingling and co-mingling until they acquire the ability to pass their energy on and to mutate. Which is to say, I imagine life to be a force field — a bit like gravity or some other attraction, in this case, primarily chemical. So, instead of Michelangelo's majestic vision, I see a double helix of coiled energy.

This sense of energy within is not a new idea. One of its earliest expressions was by the pre-Socratic philosopher, Heraclitus. You perhaps know him from the oft-quoted, *"You can never step into the same river twice,"* which speaks to the ever-changing nature of our world. More subtly, he saw the world of apparent stability as masking a balanced inner tension and uses the simile of a strung bow, an energy capable of projecting force beyond itself.

> *"All things are in flux; the flux is subject to a unifying measure or rational principle. This principle (logos, the hidden harmony behind all change) bound opposites together in a unified tension, which is like that of a lyre, where a stable harmonious sound emerges from the tension of the opposing forces that arise from the bow bound together by the string."* —Heraclitus.

You and I, dear reader, are the most complex bundles of energy yet evolved on this planet. I say "yet" because there are surely more to come. The balanced tension — the complexity of the hummingbird, the urchin, the pine tree — pales when compared to our 86 billion neurons packed into just over the volume of a quart (and you thought your iPhone was impressive!), folding and re-folding upon themselves to create virtually incalculable linkages.

We are, I think, complex, tensioned bundles of energy like Heraclitus' bow. It is that coiled energy that we call life and that, in its infinite complexity, makes each of us the unique person we are. There will never be another self-tensioning combination quite like you or me or more to the point, like Susan. But, as it happens I further wonder how we are capable of blending, folding, complexifying our energy with that of another to produce a new, different, independent bundle of energy. And, in spite of my philosophic bumbling, Susan and I have managed to send two bundles named "Rick" and "Matt" to the future.

I imagine death to be the releasing of Heraclitus' tension, the relaxing of the bow whose internal dynamic has been part of us each from the beginning and which comes, in fact, as a "release." Given Susan's present suffering, I like that thought. Not that she will live on to watch us "from above," but that the natural tension that is life will be released and she will dissolve like a dream into her component parts — which are nothing without the tension that formerly united them. Except, in their moment, they managed to create, to achieve, to laugh and cry and hope.

Heraclitus believed that opposites are necessary for life, but that they are unified in a system of balanced exchanges. The world itself consists of a law-like interchange of elements. The world is not to be identified with any particular substance, but rather with an ongoing process governed by a law of change. If objects are new from moment to moment so that one can never touch the same object twice, then each object must dissolve and be generated continually. It follows that an object is a harmony between a building up and a tearing down. Heraclitus calls the oppositional processes "strife," and hypothesizes that the apparently stable state, or "justice," is a harmony of it: *"We must know that war is common to all and strife is justice, and that all things come into being through strife necessarily."*

As Diogenes later explains: *"All things come into being by conflict of opposites, and the sum of things, "the whole", flows like a stream."* In the bow metaphor Heraclitus compares the resultant balance to a strung bow held in shape by an equilibrium of the string tension and spring action of the bow: *"There is a harmony in the bending back as in the case of the bow and the lyre."*

Think of that stationary pine, the one with the eagle in its top branches. Think of the dynamism it hides: of the flowing sap, the grasping roots, the lifting limbs. The law of change will bring it down, as it will us. But until it does, let us stretch as high and as far as we can. Let our stability conceal tensions and hopes and a hunger for new challenges.

* * *

Thoughts While Dying (October 2017)

There's an old joke:

> An elderly woman has died in a small Maine town. Friends and neighbors come for her funeral. Afterward the mourners join the 90-some year-old widower on his rickety half mile walk to the cemetery at the edge of town. Burial complete, they are slowly walking back with the feeble old widower. A young girl strikes up a conversation with the grieving gentleman: "Gee, mister," she says, "it's hardly worth your walking back to town."

And so, it is: we know our own mortality, but do not talk about it in polite conversation. The little girl is surely right, but the joke comes from her saying out loud what we all recognize — at least in principle — but do not utter. What follows are some thoughts about dying. I share them in part because this outcome awaits us all, regardless of wealth, race, gender, or social status — and yet we do not talk about it. My credentials in this conversation are exactly that same as yours. That is to say, none. Neither of us has died; each of us is going to die.

When I was young I embraced Dylan Thomas': "*Do not go gentle into that sweet night. Rage, rage against the dying of the light.*" I loved its defiance; its passion for life. It is, of course, a wonderfully thrilling call to arms in a romantic sort of way. But it's a call for someone else, in this case his father, to take arms — not oneself. It's the cry of the son, not of the father. The expression of an uncompleted life rather than a completed one. Now, in old age, I think the measure of a life is not in its length, but in its productivity and especially in its struggle to advance the human experiment.

The question must always be what have you done with the light you've had. Think Milton's, "*When I consider how my light is spent...*" And if, it happens that you have used that light well; reflected some of it back on others and on the world; lit a path for others; used that precious light to illuminate your inner self; then death is not so hard. Yes, physically the body cannot help itself in its struggle, but mentally you can be at peace.

A strange phenomenon: most fears increase as the object of that fear draws near. Are you afraid of spiders? Not that one over there, but rather the one descending from above your head. Fear of heights? Not when the ledge is even a few feet away; the fear expresses itself when you stand at the precipice. But in the case of death it is well-documented that fear is greatest not in old age when it is near but rather in youth when it is presumably far away. Why?

Being a philosopher, I have a theory. The adolescent has just recently become self-aware. Has just recently discovered his/her life. The thought of that life ending before it can begin, or ending deeply incomplete is terrifying — at least it was for me as a young man. But now, having lived a life, the thought of death is not so scary. More than that, as a young person your world is pretty much limited to your emerging self. You have discovered no causes or values beyond yourself, have not yoked your energy to climb toward something that exceeds your grasp. In short, it is still all about you — and hence the thought of you being no more is unbearable. Advancing age provides another perspective. It is no longer all about ME. Now we have merged our energies with others and with causes larger than ourselves. In short, we have become part of entities/movements/ causes that will continue on after our death.

In fact, when finally confronted (perhaps by the diagnosis of a terminal disease), with our own impending demise we often can and do reconcile ourselves. Not overnight, not all at once, but it does happen. We begin to withdraw from life, to reflect on the experiences we have had, the people we have known, the things we have done, etc... And strangely enough, no matter what our circumstances we usually discover a wholeness, even a "logic" to the life we have lived. If we are lucky, as we approach the end we see achievements, and experiences and pleasures enjoyed — all of which gives us some ability to "wrap it up" and set life aside as a completed whole.

Sartre points out that we are free right up until our death. Free to renounce our former self and invent another. Free to have a "deathbed conversion." I understand his point, but old age is not like that. We are not likely, having run the race, to now switch to another sport. I think the reality of old age is closer to Aristotle's discussion of character. Aristotle tells us that character is formed by habits which are in turn formed by repeated actions. Having lived the life, i.e. repeated actions, of an educator I am not likely now to turn my back on that experience. Indeed, I am more likely to affirm and reaffirm it. I do not long for death — life is too sweet and too beautiful to willfully let go — but I no longer fear it either. What about the title of this essay, "Thoughts While Dying???" Nothing special, just that *a fortiori*, all thoughts are thoughts while dying.

4. SAN DIEGO STATE UNIVERSITY

I love universities. At their best they are the driving force of our world: the birthplace of our science, engineering, technology and economics. Repositories of history and culture, of arts and literature. Simply put, their purpose is human growth and development: not only the enculturation, stretching and inspiration of rising generations, but also the cauldron from which our human experiment itself draws strength and energy and ultimately its progress. I spent my entire adult life in universities. In each one I found delightful colleagues, patient mentors, role models, and educators committed to their students, their disciplines, and their colleagues. My last 15 years were invested at San Diego State University – a wonderful place to be an educator. Not because of the beaches and palm trees, but because San Diego was urban, diverse, hi-tech, Pacific rim and Latin America. In short, the ingredients of the 21st-century. An educator could not have hoped for a better playground.

Aristotle (May 2015)

Much of Greek philosophy sounds as if it was written by nine-year-olds crimping it from their mothers. Pearls like, "Nothing in excess." My mother's version was, *"Don't make a pig of yourself."* Or, "No man knowingly does evil," which Mom authored as, *"He didn't mean it."* Heraclitus: *"You can't step into the same river twice."* Mom's: *"It's a new day."* You get the idea.

But Aristotle taught me a valuable lesson when I was in college. I was naturally reticent and was not happy being so. I wanted to be more outgoing, more gregarious — but it simply was not me. Then I read in Aristotle that individual actions repeated turned into habits and that habits cluster into character. I don't mean character as in probity and moral fiber, I wasn't aspiring to that, rather character in the sense of being a certain kind of thing (e.g., in the words of the old joke), that it is the character of a scorpion to sting.

I wanted my character to be less shy, more outgoing. But, of course, that was not who I was. What to do? Answer, thank you Aristotle, say "Hi," to this next person coming along the campus walk, and then to that one, and another. Do it again tomorrow, the next day and the day after that. Soon you will cultivate the habit of saying hello to people, or at least nodding your head in acknowledgment/recognition. When people used to ask in a reflective way, "How ya do'in?" I would instinctively respond, "Fine.," but walk away wishing I had added, "And you?" So, following Aristotle....

Now I know this is pitiful, that you and others do not need Aristotle to guide you through life, but what can I say, I did/do. Fast forward to the mid-18th century when the Scottish empiricist, David Hume, taught us almost as an aside that memories become stronger as you approach their source. That is to say, that you will not remember roads, names, smells, etc, from your past until you come close to the place where those memories were formed, and then they will magically (re)appear. Try it; you will see that Hume is right. Susan and I used to enjoy birding at the Tijuana estuary. If you were to ask me now how to get there I could not tell you. But when I get to San Diego, I will know. I cannot now, in my mind drive from Stony Ridge, Ohio to BGSU, but when I am there, I can. So why do I burden you with this? Because I am now in the Philadelphia airport on my way to San Diego and I notice a strange thing: I find myself walking through the airport saying "Hi" or nodding to perfect strangers — most of whom seem surprised/puzzled by this behavior. And it occurs to me that I am unconsciously, which is to say naturally, donning my San Diego personality/character. Aristotle would approve.

The Stoics prided themselves on being fixed and constant, the same in every situation. We might say, being "unflappable." But we are not constant. Different situations/circumstances call forth from us different natures. I am not the same person in San Diego as on Hancock Point. I was not the same person professionally as in my private life. As I write this I think of friends who seem to be the same privately and publicly, but truth-be-told I do not know them privately, do not know what it feels like to be them, do not know what comes naturally, or what was acquired, what they, like I, owe to Aristotle.

I am not a solipsist: I do not believe that I am alone in the universe, that all the world and its people are figments of my feverish imagination. But I do believe that it is exceedingly difficult and rare to know another person — indeed, it is hard enough to know oneself. So, as this A320 begins its descent into San Diego I prepare to don another self — not a false one, just one of many, or at least of several. It is kind of fun to be capable of change and of surprising yourself after all these years. I can feel a "Go Aztecs" coming on.

* * *

Pride and Praise (August 2015)

Please forgive the autobiographical quality of this essay. There is a philosophic passage, I can't remember where I encountered it — Aristotle, perhaps, devoted to a discussion of pride and praise. Basically, it tells us what our mothers did: you are proud of things you do yourself (not all things you do yourself); you praise worthy things done by others.

The other day I was told, "You must be proud of...." and my first thought, (thanks, Mom), was that I had not done it myself and hence ought not take pride in it. Then I got to thinking that this ill-remembered philosopher and Mom had the distinction between pride and praise only partially right. The world is not divided into things done by you or me and things done by others. There are many things that are done by us together. That, in turn, led to the recognition that most of the things of which I am proud were not done by me, but done together with others. However, I am getting ahead of myself.

Let's back up and think of things of which we are each individually proud. I am sure your list is extensive; mine is relatively short. I am proud of the care I gave Susan in her final months, of some furniture I have built, some drawings/paintings/carvings/photos I have produced, my gazpacho soup — now I am beginning to stretch. I suppose I am proud of the way I have survived Susan's death, of keeping relatively fit, of some of my writings. I like my taste in art. But that is about it.

What I find upon reflection is that I am most proud of things I have done together with others. First and foremost, of the relationship I built with Susan, of the sons we raised together. I would say I am proud of my career, but I am deeply conscious that it was largely luck and that as the Beatles would say, "I (got) along with some help from my friends."

I am proud of my teaching at the University of Maine, but I had good colleagues/mentors who helped me along the way; of my work there as Assistant to the President, but I was the most junior of colleagues, just one (two?) of several hands-on multiple oars. I am proud of the general education reform we accomplished at Fairfield University, but truth be told I merely initiated it; the heavy lifting was done by a committee. At St. Cloud State I was proud of our enrollment growth, but there, too, I certainly did not do it myself. Even at Oswego where I was proud to be part of healing a traumatized campus, I was only part of that process.

Upon reflection, most of my pride resides in San Diego State, which is perhaps why I am wearing one of their tee shirts as I type this. But, there too what I am most proud of is being a part of it, of playing my role in a cast of thousands. I had vice presidents who were literally extra-ordinary, who suggested successful initiatives and who carried them out.

Occasionally I am praised for the growth in the size and quality of SDSU's student body, for the increased diversity, for the nation-leading improvement in graduation rates, for improved relations with faculty and students, for the building boom, for increased fund-raising, for more successful athletic programs. But in each case, I played a relatively minor role. It was Nancy's office of Academic Affairs that accomplished the work of transforming our student body — and our faculty; Sally's office of Business Affairs that built the campus and led us through the pernicious budget cuts; Jim's office of Student Affairs that improved and maintained student relations and helped with athletics; Mary Ruth's division of University Relations and Development that raised the money, grew community relationships and told our story. It was a campus-wide committee that worked so effectively on graduation rates. Spectacular Senate leadership made faculty relations so productive and such a pleasure. The list could go on, but you get the point. Even in "my" strategic planning initiative, "Shared Vision," I did little more than see the need; others devised a process, engaged our campus, captured the input and implemented the suggestions.

I am old enough that, at this point in the game, I am rarely discovering new things about myself. But coming to understand that I am most proud of achievements made together with others somehow pleases me. It is nicely the opposite of Ayn Rand who has been in the news recently as fools *du jour* trumpet the virtue of selfishness.

I receive daily emails from the liberal website, "Daily Kos;" a few days ago, this one came across the ether:

attribution: Elaine Thompson, AP

Snohomish County firefighter Ken Lawless, left, and Lt. Brandon Gardner being thanked by a man near Omak after firefighters saved his home from a wildfire. From Daily Kos: "The gentleman on the right, his shirt says "Lower Taxes + Less Government=More Freedom." Yeah, freedom to watch your home burn to ashes. Freedom to rebuild from the bottom up, or not …. I grant you, that is somewhat simplistic -- as are most such self-congratulatory posts, be they from the right or the left. Nonetheless: nobody fights fires alone. These firefighters were obviously part of a team; they were surely supported by other teams, by equipment, dispatchers, perhaps aerial tankers — and ultimately by us, the taxpayers.

Safer though it surely was, my teammates and I were fighting the wildfire of ignorance that is spreading throughout our country. We were supported by parents, by hard-working, under-appreciated K-12 teachers, by thousands of colleagues at SDSU, by generous donors and ultimately also by taxpayers. We had some successes; we had some failures. But I take pride in the fact that we fought the fight and that we did it together.

It is, I suppose, about being part of "something larger than yourself." As I age and the limits of self become increasingly apparent, the extensions of self through energy invested in partnerships such as San Diego State take on greater meaning. I feel no special need to be remembered, but I like the thought that some of the partnerships/institutions to which I have devoted time and energy will persist — and I hope/trust, continue to prosper.

* * *

Courage (March 2015)

Athletics, like life, teaches many lessons: teamwork, hard work, self-discipline, sportsmanship, perseverance, etc... We associate these lessons with winning and winners. And yet, losers learn important lessons as well. They too work hard, value their teammates, persevere. Losses teach that talent and hard work aren't always enough, that teamwork will sometimes not succeed. I was reminded of the lessons of losing last night as Air Force played San Diego State in men's basketball.

Air Force came into our arena with a 10 and 13 record, overall; 4 and 8 in the Mountain West Conference. SDSU came into the game 21 and 2; 10 and 1 in the conference. San Diego State was then ranked #5 in the country though that will change after the loss to Wyoming earlier this week. (Wyoming broke our 20-game win streak the prior Tuesday in Laramie.) SDSU was not in a charitable mood. And, of course, Air Force asked for no charity in spite of the fact that they faced a sold-out crowd of fanatic Aztecs, led by our rabid student section, "The Show." They were greeted by boos as they first took the floor. I wish fans didn't do that, but they do. Every mistake Air Force made was greeted by chants like "Air Ball, Air Ball..." Meanwhile, we could do no wrong. Fans cheered every basket, booed every call that went against us.

As a rule, Air Force is undersized. It makes itself competitive through intelligence, discipline and teamwork. In football their perfected execution of the triple option is almost impossible to stop, especially early in the season. In basketball, they work patiently, working the clock. waiting for the open shot. Lots of assists. But, valuable as they may be, none of these lessons caught my attention last night so much as another: courage. What strikes me is that the team from Air Force knew all this awaited them; knew they were overmatched; knew it would take a miracle to win.... And yet, they showed up, took the floor, played their hearts out right to the end of the game.

We have all had tough days at the office, all have faced emergencies, institutional meltdowns, hostile critics. In my experience, at least, bad as they might be, like three members of our engineering faculty being murdered on campus, or a fire in a resident hall, the hardest ones to deal with were always the ones I knew were coming; the ones made worse by anticipation like a pending drug bust, an upcoming fight with the system office, or a confrontation with student demonstrators.

When you are caught up in a crisis adrenaline is flowing, you are fully engaged in the moment, all your faculties are directed toward finding a solution. In short, there is no time for reflection, no time to tell yourself, "This is really bad." You are fighting against the situation, not against yourself. But when the disaster presents itself in prospect, when you know it is coming and can do nothing about it, when you are alone with your thoughts, THEN you are up against not only the crisis, but against yourself and your fears.

These athletes from Air Force not only faced a disaster; they knew that disaster was coming. They had time to think about it as they packed their equipment, as they boarded the plane, as they walked into the visitor's locker room, as they did their shoot-around before the game. And yet they did not flinch.

One of the many lessons athletics teaches, one that is too often overlooked, is courage. I admire the courage it took for Air Force to walk out on that floor, to face that crowd, to play against superior athletes. Courage for us and for them rarely looks like Sylvester Stallone, it sometimes looks like showing up at the office on what you know will be a bad day.

* * *

Radio, Recollections of an Old Man (March 2015)

I am old enough that radio was my initial window to the world. The particular radio was a huge, maybe 27" high and 14" wide, wooden radio with glowing tubes that cast a faint light on the wall of a darkened room. It had seven radio bands allowing us to listen to the world, and to convince ourselves that the warbly whistles we heard were signals from distant submarines.

The first shows I remember were "The Shadow" and "The Green Hornet," but there were others, after chores and homework were done. By far the strongest memories were listening to our high school, (Troy-Luckey—Yes, "ey"), basketball games on cold winter evenings. In those pre-drivers-license days I could rarely go to the games. Our school as division C or D, the smallest of Ohio schools, think "Hoosiers," but we were very good, regularly competing in divisional or even sectional year-end tournaments. Needless to say, the "we" I refer to had nothing to do with this then pre-geek. We had a great coach named "Frenchy Filiere" who was known for his hot temper. He was my biology teacher.

That old radio was inherently suspenseful, waves of static would wash over the crackly sound and technical difficulties were endemic as they broadcast from tiny gyms via equipment not much more sophisticated than a tin can. Now, here I am in Dunedin, New Zealand, forty-six years later listening to a radio broadcast of "our" men's basketball team. It is San Diego State (ranked 22nd) against UNLV (ranked 12th) and I am listening to Ted Lightner on KOGO via the Internet. Of course, I am dressed in my SDSU sweater.

The game began at 1:00pm on Saturday in San Diego, 10:00am here on Sunday. The tube radio has been replaced by an iPhone and ear buds. I am

9,000(?) miles away picking up a broadcast that is bouncing off satellites like a three-cushion carom shot. None of which would have been remotely imaginable in my former radio days, even on "Space Cadets." The dark bedroom has been replaced by a McDonald's Internet cafe where I am nursing a cup of now cold tea.

SDSU is up by three with about three minutes to go in the first half. At halftime I will head to the University of Otago library. It will then be open. I will grab a study room and listen in a place where I do not need ear phones, and will no longer need to suppress shouts.

Half time: SDSU 34, UNLV 29.

I take a nice walk to the university which is about a half mile. I am now ensconced in a soundproof study carrel. What a game! They came back and narrowed our lead; we re-established it. The crowd was roaring. In between typing, I am pacing around in this small glass cage shouting. In the waning minutes UNLV has taken a slim one-point lead; now we have retaken it. We opened up a six-point lead with only minutes to go, but could not hold it. AT LAST, we went ahead with .3 seconds to go. UNLV made a desperate last-ditch effort, but to no avail. Final score, which was hard to hear over my own screaming: SDSU, 69; UNLV 67. I need a glass of wine, but that is no more allowed in this library than it was forty-six years ago in my upstairs bedroom.

There is a mystery as to why athletics can move us so. I think it is because we admire all-out effort and total commitment. Much of life requires that effort, but it is rarely so visible. Rarely are we publicly allowed to root for others and applaud their excellence. Just as I did so many years ago, I sit here alone, but feeling part of something far away and exciting. Strange also, how I will walk a bit taller as I head to the bus stop. Chores are done. Steve Fisher and his team have given me a vicarious treat that still resonates in spite of the intervening distance and years.

GO AZTECS!

* * *

Celebration (July 2009)

Part of what Susan and I like about San Diego is its diversity. Last night offered such a moment. I was invited to a surprise party for Rhonda Welch-Scalco, hosted by her proud father.

Rhonda became a friend when she served as Chair of the Barona tribe — a huge complex enterprise of casino, hotel, and golf course employing hundreds of people, not to mention all the social services such as schools and clinics and museums, or the infrastructure of roads, fire stations, etc... In the midst of her service as Chair Rhonda was raising two small children and studying for her Ph.D. in Philosophy of Education at UC Riverside. It was in the latter capacity that I came to know her better because she did much of her research at SDSU. We were gathered to celebrate completion of her doctorate.

Last night's event was held at the Manchester Grand Hyatt on the bay front. It is an elegant hotel. I arrived properly late, but still too early for what was in reality a family celebration. As I loitered while we waited for the soon to be surprised guest of honor I strolled through a Philippino wedding reception complete with orchid leis.

Due to Rhonda's party being a family affair, I only knew half a dozen of the 120 or so guests including her brother, now Chair, and the Chairs of the Sycuan and Viejas tribes each closely related in a cousin sort of way.

The dinner began with a song/chant. They invited Rhonda and her two children to come forward and stand at the front. She, in turn, invited two adolescent nieces to join them. Then Anthony Pico and a second man with a rattle began to chant in deep resonate rhythmic tones. We were all standing, dancing our weight from leg to leg in a shuffling sort of way. Even a German could do it! It was magical. Then an elder was called forth to offer a prayer — wonderfully wise, sensitive, appreciative and proud. A little later, after the meal had commenced, the Sycuan Tribe presented Rhonda with a blanket that they joked about having bought at K-mart.

Their Chief, Danny Tucker, who is an accomplished singer, then invited Rhonda and her children back up front as he sang, "What a wonderful World." There were, of course, speeches and the obligatory slide show. But most of all it was a family gathering to express their pride in an accomplished daughter who has won one of the .00074 of the doctorate degrees in this country earned by Native Americans. This job has given me some extraordinary/delightful experiences all over the world — none sweeter and more humane than last night. It was an honor to have been invited.

* * *

Weeds (June 2017)

Much as I enjoy my gardens, I have always been fond of weeds. That I can work so hard, and go to such expense, to create islands of beauty when all around me beauty tumbles forth unbidden… It is a wonder. E.g.:

My dictionary tells me that a weed is: *"a wild plant growing where it is not wanted and in competition with cultivated plants."*

So, perhaps these are not weeds. They are surely not competing with my gardens, nor are they "unwanted." Rather they are reminders that sometimes the most compelling beauty is most humble, most unexpected. So it is with human beings. Some of us have odds greatly stacked against us, be they the poor soil of poverty, ill-health, traumatized childhoods, addiction of one sort or another — and yet, like these weeds we succeed and throw our little bit of beauty into the world — recognized or not.

There is much talk at the moment of "winners" and "losers," as if some plants were "winners" because they came from the hothouses of nurseries, while those for which we paid nothing are "losers." I think the opposite may well be the case.

At San Diego State we had a program for foster children called "Guardian Scholars." These were young people who had just been disgorged from the foster care system as they reached eighteen. In spite of being shifted from home to home, sometimes being homeless, sleeping in cars, roaming the streets, perhaps being abused, these "weeds" had succeeded in obtaining a high school diploma and in compiling the grades necessary to enter SDSU. No hothouse for these Guardian Scholars, and yet they do better than our highly selective student body as a whole.

I have the pleasure of serving on the Board of AVID, a national non-profit serving primarily low-income, first generation, students of color. "AVID" is an acronym standing for "Advancement Via Individual Determination" — i.e. regardless of the soil in which you are planted. These "weeds" not only do better than their peers, they do better than the hothouse kids from the suburbs, regardless of race and social class. The carefully cultivated plants in my garden will fail if I do not "hold their hands," do not water and feed them, but their wild cousins in my meadow are strong and tough as well as beautiful. They have persisted and bloomed in spite of their hardships. Now, I ask you, on which would you place your bet: the wild plant or the cultivated one?

* * *

Good Word Gone Bad (July 2017)

Our word "administrator" is defined in Webster's New World Dictionary as: "*to manage, conduct, direct, control.*" It goes on to identify "administration" as: "*the direction of affairs, see management.*" Upon looking, I note that "management" refers to: "*supervision* (literally, viewing from above), *command, order, power, control.*" My Oxford Compact Thesaurus lists: "*direction, control, command, supervision, overseeing,*" as synonyms.

So, understood we think of administrators as CEO's, as bosses, as management. It is not too far a stretch to think of the dichotomy between "labor" versus "management." But this is an almost topsy-turvy sense of a word which began its life denoting "service." Cassell's Latin Dictionary defines "*administrare*" as, "*to help or to assist*" — an unlikely root from which "command" or "control" might sprout.

My O.E.D., (without which no child should be), cleaves* more closely to Latin origins when it defines administration as, "*to minister to, to serve, to manage as a steward, one who ministers to others...*" (*Is it not strange that the word "cleave" means both "to cut a sunder" and "to stick fast to?" It is in the latter sense that I employ it now). What a strange and tortuous route this word has traveled. Is it any wonder that some people go into "administration" for the wrong reasons? wanting to be bosses rather than servants; relishing "you're fired" more than "well done"; elevating themselves above those whom they serve.

I have long been a fan of Robert Greenleaf's, *Servant Leadership: A Journey into the Nature of Legitimate Power and Greatness*. In it he writes:

> "*the servant-leader is servant first... It begins with the natural feeling that one wants to serve, to serve first. Then the conscious choice brings one to aspire to lead. That person is sharply different from one who is leader first, perhaps because of the need to assuage an unusual power drive or to acquire material possessions...* "*The difference manifests itself in the care taken by the servant-first to make sure that other people's highest priority needs are being served. The best test... is: Do those served grow as persons? Do they, while being served, become healthier, wiser, free, more autonomous, more likely themselves to become servants? And, what is the effect on the least*

> *privileged in society? Will they benefit or at least not be further deprived?"*

This idea of servant leadership is not new. Some of you will hear echoes of it in Mark, 10:42–45 in which we read (I like the King James version):

> *But Jesus called them to him, and saith unto them, Ye know that they which are accounted to rule over the Gentiles exercise lordship over them; and their great one's exercise authority upon them. But so shall it not be among you: but whosoever will be great among you, shall be your minister: and whosoever of you will be the chiefest, shall be servant of all. For even the Son of man came not to be ministered unto, but to minister, and to give his life a ransom for many.*

I suspect there is no truth to the claim that Jesus stole this thought from the 6th century BCE Chinese philosopher Lao Tzu. None-the-less, I prefer his version:

> *The highest type of ruler is one of whose existence the people are barely aware. Next comes one whom they love and praise. Next comes one whom they fear. Next comes one whom they despise and defy.... The Sage is self-effacing and scanty of words. When his task is accomplished and things have been completed, All the people say, 'We ourselves have achieved it!'*

Other behaviors follow from servant leadership, Listening: you cannot serve if you do not listen. A servant needs to know what those being served need, want, hope for, fear. Caring: putting needs of others ahead of your own. A corollary of caring is doing your homework: you cannot serve from a base of ignorance. Humility: as Lao Tzu said: *"The highest type of ruler is one of whose existence the people are barely aware."* Standing up — in the phrase of the day, "leaning forward:" the servant leader must accept responsibility — which means literally being answerable — especially to those whom he/she serves.

There can be great satisfaction in an administrative life, a life of service. It can be stressful, but the stress derives from your desire to be helpful and to bring events into a constructive configuration. I used to joke that administration was good work for someone, like myself, with a short attention span. But, in fact, that busyness reflects the variety of interests/concerns this work embraces and the upward growth curve that keeps one fresh and engaged.

I have a friend who is about to start her life as an administrator. I think she will be good at it. She has been a teacher, another kind of service; now she is about to pick up the mantle of administration. She wants this for all the right reasons: to be of help, to serve, to make a difference in the lives/well-being of others. Her primary duties will be fostering leadership and community. I thought of her when I re-read Greenleaf's; *"The best test ... is: Do those served grow as persons? Do they, while being served, become healthier, wiser, freer, more autonomous, more likely themselves to become servants?"* She will literally be devoting herself to Greenleaf's challenge of seeing that those served "grow as persons." She will pass Greenleaf's test and many others. I envy her starting on this path. May it lead to the continuing growth of those she serves and of herself.

* * *

Beyond "Price" (November 2018)

There are many reasons why I am grateful to San Diego State. High on the list are the opportunities it provided to meet extraordinary people — people of intelligence, vision and compassion. Two such people were Sol and Robert Price. Sol founded Fedmart that became Costco; Robert is his son, an accomplished business man in his own right.

Sol had the audacious idea of turning around an entire community: City Heights, one of the poorest and most violent neighborhoods in San Diego. His comprehensive vision for renewal embraced public safety, schools, recreation, libraries, civil discourse, jobs, housing: all the elements that make for a healthy, functioning community. One of the most memorable days of my presidency was when Sol Price called me into his office and asked if San Diego State would be a partner in transforming City Heights.

From our very first meeting with Price Charities, Robert was at the table. I don't just mean sitting there. He was an active force in shaping Sol's version and in perfecting its scope and detail. That transformation was not an easy or simple process. Sol and Robert were attempting something that had never been done before by a private party on such a profound scale. My colleagues and I at San Diego State were eager to participate. For us it was a chance to serve, a chance to learn and a chance to grow. We began having frequent meetings with Sol and Robert.

Sol was fond of saying that his major contribution to the City Heights effort was not financial, even though by now it is surely over $100M, but rather critical. And Sol was as generous with his criticism as he was with his money. Sol could ask penetrating questions, sniff out the weaknesses in any plan and readily send us back to the drawing board. I think it's fair to say that, though it was never his intent, Sol was inevitably both the smartest and most powerful person in the room. He was a force not easily resisted. It was often Robert who was able to push back when this university president did not know how to constructively do so himself. It was often Robert who would say, "But Sol," or "Let's think about that for a moment."

When the City Heights project began Sol was already telling us that he was "too old to buy green bananas." Consequently, it was often Robert who was Sol's eyes and ears on the ground. Robert was out in our three City Heights schools, Rosa Parks Elementary, Monroe Clark Middle School and Hoover High, almost daily. He knew the principals, many of the teachers, many of the students as well. And Robert brought the same attention to detail (sometimes lacking among academics like myself), to City Heights that he had previously directed toward creating a retail empire. Was there a dirty restroom? If so, Robert would find it and call it to our attention. Graffiti on a trashcan? Robert was on it. A cracked windshield of a school van? Again, Robert saw it and insisted that it be made right. In short, these were not "handle it" philanthropists who write a check and move on; they were deeply involved. All this, at the same time that Robert was Chairman of the Board and, subsequently, Chief Executive Officer of Price Smart.

Over time, as Sol's leadership of the project became increasingly big picture, his reliance on Robert's leadership grew as did his confidence that Robert had a firm grasp on both the vision and its implementation. Through Sol's vision of profound social change, and Robert's commitment to the implementation of that vision, literally tens of thousands of lives have been made better. The three public schools in City Heights that San Diego State came to administer were profoundly transformed, as were the lives of the 5000 students studying there annually and the careers of hundreds of teachers whose professional experience became one of pride and accomplishment.

Universities are in the "business" of human growth and development; entrepreneurs are typically not. In my 15 years as president of San Diego State I never encountered colleagues, in or out of our university, more committed to the realization of human growth and development than Sol and Robert Price. Their commitment was not just financial, though their generosity was awesome, but deeply personal. It sprang from a genuine concern to help those less fortunate than themselves, to transform a community and, in the process, to transform our university.

One ought to resist the temptation to categorize remarkable people like Sol and Robert, but if I were to attempt to explain Sol and his generous vision, I would suggest that he was a 1930's socialist. He believed in the common good and never lost sight of that vision. When his genius brought wealth, he used it to make a community better.

Let me conclude with a favorite Sol Price story. As noted earlier, Fedmart eventually became Costco — led by an SDSU alum named Jim Senigal. He had started with Sol as a box boy while studying at SDSU. I had the pleasure of conferring an honorary degree on Jim. The night before the ceremony we celebrated with a small dinner at University Club. Knowing Jim's fondness/respect for Sol, I invited his mentor to join us. Not long into the meal Sol turned to Jim and inquired, "So, Jim, did you learn more from San Diego State or from me?" Vintage Sol. No slouch himself, Jim immediately answered, "From you, Sol, from you." I have no doubt that was true.

* * *

Anonymous (October 16, 2012)

As I write this there is a young girl named Malala Yousafzai who is battling for her life in a London hospital after the Taliban hunted her down and shot her on a school bus at point blank range. Why? Because she had the temerity to call for educational opportunity for girls in Pakistan. I had originally written "argue for" but argument is not allowed for girls. Malala lives in a country where freedom of speech is unimaginable, and where if such a notion were to be conceived it would be judged unethical and blasphemous. Beyond that, she lives in the Swat Valley which is a region of Pakistan that has been the locus of particularly intense and vicious fighting. But still she spoke out, even after having been threatened.

The name "Malala" is an honored one in the Middle East. Her namesake, and her shepherd father supported Ayub's army in their effort to expel the British from Afghanistan. When the tide of battle (July 27, 1880) seemed to be turning in the favor of the British, young Malala took off her veil raised a flag and shouted: *"Young love! If you do not fall in the battle of Maiwand, by God, someone is saving you as a symbol of shame!"* Though Malala was killed, the Afghans rallied to defeat the intruders. This is a well-known story in the Middle East. It is probably why her parents chose this name for Malala; more importantly, her name probably propels some of her self-expectation for courage.

Contrast Malala's courage, present and predecessor, with the letter I just received. Although I am retired, my former office occasionally bundles up letters addressed to me and forwards them. Yesterday I opened one of those letters to find an anonymous author raising concerns about an athletic coach.

Here, we are in a country renowned around the world for its free speech, a country in which the framers of its constitution recognized the importance of free speech almost 250 years ago. And the letter is sent to a university, perhaps the most jealous of institutions with regard to free speech. And yet, this coward is afraid to sign his own name. I assume the author is male because in my experience women are not so cowardly and typically have more important things to do with their time than to pen a letter that is just an expression of opinion about an athletic coach. What are the odds that if he had had the courage to sign his name the university president would have tracked him down and shot him? Malala actually faced such a threat and continues to face it.

I must confess that as much as I loved my work, I hated anonymous letters such as this one. Usually, the writer was simply ignorant. Had an address been available I could have at least provided some facts and perhaps another interpretation of events. In over 35 years of administrative work in a variety of universities I only received two or three anonymous letters that were actually informative, that brought information to my attention I might not otherwise have had. Because of that remote possibility, such letters must be read, and this one will be dutifully returned to the office for which it was intended, but for every anonymous letter that might be genuinely helpful there are a hundred written by cowards such as this one.

So, here I am admiring the courage of Malala and lamenting the pusillanimous no-name who hides behind anonymity to criticize a coach. There is a phrase that one hears around athletic locker rooms which my dictionary identifies as, "*an offensive slang term referring to female genitalia; it is used to express contempt for males who have displayed a lack of strength and/or courage.*" Were I to know the name and address of this letter-writer I would be tempted, now that I am free of the constraints of office, to use that term in describing his anonymous letter. I think of that term in this context in part because it is the young girl who is showing courage and strength. Even the Taliban have the courage to stand up for their twisted views.

* * *

Charge to Graduates

For the 23 years I had the responsibility of serving as a university president I had the privilege of presenting a "Charge" to graduates. In round terms I presented this charge to approximately 180,000 students. Now I present it to you:

I give this charge to you — our newest graduates — not just as President of San Diego State University, but as one more proud parent who has watched his sons cross a stage such as this. I wish for you what I wish for them: that you may find challenges worthy of your talents and energies. I trust that you will have occasion to use, test, and eventually surpass the lessons you have learned thus far. I expect that you will come to feel and appreciate the rhythms of life, and that you will learn to walk more lightly on the earth. I trust that you will continue to discover yourself and that you will consider that self a work in progress.

I hope that you will learn how to value the wondrous diversity of the human condition, and that your mind and spirit will always be open to the thoughts, abilities, and needs of others. And finally, I hope that years from now, when you sit in a ceremony like this one celebrating the achievements of a child or friend, you will be able to look back on your own life with the satisfaction that comes from knowing you have endeavored to make this world a better place; endeavored to elevate rather than diminish the human spirit; endeavored to discern the movement of the human struggle — and that you have been a player in it.

6. LOVE
*Most of these essays are about Susan, my particular love.
However, they are also about love itself.*

Not Nostalgia (July 2013)

Last night Susan and I were up in Orono — home of the University of Maine, our first academic post. Susan went to visit an old friend; I went to give a talk about, "Building a Better University of Maine System." It's an hour and a half drive to Orono from the Point. Weather here has been unseasonably warm, 90 degrees, almost 100 in Orono. It was nice to get away for an evening's drive.

Susan's friend, Polly, used to be a neighbor — about 10 years older than we, full of wisdom and helpfulness for a young couple with their first child. Her husband, Paul, a physicist, and I used to sit by the fire on winter Sunday afternoons talking university. Polly is recently widowed, and doing great. She and Susan have reignited the friendship they shared thirty-five years ago. I was speaking at Dirigo Pines, a retirement community in Orono; it was a pleasure to see some old friends and their no-longer-familiar faces in the audience.

It was a little after 8:30 when I picked up Susan from Polly's condo:

"Okay if I put the top down?"
"Please. It's so hot!"
"How about we stop in Brewer (on the way home) for an ice cream cone?"
"Perfect."

There are few pleasures more seductive than a convertible on a sultry evening. We drove to Brewer, about 20 minutes, Susan rehearsing her evening with Polly, I telling her who was at the talk, questions that were asked, inventing brilliant post-facto responses etc... Nothing fancy. We stopped at the McDonald's drive-by window for our cones: Susan's dipped in chocolate, mine not. A couple minutes in line and we were off, furiously licking our ice cream cones to keep them from melting in the warm air. The lights of the "big city" fell away as did our conversation as we entered the Maine woods. We each attended to our cones, enjoying the quiet, the fresh air in our hair, the evening we had had.

Now more than halfway home we passed through Ellsworth, cones long since gone. Nothing on the radio so I turned on the CD player. As it happened, the disc was "Momma Mia." I am, of course, not smart enough to have planned it, but that was just the right music for two creatures of the 60's driving through the night. The music was loud, a function of having the top-down and perhaps of our fading hearing. As we turned onto our dirt road it was nearing 10:30. I felt the need to lower the volume as we snuck past our neighbors' open windows.

Top up. Down the stairs. Home. As we were getting ready for bed, I said to Susan: "I was thinking of our college drives home from Lake Erie." Those memories after a summer day at the beach; top-down; ice cream cone in hand, or snacking on a tub of Bing cherries on a hot, pre-air-conditioning night, nearly fifty years ago. She answered, "So was I." Nothing could have pleased me more. It is a rich and creamy, chocolate-covered thing to have shared life together — recalling shared experiences, moments of joy and happiness.

Our dating was no different from anyone else's — except perhaps for my clumsiness. We shared special songs, like "Moon River"; special places, the Lake Erie shore; Cranbrook; a parking spot by the Portage River, special moments, waiting for a long Midwestern train to pass as I was rushing Susan back to campus for her evening's date --not with me; an evening alone on the shore of Lake Superior, our trip to Stratford Ontario for the Shakespeare Festival.

There was a point, perhaps on those drives back to Bowling Green State from Lake Erie that we recognized how comfortable we were with one another, how easily we could share a laugh. Somewhere along the way we recognized that we could spend our lives together. Sometime later (after she had dumped me for a football player, another story for another morning, and I had "screwed my courage to the sticking post"), we decided that we would spend our lives together.

Of course, that is a presumptuous, youthful decision full of unwarranted confidence in love and in benign fates. In fact, however, that youthful presumption has been fulfilled: love has lasted; *fortuna* has been kind. Susan and I have been together, except for the football player episode, since the summer of 1962. Now we find ourselves sharing memories more than expectations, enjoying recalled moments more than seeking new ones.

The feeling I was experiencing last night and again this morning is certainly not "nostalgia," at least not in the etymological sense of "homesickness." We are perfectly "at home," perhaps more so than at any time in our lives. For it to be nostalgia one has to be longing for past moments. This is, instead, finding oneself satisfyingly at home in the present — a present enriched with an overlay of moments past. Not so much a sickness as an enhancement. Not a daydream, but a dream fulfilled, refreshing in itself. What we need here is a new phrase. I nominate "momentus augmentus" from my patched together Latin for "heightened moment." May your moments be rich and creamy and chocolate-covered. And may they occasionally be enhanced by the whiff of a treasured past.

* * *

Neatness

I remember a laughing conversation Susan and I had well before we were married. Susan mentioned her mother's sage advice: *"Always wear clean underwear; you never know when you are going to be in a car accident."* My immediate unexpressed thought was that I might have HAD clean underwear, but.... In any event, it serves as a reminder not only of mid-western wisdom, but also that we are each conscious of the fictions we maintain and wary of being found out. We live public lives different in more or less serious ways from our private ones. We are each conscious of how we will be viewed/judged by others.

Susan used to always keep the house relatively "picked up." Neatness is a common human fiction. She did this as a matter of routine, of habit, I think at least in part because she was aware that someone might drop by. I on the other hand was oblivious. Why? Was it just my slovenliness? Maybe, but I think it was also that, in this regard at least, I lived in a blame free zone. Had someone in fact dropped by, the mess would not have reflected badly on me (its maker) but rather, unfairly, on Susan (its "unmaker"). I am aware of this now, after Susan's death, because the mess, were I to allow it to persist, would reflect on ME. I have gained a similar awareness about entertaining. Are these cups right? This teapot? Would cookies be appropriate? Nuts? Wine?

Recently I was present at a lovely meeting of "Bridges," a woman's group Susan founded in San Diego and which happily persists to this day. The meeting was at Jane's house. I was the only male except for Richard, Jane's husband, who kindly assumed car-parking duty complete with tags for each set of car keys. These Bridges members are each remarkable, accomplished ladies. They enjoyed Susan and discovering other impressive women through her.

In any event, that late-afternoon "Tea" was an occasion for me to reflect on how I have changed/evolved since Susan's death. Now, occasionally being a host myself, I was aware of Jane's fine, ivory and blue, china cups, the small folded cloth napkins, the tasteful (in both senses) snacks. I was also aware of how beautifully each of the women was dressed — and was silently relieved that I had worn appropriate clothes.

Susan used to always take care of my clothing choices with a consciousness that they reflected on San Diego State. Of course, they also, again unfairly, reflected on her. I am still occasionally being complimented on a sweater or a sport coat to which I inevitably respond, "Susan chose it."

Why do I burden you with these reflections? Because they lead to another one. It is a cliché to suggest that a widow/widower is diminished by the death of a mate. In many ways that is true, but in many other ways one grows, becomes more aware, develops new capacities/abilities that were formerly not needed because one's partner handled them (e.g. entertaining, cooking, laundry, neatening up the house, etc...). I have not shrunk after Susan's death; I have grown. Perhaps that is still another gift she has given me.

* * *

A Halloween Memory (October 2016)

Susan and I married in June of 1965 in her hometown of Urbana, Ohio. We honeymooned on Cape Cod; briefly returned to Ohio to load our meager belongings into a U-Haul trailer; hitched it to Susan's blue Volkswagen beetle (with sunroof) and headed west to Boulder and the University of Colorado — the magic of it all sprinkling pixy dust in our path. Once in Boulder we settled into a furnished, one bedroom, married-student apartment and began "playing house."

It was, of course, a time of discovery. I used to tell parents, concerned about their children living in residence halls, that this was part of their education, a chance to learn that not every family behaved as theirs; that some showered daily, others not; that some put the cap back on the toothpaste, others not; that some.... Well, you get the idea. There are many ways to invent the human condition.

Newly-weds go through a similar process of discovery and adjustment. Susan and I were relatively young, 23 and 24, so there was much to discover, less to adjust. Which brings me to my story. We had settled into our married routine: Susan teaching Junior High (now Middle School) near Denver; I was studying philosophy. There was the weekly grocery shopping, the figuring out (i.e. adjusting) budgets, the parties with other graduate students, making new friends, etc...

I should interject that Susan's father had owned and operated a small gift/stationary shop in Urbana. Part of the life of a gift shop is the celebration of holidays. Did you know, for instance, that there is a "Sweetest Day?" Well, there is. You can look it up, third Saturday in October. And a newly-wed husband ought not forget it, even if he never knew it. Susan was aware of holidays in a way that I was not, part of my adjustment. Having blown Sweetest Day, I should have seen Halloween coming, but of course being an obtuse graduate student, I did not.

One afternoon Susan came home from school with bags of candy for the marauding neighborhood ghosts and goblins — and a large pumpkin. Our evening project would be to carve the pumpkin. Dinner complete, we spread newspaper on the Formica-topped kitchen table, turned up the brightness of the overhead light, picked a sturdy knife... Susan: "Why don't you get started while I finish up these dishes?" "OK," I responded, getting into the spirit, no pun intended, of the occasion. I went to my modest built-in desk, extracted a small, flexible plastic ruler and began drawing the projected Jack-o-lantern face onto the still-pumpkin surface. All the sudden, from the area of the sink came a horrified cry, "What are you doing?" "Making a Jack-o-lantern," I responded. Susan, mortified and incredulous: "With a ruler!!!"

She stepped to the table, pushed her wonky husband aside, and said, "Here. Let me show you," she suppressed fool, "how to make a Jack-o-lantern." Where upon she grabbed the knife firmly and with purpose plunged it into the innocent squash. I share this Halloween memory in part because it is the season, but also because it reminds me of the wonder of two lives experiencing one another, shocking one another, pleasing and displeasing one another — and literally educating ("leading forth") one another.

I loved sharing those experiences with Susan; young and old they continued throughout our marriage. I had never thought I would have the opportunity to share such experiences again, to experience another human being when we are not each wearing our public faces. Now I have such an opportunity. It is full of wonders, and surprises, and lessons learned. My ad-hoc, improvised, free-hand Jack-o-lantern glows brightly this Halloween eve.

* * *

Poem for Susan

<u>For Susan</u>

Two butterflies flutter together
    from distant regions of the garden.
They circle, rise and fall in a dance
    of recognition and wonder,
So alike, yet so different
    sharing the echinacea.
A gentle breeze bows the flower,
    they lift off, but settle back
    held together not by the nectar
    but by the sharing of it.

Time passes; the sun drops lower,
    shadows stretch across the garden.
Still, they are together, their flight
    no longer the frantic flitter of morning.
Now slower, more knowing
    ripened by time and sharing.
Mutually confident their circles broaden
    one samples the flax
    the other rides the liatris
Yet they are drawn back to the echinacea
    not by the nectar
    but by the sharing of it

Never again to be
 one and other
Each forever changed.

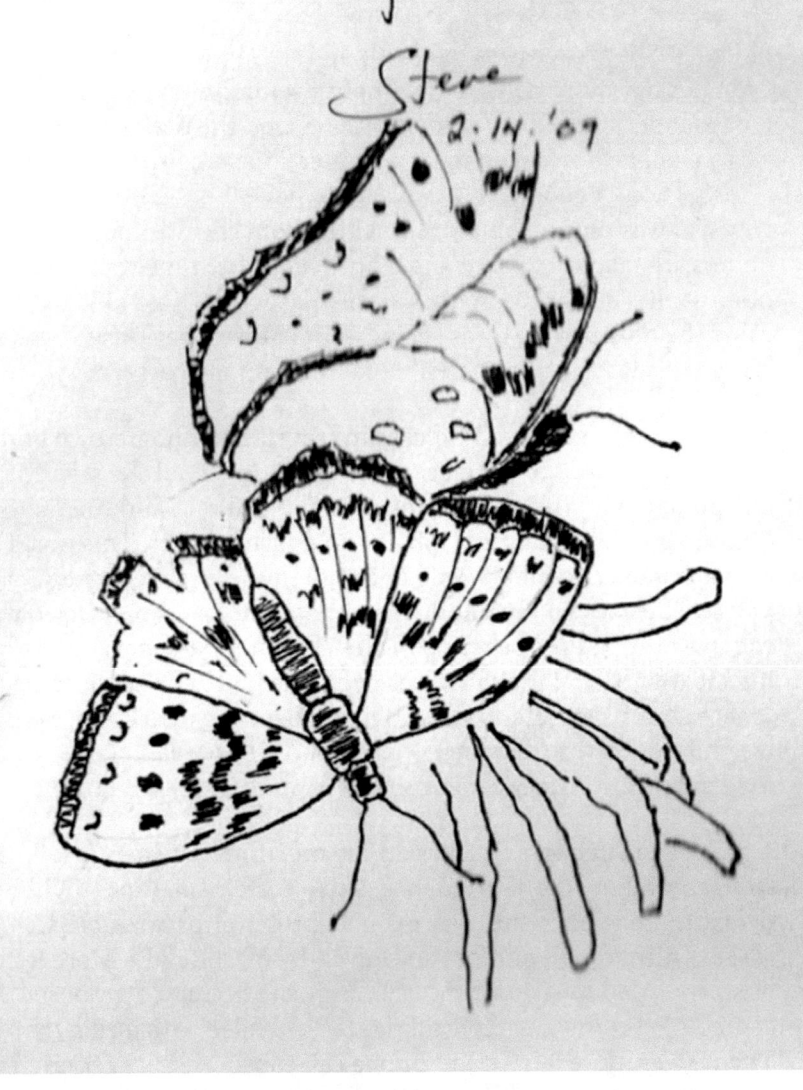

Steve
2.14.'09

* * *

Compact of the Heart (February 2002)

Lives are formed in mysterious ways. Mine began to take shape, without my knowing it, in a Modern English Poetry class at Bowling Green State University. There I encountered a pretty face with clear, intelligent if sleepy eyes, a strong chin (I had no idea what that would portend!), and the most delightful laugh I had ever heard. I was smitten. Some cups of coffee, a few well-planned accidental meetings, one or two pitiful efforts to display my intelligence in class, and a first double date soon followed on July 4, 1962.

I liked it. She was easy to talk with, fun to be with, self-confident, and interesting. A few more dates and without ever quite discerning the beginning, a compact began to form. Somewhere beyond the dating dance at which I was so inept there began to be a connection, a discovery of shared interests, a perception of goodness, a capacity to have fun together — a compact. Of course, I was not the only suitor with whom she was having fun, but philosophers are taught to share and a little bit of her time was far better than none at all. Four or five more dates, at last a kiss (just kidding), and she became the only person I was seeing –- of course, previously I was seeing no one so this was not a remarkable sacrifice on my part.

There followed contrived excuses to travel to her hometown and idyllic dates on the shore of Lake Erie. I was pulling out all the stops. But she was just pulling out: first to Wisconsin for the summer and then to Grosse Pointe for her first fulltime job as an English teacher. This was, I told myself, inevitable; I could handle it. But then there came a fateful day. I can still see it clearly in my mind. We were sitting in a small Detroit restaurant, she in a cruel (in retrospect), off-the-shoulder peasant blouse. She was telling me that our relationship was over. She had been seduced by the "charms" of a football player and hence sent the philosopher packing. But we philosophers are a patient bunch; though football players can be a passing fancy even a cheerleader can sow only so many wild oats.

A year or so later, after a few midway meetings between Toledo and Detroit, continuing correspondence, and a certain amount of whimpering on my part, the relationship was resumed, the compact restored. But now it was my turn to pull out for the University of Colorado. More letters. She was persuaded to visit for the Thanksgiving holiday. I proposed. She accepted. The compact grew still tighter — sealed with a ring that Christmas. Then it was more letters and phone calls until we were reunited when I came back from Colorado and she from Grosse Pointe.

The wedding was on a hot day in June, the 27th to be exact, in her hometown. No cold feet. It felt right from the first minute. The compact had long preceded the wedding, which was merely its formal acknowledgment. Honeymoon in New England; back to Boulder for another year at the University of Colorado; then three years at Notre Dame. She working; me studying while all the time realizing that this compact was not only making me happy, it was making me better.

Next came Maine. Wallpapering at Mr. Kelly's house showed how strong the compact was. And our first trip to Europe showed us how much sheer fun and adventure it could be. Life-long friendships were formed. We bought our first home. Son Rick soon joined us. Now the compact had expanded to three and let us grow into caring for and teaching our own child. Then son Matt joined us: completely different, except in loveability. What fine memories.

We took our expanded compact on the road. It prospered in Connecticut just as it had in Maine. While the kids grew and developed and overcame threats by neighborhood bullies, Susan and I sat through Cub Scout meetings and Little League games. The compact was reinforced. We screwed our courage to the sticking post and bought the Maine property on Frenchman Bay, which has come to mean so much to us all through these years.

In Minnesota Susan was not only a working mother, but increasingly a community leader, beginning a long line of civic involvements. Rick and Matt continued to thrive: good schools, a wonderful town in which to roam and grow. And, perhaps most of all, they achieved their first real sense of excellence via swimming. Now our compact was tempered as we watched swim meets in hothouse pools and then froze as we dashed to a frigid car in the dark Minnesota night. You know the compact is strong when you roll out of a warm and cozy bed at 5:00am to drive Rick around his paper route in minus 30-degree weather.

In many ways, I think the days in Oswego were the best of all. Rick and Matt were growing into fine young men. Swimming persisted with "Weber" beginning to dominate the record board. We treated them to their first visit to Europe. Susan was busy teaching and leading in the community; I was busy "presidenting." The campus and community understood and appreciated the contributions we made. Matt and Rick found some ways to test us, but the compact was strong enough to hold them and we all escaped without serious damage, except for a few parental gray hairs. The hardest part was the semester I spent at the system office in Albany while Susan held down the fort in Oswego. That was hard, but the compact was strong and saw us through. The next semester Susan joined me in Albany.

Then, just when the kids thought we could no longer surprise them, we were off for San Diego and southern California — and the culture shocks that came with them. It wasn't easy at first and it's still not easy, but once again, in spite of our advancing age, we grew to take on new challenges and opportunities. The university prospered. Once again, Susan emerged as a community leader.

Now here we are, Valentine's Day, 2002, in a strange and foreign land. Our compact has expanded to include Kath, a great addition who helps Rick grow just as Susan helped me. The adventure continues, as does the compact. Susan is more active in the community than ever before and doing a world of good. I get to play with a really big train set. We are both able to use the talents and abilities we have acquired over the years to good and important purposes. Rick and Matt, full of intelligence and decency, are launched on good and productive lives.

So, my love, when you open this little Valentine "sus" remember that the reason I like to give you compacts* is because you have given me such a wonderful one.

Happy Valentine's Day.

As ever,**

    steve

* I used to give Susan antique compacts, i.e. small shiny cases containing a mirror and powder, when I returned from my travels.

** There is a story behind this closing. When we were dating I would frequently write Susan long tortured love letters. They would end with affirmations of "undying", "aching", "unconditional" (Thank you Paul Tillich.), love. She, being more mature, and perhaps less desperate, would sign her letters "As ever."

Sigh.

* * *

Picnics (May 2013)

Susan has a genius (you will come to understand why I use that privileged word) for picnics.

Our first date was a picnic at a Fourth of July celebration on the banks of the Maumee River. We doubled dated with my cousin Doug. While Susan and I were in summer school at Bowling Green State we would occasionally escape on a Saturday to the beaches of Lake Erie in my 1957, pink Olds 98 convertible. We would drive east on two-lane roads: 105 to 163 to Rt.2 through Oak Harbor, Port Clinton, and Sandusky (birth place of Doris Day) toward the beaches that were then unspoiled, as were we, cupping clear, clean water.

But we would not go directly, no matter how hot it might be or how eager we were for a summer swim. First the treasure hunt: we would stop at a farmer's market. Susan would choose sweet cherries, perhaps a plum or two, maybe some apples. There was a cheese shop a few miles farther down the road. We would stop for some cheddar and crackers, perhaps some coke or cold beer. Then, and only then would we proceed to the beach. A towel was spread for each of us and one for the picnic feast. I don't remember anyone else on the beach — which is surely not possible on a summer weekend in Ohio. In the lingering evening we would drive home, perhaps with the open basket of cherries between us on the seat, Susan's long white scarf (wrapped Audrey Hepburn style around her head) trailing in the breeze. I drove as slowly as traffic would allow, not wanting the day to end even with the prospect of a chaste kiss waiting on the sorority house steps.

Perhaps my favorite picnic was on the remote shore of Lake Superior. It was the summer after Susan graduated from BGSU. She was a counselor at Camp Minong near Hayward, Wisconsin. I was again in summer school. I drove up to spend a weekend with her. Susan had learned from other camp counselors of a remote beach on Lake Superior — perhaps an hour away. But, not surprisingly, half the fun was getting there and building our picnic along the way. We bought the usual fruit, and cheese and crackers and this time a bottle of wine. But wine ought not to be drunk from paper cups so we drove all the way into Duluth to find wine glasses. I ended up buying two used Martini glasses from a bar.

The beach could only be found if you knew where you were going. Smaller and smaller back roads, finally a dirt road, then a path over a dune — and there was Lake Superior spread before us and the deserted beach. This time there actually were no other people there. By now it was late afternoon. We swam a bit in the frigid water, then dried off in the sun before enjoying our picnic once again spread out on its own towel. I gathered driftwood for an evening fire. It would not be dark until well after 9:00, but the fire was warm and cozy. A stray dog joined us, laying just beyond the penumbra of the fire, its head resting on crossed paws. I still have a picture of Susan in her black and white swimsuit leaning against some driftwood.

So, a few days ago, fifty years later, Susan's picnic genius once again reasserted itself. We had invited some friends over for sake. He is a Ph.D. in English Literature from SUNY Binghamton; she is a certified Master

Gardener. As it happened we could not find a date that worked and ended up going to their house last evening, which happened to be Memorial Day. I thought: what a shame that they cannot enjoy the way Susan would have entertained. Susan thought: Japanese picnic!

So we went to town to buy some good sake and to order some fresh, sushi and sashimi. Susan chose just the right basket into which she put a handmade pear wood box by Wendy Maruyama filled with tiny linen napkins. Lacquered Japanese, not the bulkier/blunter Chinese, chopsticks were added for all, along with carved jade chopstick rests. Wasabi and ginger were arrayed on a lovely sculpted Japanese plate in the shape of a reclining princess. Tiny cruets of soy sauce and sweet sauce stood by. Two sake pitchers, each with two matching dollhouse cups, were added as were miscellaneous Japanese bowls, a tiny oriental vase filled with that afternoon's wildflowers and some bleeding heart from our garden filled the last crevasse in our basket.

Our friends supplied a lovely home, an old cobbler's bench table around which to gather, stimulating conversation and a homemade spring rolls with homemade peanut sauce. Not all picnics have to be on the beach. I could not resist taking some photos:

Now, if only I could figure out how to share that photo of Susan in her swimsuit!

* * *

Yesterday (June 2015)

The instructor on my morning Tai Chi DVD tells me that, "The beauty of Tai Chi is about change. Everything around us is changing constantly. We do not stop the change, but have to harmonize ourselves with the change." You can hear in that a similarity between ancient Chinese wisdom and western Stoicism. At another spot on the disc he cautions us about being too aggressive (no, not for you youngsters), in a challenging, move: "It is based on what we can do, not on what we want to do." And so, it is that I adjust and do what I can.

As I have worked to invent life without Susan I have shied away from outward signs of grief. Kierkegaard is contemptuous of those who wear Christianity on their sleeve, arguing that it is a properly inward thing. So, too, is grief. I have some black shirts that I would normally wear, but I do not want them to be taken as a cheap sign of grieving; they hang silently in the closet waiting for next summer when the danger of misunderstanding will have passed. I try to involve myself in life, serve on committees, participate in conference calls, do my volunteer tasks, enjoy friends not as substitutes for grieving, but as expressions of normalcy. And there are some activities that make me feel especially close to Susan: filling our bird feeders, walking the shore, tending to the garden, reading on the deck.

Yesterday was Susan's birthday. I needed to mark the occasion. To do so I decided, well in advance, that I would suspend my normal activities: no Y, or grocery shopping, or Post Office. Instead, I would stay at home with my thoughts and devote the day to things Susan. I began, I know this sounds silly coming from an atheist, by lighting a candle on the fireplace hearth that would burn with two substitutions through the day.

I have been working on arrangements for the Celebration of Susan's life that we will be doing here on the Point a month from now. I have to revise my remarks, originally intended for a San Diego audience, to better suit friends on the Point. While San Diegans did not know the younger Susan, and it was fun to share her with them, "Pointers" do not know her life "away." In some ways it was the same Susan in each role; in others, not. Both Maine and San Diego knew her laughter and her conversational skills, but Pointers do not know her competence, her accomplishments, her organizational wisdom. I will try to share some of that with them. Here on the Point Susan was relaxed, unhurried, deeply appreciative of the natural beauty. She enjoyed friends, but not the social activities that were so much a part of our professional lives.

As I write I am reminded of a moment that sheds some light on this difference. In San Diego, and Oswego before, entertaining was often on a wholesale scale. Susan would work with staff to sort out arrangements, making sure that everything was just right, being conscious of representing the university well and gracefully. But, of course, we did not do the actual food preparation or the subsequent clean up ourselves, as we had earlier in our lives. I remember with pleasure those former late nights as junior faculty members, the glow still lingering after a successful dinner party, washing dishes at 2:00 a.m. and not being the least bit tired; just reliving the occasion, re-enjoying our friends' conversation. Laughing. Susan enjoyed preparing for those meals. They were occasions not only for hospitality but also for creativity. As their scale increased through the years, Susan's direct involvement necessarily decreased. She missed that.

I recall an occasion in Maine, after retirement, when Susan put together a spectacular occasion around a Japanese theme for a couple she knew would appreciate it. She served several kinds of Sushi, all on Japanese china — including a small Japanese dish holding fresh ground Wasabi. Japanese chopsticks, not Chinese, were at the ready. Saki was served in small Japanese carafes each couple having their own along with two tiny/matching cups.

Japanese flutes sounded softly from our CD player. A Japanese vase from Kyoto sat in the center of the coffee table where we shared the meal before our fireplace. A bouquet of flowers, delphinium and bleeding hearts, from our garden recalled the Japanese aesthetic. It was almost like kids playing at tea, which Susan served at the end from a Japanese tea set.

In San Diego, many, many people told me how much they appreciated Susan's ability to make them feel welcome, special, attended to. Those skills took a different, no less appreciated, form here in Maine. So, I am looking forward to sharing the "wholesale" Susan with friends who know only her "retail" expression.

Another thought from yesterday in at least two senses: I mentioned that I had a single taper burning on the fireplace hearth. Were you to look up you would see a wall, punctured by windows on either side of the fireplace; we called that our "wall of strong women," one of many appreciations Susan and I shared.

Let me walk you through it: Upper right, a painting entitled, "Bringing the Pipe" by a friend of ours, Michael Lewis, from the University of Maine. Beneath it, a painting by another friend, David Baker. You know David as the artist who painted Susan's portrait. Below that, resting on the window frame is a beaded mace Susan brought back from Africa. To the left a large ceramic plate fashioned by an African American Artist from Syracuse. Beneath that a faded print of a spectacular painting by Paul Cadmus entitled "Hommage to Reynaldo Hahn." A better view...

Paul kindly inscribed it, "To Steve and Susan." The large painting in the center is, "The Ponderer" by a Maine artist named Leo Brooks; it was Susan's favorite. To its left, two more paintings by David Baker.

I have left out a few things. At the extreme right is a citation from the California State Board of Trustees authorizing the "Susan and Stephen Weber Honors College" at San Diego State. I have hung Susan's portrait at 90 degrees contemplating the citation and the "wall of strong women." Beneath the citation is a small, framed medal, a gift from Matt to Susan, from the Soviet Union presented to citizens who had given birth to 25 or more children — strong women, indeed!!!

On the mantel is some dried sea heather from our beach, a piece of obsidian from the Salton Sea, and, illegal to possess, an eagle feather that an eagle discreetly dropped on our forest floor. That is Sisypha, not Sisyphus, on the coffee table. She is pulling rather than pushing the stone. Put the pulling and the pushing together and (if you will remember the myth), the gods don't have a chance. As you can tell, the house is full of memories. They are pleasant, gratifying; mostly they make me smile at my good fortune to have shared this life with such a woman.

My quiet, June 24, included baking a rhubarb pie. Susan was a great cook -- though in later years she rarely had time to indulge her skill. One of our favorites was rhubarb pie, from our own rhubarb, of course. Susan used to make a wonderful pie crust. I have the recipe, but not the skill/courage to attempt it. Instead mine is a homemade filling poured into a store-bought crust. Instead of Susan's double crust, mine has a crumble on top. It turned out quite well, if I do say so myself.

Yesterday afternoon I had a lovely call from Jane Haskel, Susan's best friend. How kind/thoughtful. We shared memories; laughed a bit; cried a bit. In the evening as the wind died down, as it tends to do at that time of day, and the Bay settled, as it tends to do at that time of day, I paddled out to the center of the Bay where Rick, Matt and I had scattered Susan's ashes and just floated quietly beneath a pink-blue sky, looking south to the open sea with a setting sun over my right shoulder.

As darkness fell I watched a bit of TV and then read as Susan's taper burned lower and lower. I waited for it to extinguish itself. When finally, it began to flicker, I set down my book, turned out the light and sat alone in the dark with the diminishing flame. When its light ended I looked up, out the south-facing windows to see scores of fireflies picking up the flame and sending it forth on new adventures.

My Tai Chi disc instructor is right: life is change; we must harmonize ourselves with it. As he would also say, but in another context, we must find our balance. Yesterday was a day of finding balance, of memories, and of gratitude. I assure you I am fine. I am not wallowing in despair or self-pity, or anything stickier than rhubarb pie. I just felt like a quiet day of reflection. Thank you for sharing it with me.

* * *

Home Alone (January 2016)

No one waiting for me
As I shoulder my way through the crowd
of other-directed
greetings and hugs.
No one with whom to share tales of the adventure
on the long drive home,
or to lie to about the hazards of travel.
No one to catch me up on the local news and gossip.
Pulling into the dark drive of a dark house, alone.
Opening the door, alone.
Fighting the luggage, groceries, and mail into the cold house, alone.
Alone turning on the lights, one by one,
each revealing the house to be exactly as I left it.
No human activity without my own.
Upstairs a still unexplored, but a predictably cold and dark bedroom awaits.
Susan and I used to joke with one another about the pleasures of being
home alone when one or the other of us was traveling.
Having the house to oneself.
Not having to accommodate another human being.
Eating, sleeping working when you like, as you like.
Exclusively controlling the TV remote.
Since Susan died those empty "pleasures" are now all mine.
How I long for the inconvenience of another person.

* * *

Grief (October 12, 2015)

There used to be conventions about grieving: wearing black, draping crape, mourning jewelry. We are better off without such things. Kierkegaard used to say that outward signs of Christianity, (today he might be referring to tattoos of ornate crosses, fish symbols on cars — or "Jesus Loves You" bumper stickers), detract from rather than enhance true religiosity which is properly inward. So, too, is grief. Susan died a year ago today. Convention would have it that the traditional period of mourning has elapsed. This is, of course, a silly idea. Mourning is not a matter of elapsed time or of a completed revolution around the sun. But I do have some thoughts about the experience of grieving that I am now in a better condition to express.

The first moment is one of shock — no matter how recognizably inevitable the event. One is emotionally raw, disorientated because so much of one's orientation was focused around the other. There are, and they linger still, unexpected moments in which you forget and then have to remember that your loved one is no longer here. Instincts well up to share a lovely flower, the sighting of an uncommon bird, or a particularly worthy passage in a book and things less grand, like neighborhood gossip.

There then sets in a profound sadness unlike anything I had ever experienced. A sadness born of loss and perhaps a bit of self-pity. One wants time alone. Energy is difficult to summon. But in my case, at least, the sobbing ended to be replaced, when you thought it was thoroughly past, by unexpected moments of re-recognition. The days are long; the nights longer. However, the long days are not empty. There is truth in the cliché that "life goes on." There is laundry to be done, mail to answer, dishes to wash.... In spite of which, I find myself reflecting on Susan, on our relationship, on who I am and how I will re-configure myself as time goes on.

Anniversaries unexpectedly announce themselves. When I am driving south on our dirt road the now-low morning sun lights up the film on the inside of my windshield making it hard to see. When I got out some Windex and paper towels to clean off the film I realized that the last time I had cleaned the inside of the windows on the Lexus was when I prepared to take Susan down to Brigham and Women's in Boston.

Friends are particularly welcome/valuable during this time. Not that they can say much to alleviate your sorrow, but the fact that they wish they could be is somehow appreciated. As are the pieces of the puzzle they, sometimes inadvertently, supply. Their memories of events/moments of which you were not a part, but which continue to fill out the mosaic of Susan: her joy, her thoughtfulness, her wit. In the process, just as Sartre said, a finished picture begins to emerge, not to be put aside on a shelf, but as a product of the mind's constant mulling, a void that must be explored, like your tongue being drawn to the roughness of a chipped tooth.

This time of reflection and memory is not at all unpleasant. Perhaps it is a therapeutic pleasure. A friend who recently lost her husband referred to these unexpected moments as "grief bursts." I reminded her that they are not all painful. Certainly, they can be, but more often than not, I find my memories of Susan a source of pleasure. One such memory presented itself recently. I stopped by a local discount store called Reny's to buy some cheap vases to hold garden flowers to present to various hostesses here on the Point. While there I saw some large, fully-budded mums. My end-of-summer garden was looking a bit peaked. The mums were cheap. I liked them even more. I was sold.

These are large, perhaps twenty inches in diameter, mums — just beginning to open. I bought three. I squeezed two into the small trunk of the

Audi and put the third on the floor in front of the passenger seat. Business as usual, just another errand after the Y, but then an unexpected memory made me smile.

A few years ago, Susan and I were in Reny's when she saw a predecessor of those large mums and wanted it. The trunk was already full. We ended up squeezing the mum in between Susan's legs as she sat in the tiny passenger seat compartment: the flower pot between her knees; the crown of the plant filling her lap. Not much legroom, but not a long ride home.

About five minutes into our return-to-the-Point drive there was a commotion. A small bat had secreted itself in the mum. My driving or our talking had roused it and caused it to flutter forth onto our dash. It was discombobulated, as I often am upon awakening. Susan was cool as could be. "Isn't it cute? It's so tiny!" I was less composed. I pulled over to the side of the road (some might say lurched), and lowered the windows. The bat was happy to leave. Thinking of this little — otherwise forgotten event — made me smile, even chuckle at Susan's calm and my lack of same.

There are several things I have come to understand/appreciate about Susan. First, what a feminist she was. Not in the bra-burning sense (though I encouraged that!), but in the sense of self-confidence, in being comfortable with who she was, and her interest in supporting other women — especially promising/talented young ones. Her work with the YWCA and with Bridges are examples of this, but also her one-on-on interactions with so many other women.

Strangely, we have the phrase, "a man's man," but not its converse. Susan was, "a woman's woman." She particularly enjoyed the company of other women; celebrated their successes; held their secrets. Susan was literally capable of treating everyone the same way — heads of state, celebrities, the wealthy, school kids, tradesmen. Perhaps that is why they all enjoyed her so much. She, unlike me, did not have an agenda other than making that person feel welcome and comfortable. She was genuinely interested in other people.

Another clarity emerged from reviewing old photos in preparation for our celebration of her life. I was first attracted to Susan by her laugh and her smile, then by the person I came to know. As time went by I recognized her wisdom and competence. I always knew she was an attractive person, but now, when I look at some of those old photos I recognize to my embarrassment that she was gorgeous.

Look at this:

or this ...

and this ...

Or this one that is still a favorite of mine ...

So, it turns out that Stevie Weber was sleeping with a "babe" — when he (clueless to the end), just thought it was his Susan.

I mention these revelations because they are the product of this period of reflection and introspection, a period that is surely not complete, regardless of the just completed revolution around our sun. The raw emotions heal; the sadness lessens, and lessens; the memories, the thinking about, the missing linger. I hope and expect they always will.

Last winter I wanted to be alone in a cold and dark place, though I could not have articulated why. I now think there was a subconscious wisdom in that. There is something beneficial about living with the cycles of nature at such a time: seeing the ducks raft up for their flights south, enjoying the hillsides painted crimson and yellow, watching the first snows spread white across the evergreens, feeling the plunging temperatures, experiencing the shortening days.

And, of course, the reverse with the coming of spring: the return of the robins, the lengthening/warming days, the appearance of the crocus and daffodil. It reminds one of the cycles of which we are all inevitably a part. That those cycles are natural. That, as the Stoics taught us:

"Never in any case say I have lost such a thing, but I have returned it. Is your child dead? It is a return. Is your wife dead? It is a return. Are you deprived of your estate? Is not this also a return?" — Epictetus

When people ask, less frequently now, how I am doing. I respond: "I'm doing well." Turns out that response is not only socially acceptable, it is true. I am doing surprisingly well. If people inquire further I add that: "Susan did not raise me to be a wimp." Also true.

I have grown a lot in this past year: discovered some things about myself, that I am stronger and more self-reliant than I suspected, learned some new skills, become a better friend and more a part of Point society. It has, truthfully, been the longest year of my life. But in strange ways I could not have anticipated it has also been a year filled with growth. I write not only to note the celestial moment but also to thank you for sharing, via these essays, this year with me. I miss having Susan to talk with. You have filled some of that void, for which I am most grateful.

* * *

YES (April 2015)

Sometimes the things we most admire are right in front of us but go unrecognized. Like the father who preaches courage but does not recognize it in his eight year-old son who walks to school every day knowing that he will be accosted by bullies on the way home; or the man who admires athleticism, but cannot see it in his daughter's ballet lessons; or the daughter who does not see her mother's courage as she descends into old age; or... Enough, it is often easier to embrace a virtue in principle than in its instantiation. This is what Aristotle was getting at in his "Practical Syllogism" when he said, in effect, that it is not enough to condemn stealing, you have to recognize it in the tax evasion you are contemplating and, beyond that, in this questionable deduction.

And so it is with me: the forest sometimes escapes me for the trees. One of the philosophic concepts I most admire is Nietzsche's "Sacred Yes." Some quick context: Nietzsche asked what if time were infinite and hence eternal and physical reality, finite? Then each and every combination of those finite elements would have to be repeated (recycled) time and time again. This is what he meant by the "Eternal Return," (don't get hung up on it; it is just a conceit to get where he is going). He reasoned from this that each of us would not only come back to relive our life again and again, but that we would be forced to relive each and every part of our life: the tedious committee meeting yesterday afternoon; our adolescent humiliations, the dumb/vindictive boss, even those weeks with mononucleosis.

His point was that if you could not say "Yes" to it all, then you have not fully lived; not fully said "Yes" to any part of it. You have harbored false hopes that the next time will be better. As he put it, "*On the tree future we build our nest.*" Which is to say, we do not live in the here and now. Which is to say, we do not live. It is only by saying "Yes" to it all, that we say "Yes" to any of it."

In the past few months I have been thinking a lot about Susan and what made her so special. Many of you have helped me in those reflections with your thoughts and remembrances. Of course, Susan was smart, and gregarious, and full of good humor. But there was something else, something more. And, I am ashamed to say after knowing her for 52 years, that I have just come to recognize it. And "it" is precisely what I have so long admired in the abstract: Susan said "Yes" to it all. Yes to the spiders as well as the butterflies; yes to the crows as well as the eagles. She used to say, "People would be more struck by the beauty of crows if crows were not so common."

One of the cards I recently received marveled that just after having been diagnosed with a fatal illness, Susan listened to a friend's minor physical complaint without saying a thing about her own challenge. That was typical. Indeed, Susan never complained about her illness; never lost sight of our good fortune or of the goodness and beauty spread across this globe. It was right there in front of me and I did not see it. Susan truly said, "Yes" to it all. Perhaps that is why she was so happy and so fulfilled. In any event, having preached Nietzsche for over fifty years, it is now incumbent upon me to also say "Yes."

* * *

Intimacy (November 2014)

I wrote this essay a month or so before Susan died, and put it aside, only to pick it up again now... I have been thinking a lot about intimacy lately perhaps because I am experiencing so much of it and am hungry for more.

My Onion's Dictionary of English Etymology tells me that our word "intimacy" comes from the Latin, "intimatus" meaning *inmost* — hence inward, essential, intrinsic. When I was young I thought a lot about intimacy — mostly about breasts and crotches. The word clueless does not suffice. Later, when Susan and I were first married, we were much more like kids playing hooky, or house, or doctor, which is to say happily enjoying ourselves and one another, but hardly intimates. What was missing?

One has to achieve personhood oneself before intimacy is possible. One has to have an "inner" before it can be shared. And (though Susan was surely ahead of me on that path) we were not yet there. I was still a graduate student; Susan a high school English and Communications teacher. It was a great and grand adventure, but mostly directed outward. I don't think we became truly intimate until after Rick was born. That intimacy was then rooted in my dawning comprehension of Susan's prodigious competency. How did she unerringly know what to do? Where did these instincts come from? Playmate turned into admired colleague. And, then, of course, as time moved on, she was the rock: calm, unflappable in the midst of every domestic and professional emergency. Susan had an "inner" and it was solid steel.

Yet, we were still young. Neither of us set out to live the lives that finally presented themselves to us. Susan was happy to be a school teacher; I to be a philosopher. But unexpected opportunities presented themselves along the way. We would sit up all night in bed talking them over, deciding whether or not to set sail on each new adventure. An old colleague recently wrote to me, having learned of Susan's illness. He did not know her well but recalled what a great hostess she was. That was true from the beginning. When I was still a faculty member and Rick had just been born, Susan and I used to host an Open House each fall. Perhaps 75 people would gather in our first home by the Stillwater River in Orono. Even then Susan was as spectacular a host as I was an inept one.

And the dinner parties! Young professionals, just starting careers and families. Susan preferred to invite three couples. The eight of us would sit around our round oak table in the dining room. She would serve a fresh garden salad to start, accompanied by toasted home-made garlic bread sliced into 2x1x5 inch beams. The main course would be a delicacy such as made-from-scratch beef bourgeon, (thank you Julia Childs), or perhaps beef stroganoff (those were the red-meat days!). For dessert Susan would bring a home-made, flaming Baked Alaska into the candle-lit room. The laughter, the friendship, the shared moments of our young lives: it was bliss.

Afterwards, when our friends finally left well after midnight, Susan and I would be up late in the kitchen cleaning up, reliving the evening. I say this because Susan comes by her hostess qualities naturally. They are intrinsic. She loves people; she listens well; she has a great sense of humor.

When you think of it: how does a small-town girl from rural Ohio become such an accomplished "First Lady" of universities? I think intrinsic is wrong. She paid attention, she watched and she learned. She did not have to learn to be gregarious, or how to make people feel at ease, but to understand the complexities of university entertaining — to host thousands of people in a single year — that was surely (and well) learned. Once again, my admiration and our intimacy grew.

As our lives unfolded, it turned out that Susan was wonderfully suited to the role of Dean's wife, of Academic V.P.'s wife, of President's wife, everyone could see that. What they could not see was her support and wisdom, first in moderating my enthusiasms, but most importantly in being my chief guide and consultant. Part of our intimacy has been the fact that we ended up working as partners. Susan once said she could imagine no worse life than that of a pastor's wife but, of course, the life we had was similar in many ways. She made my business her own. Susan knew the universities we served almost as well as I. She was a great reality check as my capacity for self-delusion would occasionally threaten to overwhelm.

Perhaps part of true intimacy is knowing another person better than he knows himself. But it is more than just "knowing"; it is acting on that knowledge. A profound, existential trust, the placing of your life in another's hands. You must have first assumed responsibility for your life — i.e. become an adult. But then, to pass that responsibility to another, to ask him or her to guide your decisions, that is intimacy. An intimacy in which you rely more on the other than on yourself, when you know that she sees better, farther, more clearly. And you do not doubt for an instant that, no matter how unwelcome the advice may be, she has your best interest at heart — and knows that best interest better than you do.

If being a whole person is a criterion for intimacy, the consequence of prolonged intimacy is becoming a changed person. Susan and I now often comment on how alike we have become, how I seem to have become more social and she less so. The inwardness of intimacy transforms, what was "intrinsic" to one now becomes intrinsic to the other. Onions speaks about intimacy involving "inmost thoughts"; it does not say that those thoughts are no longer the ones with which you started. It was at this point that my nascent essay broke off. I return to it now thinking that there is a powerful intimacy in death; an intimacy that does not require words. Perhaps this is why it hurts so much. Because she seeped into my bones, literally became my (clichéd) "better self." In that sense Susan is still deeply, intimately with me. Because the "me" I am is now (happily) mostly her.

* * *

Sons, Brothers, Friends.... (October 2014)

Susan died at 1:15 Sunday morning. Rick and I did not get to bed until about 4:00. After a brief and fitful night I was up at 8:00 or so — bleary eyed from tears and lack of sleep. I fumbled around the kitchen trying to pull together a cup of tea and a bowl of cereal.

Then, from the north window above the kitchen counter I saw a small gold/green puff of feathers in the Rhododendron. My immediate suspicion was that it was a Kinglet; a common bird, but rarely seen.

© _Ken Schneider_

Kinglets are very tiny birds, usually moving quickly through trees and shrubs, very hard to spot, with fall coloring not unlike a female Goldfinch. Sibley tells me that they are tiny, drab insectivores; active, flitting; often hovering at the tips of branches gleaning insects. I had never seen one though we are in the midst of their territory. For me it was a "life-lister."

I am not trying to suggest that Susan's spirit had returned as a Ruby-Crowned Kinglet, though she was fond of rubies, crowns and small kings. My point is a different one. Immediately my first reaction was to call Susan to the window, to share this avian treat with her. But, of course.... One of the great pleasures of life is sharing those pleasures with others. Half the fun is not seeing the Kinglet, but sharing it.

Since that moment, only a few days ago, there have been many times when I instinctively thought to share deer, or a gliding eagle, afternoon sun on the orange-and-yellow-speckled side of Cadillac Mountain; to share a thought, or a laugh, or a memory. Now I am turning to you, dear reader, to be my bulletin board; to give me a chance to post a "Wow" or a "Thank you" or simply to share one of the many small marvels of human life. For me writing intensifies the experience of life, nails it down in the scrapbook of my memory.

The occasional essays that will follow in the weeks and months ahead require no response; no agreement or disagreement; indeed, they do not even require that they be read. The requirement is my own: that the experience of living be captured and shared. This is clearly a selfish affectation. (You have, however, each asked what you can do. You can grant me the fantasy that you are listening.) From time to time I will bring you a rounded white stone from the beach, an eagle feather dropped on the path to the woods, a perfect autumn leaf — perhaps, occasionally, a thought. Susan was tolerant of these "gifts"; I hope you will be as well.

* * *

Embracing the Bad with the Good (October 2014)

In a private moment, perhaps when I am walking them to their car, people kindly ask me how I am holding up. I know this solicitous question is well-intended, but I am always hard pressed to know how to respond. The truth is that I am so unself-aware that I rely on Susan to tell me when I should be angry or more frequently when I should be embarrassed. Caring for Susan is not a burden. Indeed, I am doing nothing for her that she would not do for me — and more competently at that. More importantly, you can't accept the good times and avoid the bad. As Nietzsche said, paraphrasing, you have to embrace it all, to accept any of it is to accept it all. And it is not as if I had something else I would rather be doing.

And, in a strange way, caring for Susan is one more way of expressing my love. She is still a delight to be around — though now occasionally more withdrawn. When she is up to it we have frank and honest conversations that reflect our almost fifty years together, share memories, discuss current challenges, savor family and friends. We joke a lot. Yesterday Susan said, "I hate to leave you." It almost brought me to tears. She does not "hate to leave." In fact, the option is seductive to her. But she hates to leave me. Which is just another way of saying, as we so often do, that life has been good to us and we have been good for one another.

Life is a series of trade-offs — always has been, always will be. You can have that cake, but you cannot eat it too. You can take a winter vacation in Rome, but to do so you must forsake Hong Kong. Now we face the trade-offs that appear near the end of life's journey. First and foremost, the possibility of a new lung, and the return of old-person health, versus the daily suffering. The relative ease and comfort of a nursing facility versus the tonic of Frenchman Bay and its ever-changing beauty.

* * *

"To Life: You've made it very good for me." (September 2014)

We have been enjoying an unusual moment here in Maine. Son Rick, his wife Kath and their two children have been visiting for the past week or so. They left this morning. That is an annual event, a great time filled with wooden sword fights, hammocks, Legos, exploring tide pools, fireworks, etc. But this year son Matt was home from Afghanistan as well, not an annual event. And so, we have all been together, a very rare event.

It has been a time of great fellowship, old stories. The grandkids love embarrassing stories about their Dad and outrageous stories about their Grandfather's childhood, especially tricks/pranks played on their uncles. I beat Colin in chess perhaps for the last time. He was within one move of beating me. We fashioned wooden swords out of oak in the garage workshop; lit fireworks on the beach, admired visiting eagles. And generally celebrated one another's company. Usually, I preform magic tricks. This year I had two, but had no time to rehearse them and hence thought better of a performance.

They have not come because of Susan's illness, but at the same time they are not unaware of it. No one is unclear about the challenges/odds Susan faces. But each did a great job in being their natural, boisterous, precocious selves. Susan reveled in their company, tiring though it occasionally was. Ours is not a family of church-goers. I do not believe that any of us imagine a future existence. I mention that because no one felt it necessary to make any speeches to Susan. Their actions expressed their love/affection better than any words might have. On the other hand, in our family as it turns out, we believe the "ingrown speeches" are for Susan to make.

Last night we all went out for dinner, grandkids included. When we were seated and wine poured. Susan was ready with the toast: "To Life: You've made it very good for me." Perfect. When Matt left, a few days after Rick and his family, there was the inevitable evening good night as Susan went off to bed, knowing she would not be up when I drove Matt to the airport and that even under the best of circumstances that she would probably not see him again for at least a year.

If you believe in the forgetfulness of the river Styx, then you know there is little point in lecturing the departing. The conversation should be directed the other way. And so, it was. Matt said goodnight and once again expressed his love for his mother. I watched wondering what Susan would say. Her reply was simple and encyclopedic, "Take care of yourself. Be good."

* * *

Goodbye (September 2016)

Let me fluff your pillow.
Some water to moisten your lips?
More morphine?
You lie here; I'll go on alone.
Yes, I'll be brave.
Someone else? Another partner?
No.
OK. I'll be open to it. We'll see.
I love you so much.
I will miss you so.
Yes, bravery.
That was always you
more than me.
But I will try.
Yes. It's a beautiful world.

7. REFLECTIONS OF AN OLD MAN

This collection of musings were written after I retired in 2011. If you are fortunate in health and wealth, retirement can be a sweet time of life, full of new experiences and the time to enjoy them.

Simple Gifts (October 7, 2012)

There are many surprises in retirement. It is one thing to realize intellectually that you will have more free time; it's another thing to live it. Last week, for instance, Susan and I learned of a lecture taking place the next day at the College of the Atlantic by a sailor who had recently circumnavigated Newfoundland. Because of our retirement we could simply look at each other across the kitchen table and say, "Let's go." And then, since in the summer and even now in "leaf Peeping" season, Mainers avoid Bar Harbor like they avoid waste, we decided to combine our rare expedition to the Island with dinner at Havana, a great restaurant with Cuban cuisine. Result: good lecture, even better meal.

The experience of retirement is hard to pin down. Its pleasure is not freedom from work since Susan and I both found enjoyment and satisfaction in our work. There is a certain relief, for lack of a better word, in the escape from responsibility, but what responsibilities we had never felt burdensome. Admittedly, I find myself enjoying the fact that I now have no ceremonial role opening or closing meetings. Having been married to Susan for almost 48 years it always felt unnatural for me to have the last word!

Our son, Matt ends his emails with the Latin "laborare est orare" — to labor is to pray. The Benedictines had that one right. Though the object of their devotion is different from my own, it is hard to imagine any better form of worship then through work toward a purpose. So, I do not value retirement in its release from good and honest work. I think, instead, that if we are lucky the pleasure of retirement lies in its simplicity; in being with a person who is right for us in a place that is right for us.

Which brings me to a fellow Mainer, the venerable Joseph Bracket. Bracket was born in Cumberland, Maine in 1797. He joined the Shakers at Gorham, Maine. He became an Elder in the movement before dying in New Glouster, Maine in 1882. Like all Shakers Joseph believed that we find god within ourselves. Shakers simultaneously embraced the pursuit of excellence with a life of simplicity — perhaps most evident in the aesthetic triumph of their furniture. They were self-sufficient and celibate. The latter perhaps having something to do with simplicity! In any event, if you know Joseph at all, you know him as the composer of "Simple Gifts," the Shaker children's dancing song that Aaron Copland incorporated into Appalachian Spring and later into his first set of Old American Songs. If you are struggling to recall the tune it is beautifully rendered by Yo-Yo Ma at the following site:

http://bit.ly/yoyoma-weber

Joseph's lyrics, both simple and excellent, are:

*'Tis the gift to be simple, 'tis the gift to be free
'Tis the gift to come down where we ought to be,
And when we find ourselves in the place just right,
'Twill be in the valley of love and delight.
When true simplicity is gain'd,
To bow and to bend we shan't be asham'd,
To turn, turn will be our delight,
Till by turning, turning we come 'round right.*

I don't want to pretend that everyone's retirement is idyllic; indeed, many are never reached, others made miserable by poverty or disease. But when you are fortunate, as Susan and I have been, to enjoy a retirement in the right place with the right person in simplicity and freedom from want it is sweet, indeed. So, I suggest, that the beauty of retirement lies in its simplicity, in its freedom and (as Joseph said) in coming "*down where we ought to be.*" Of course, to do that you have to have been paying attention, have to know where it is that you can "come down right". I would not at all suggest that Maine is that place for everyone — surely it is not. But it is that place for Susan and me.

I have always admired and often quoted Emily Dickinson's, "*Success is counted sweetest by those who n'er succeed, to comprehend a nectar requires the sorest need.*" Her point being that the sweetness of success is heightened when it follows failures. So, too, I think simplicity gains in contra point to complexity. There was a time when Susan and I lived a life of some complexity. Now the nectar of simplicity is all the sweeter. Because we have walked the Great Wall of China, walking the dirt paths of Hancock Point is more pleasurable. Because we have shaded our eyes in the shadow of the pyramids, visited St. Catherine's in the Sinai, crossed the equator and voyaged through the Northwest Passage, the simplicity of an evening at home by the fire is all the sweeter.

Perhaps part of the joy of retirement lies in the opportunity to do something different, "turning, turning 'til we come round right." When the time comes, I hope you will enjoy a full and satisfying retirement. May it be strong, pure, and simple like a long, sustained note from the cello of Yo-Yo Ma, echoing through "the valley of love and delight."

* * *

Emmett Till (January 2016)

One of the wonders of our human condition is that we are able, through the written word, to revisit our past and, if we are willing, to learn from it. As it happens, I am visiting Money, MS on Martin Luther King Day. That is not by intent or by design, but it is a satisfying way to honor the occasion.

While serving SUNY, Oswego and then SDSU, I used to say that I was, "an institutional hood ornament." That is because I was a symbol of an organization and was hence an expression that organization's values. That meant, among other things, that Susan and I would attend annual Martin Luther King breakfasts. These were good/constructive expressions of community values/aspirations with good people in attendance but they were hardly genuine. Indeed, we were collections of hood-ornaments: mayors, legislators, CEO's, civil rights activists. We raised some money, sang "We Shall Overcome," exchanged hugs, and went on our way. Money, MS is a better/deeper way to understand the evil against which MLK fought, the hope he represented, the unfinished change he portended.

Evil does not have a home in the natural world though it does occasionally visit the hearts of humans. Evil passed this way sixty years ago, on August 28, 1955. That is why it is not Greenwood, (pop. 16,000), that lures me off the Natchez Trace except for the fact that it is the closest town to Money, MS.

But before I write about Money, MS I should say a word about this road trip and some of the places in the south that I heard about when I was young, but have never seen first-hand. Of course, the reason I heard about these places was that our nation was launching a not- yet-completed civil rights revolution and that revolution was being led by my generation. It is not that I wanted to be here in the fray; I lacked the courage for that. Better to say that I was rooting for these young heroes, black and white. I am, however, not here because of those heroes; Money, MS is the home of some of the villains and of an accidental martyr named Emmett Till.

Emmett was a 14-year-old, African American from Chicago visiting his Great Uncle, Moses White, here in Money, MS. Emmett's murder is, in part, a story of culture, of what is acceptable in one place but not in another and of how hard it is to adjust to another culture. On August 27 Emmett and his cousin, Wheeler, came to the Bryant Grocery and Meat Market to buy candy. They had been warned to be careful. But, Emmett was 14, probably showing off a bit for his cousin, perhaps pretending to be older/more experienced than he was, acting like a "swell" from the big city.

It is not clear precisely what happened. The story most told is that Emmett whistled at Carolyn Bryant, the young wife of the store owner. Whatever the "offense," (perhaps just an instinctive "wolf-whistle" in appreciation for her beauty), Carolyn's husband, Roy and his half-brother forcibly extracted Emmett from his great-uncle's home at about 2:30am the next day. They drove him to Sunflower County; beat him, shot him with a .45, tied a 75-pound fan to his dead body and threw him into the Tallahatchie River.[2] The

---

[2]* Yes, that is the river you know, if you are "of an age" from Bobby Gentry's, "Ode to Billie Joe."

next day Roy and J.W. were arrested and eventually charged with murder. In spite of the eye-witness identification from Moses White, who had confronted them as they took Emmett away, Roy and J.W. were acquitted by an all-white, all-male jury after only 67 minutes of deliberation. To her great credit Emmett's mother, Mamie, brought Emmett's maimed body back to Chicago and insisted on an open casket funeral; "I want everyone to see what they did to my boy."

A few months later, after having been acquitted, Roy Bryant and J.W. sold their confession of Emmett's murder to "Look" magazine. As the nearby historic marker says, "this atrocity is often credited with starting the civil rights movement." It was just 100 days after the trial concluded that Rosa Parks refused to give up her seat on that Montgomery bus. When asked why, she said she thought of Emmett Till and could/would not be relegated to the back of the bus.

One gets a further appreciation of Rosa Park's courage when you think what happened to Emmett, just for whistling two notes. Try it. Put your lips together and whistle those familiar notes. In a different time and place they could have cost you your life. The evil does not tarry in Money, MS; as I said evil lives in hearts and not in places. But even so, there is something scary about this place.

* * *

Seventy (March 17, 2012)

I am just completing my 70th journey around our sun. It has been a nice trip, particularly this last lap. They say philosophers don't get around much, but just riding this globe I've covered approximately 40,903,536,349 orbital miles, and having lived at an average latitude of about 40 degrees, I've spun for another 357,700,000. I omit, because my math is not capable of it, the fact that our solar system is moving through the Milky Way galaxy at 220 kilometers a second. So, it is not surprising that my tires and pate are beginning to bald or that my torso has confirmed Newton's laws of gravity.

More importantly, good fortune has let Susan and me visit much of this globe we're riding, meet some of its extraordinary inhabitants, and be a small part of humankind's upward climb via education — which may be our best bet for keeping this blue/green marble viable. Even when I was a teenager studying him at Cranbrook, I resonated with Robert Browning's, "Rabbi Ben Ezra": *"Grow old along with me! The best is yet to be, the last of life, for which the first was made..."*

I recognize that my youthful attraction to a poem about old age was strange, but nonetheless... Perhaps it had to do with my father's early death. Truth be told, I never expected to see 70, and hence value it all the more. I am reminded of a favorite passage in Camus, written in the shadow of

WWII, that speaks of the good luck that avoids an early death. I have, indeed, been lucky and have now outlived both my parents. Browning goes on to write: "*Our times are in His hand, who saith, 'A whole I planned, youth shows but half; trust God: see all, nor be afraid!'*"

I do not share Browning's theism, but a do share his sense of wholeness. One of my favorite philosopher's, Friedrich Nietzsche, writing at about the same time as Browning, but from a completely different universe, reminds us that we cannot truly say "yes" to anything if we are not prepared to say yes to it all. "Yes" to craven legislators who make the many good ones stand all the taller; "yes" to these arthritic joints, "yes" to yesterday's loss in the NCAA tournament that makes the victories all the sweeter, even "yes" to the ignorance against which I fought for lo these many revolutions.

Which brings me, surprisingly, to my theme of how much Susan and I have enjoyed this past lap around the sun. Nietzsche's hero, Zarathustra, was heart struck by the poverty, and meanness of what he called "The Rabble." They seemed to be always with us, like Susan's students in Elkhart, Indiana who were marking time until they could drop out of school and raise another generation of children sitting in study hall waiting to drop out and continue the cycle. Consequently, our best efforts seemed futile. To avoid this ugly specter Zarathustra flees to the land of hope, "*On the tree future we build our nest.*" Which is to say, we will avoid the ugliness of the moment by not living in it.

But then Zarathustra rises up and realizes that you cannot truly say "yes" to a friend, or to an early morning moonset over the Pacific, or to Avocets preening on a shallow lagoon if you are filtering the experience through some hoped for better future. Paraphrasing, because I did not bring my Portable Nietzsche with me on this trip: If you have ever said "yes" to one moment, abide moment, then you wanted it all back. The moment is eternal. It is in the moment that we must live. So, what does this have to do with my 70th lap??? Just this: these past months have given Susan and me an opportunity to live in the moment as never before — not to worry about an upcoming Board meeting, or a pending gift, or how bad CA's budget will be.

Last spring this 70th lap gave us a chance to look back and feel good about our lives, about the progress of San Diego State, about our gratitude to those who made it possible; in the summer our globe spun us back to Maine, a place we learned to love 45 laps ago; and now it has brought us some quiet time together ("Grow old along with me...") — sweet moments to savor memories; leisure to plan new adventures; a chance to spend time with friends.

I have no illusions about how well life has treated us, about how lucky we have been. Were I part of Browning's universe and not of Nietzsche's I would say with him, "*Of power each side, perfection every turn: Eyes, ears took in their dole, Brain treasured up the whole.... Perfect I call Thy plan: Thanks that I was a man!"* Like Nietzsche, unlike Browning, I suffer from an ingrown "Thank you" that gnaws more insistently because it has no ready release.

Thank you for granting me the good luck to avoid Camus' early death, for the luck of being part of a good family, for having had the chance for an education, for the opportunity to serve, for friends found along the way. But also, for the little things that raise a silent thank you: after a dinner with friends, or enjoying a glass of wine by the fire in Maine, or watching our brave crocus emerge through the spring snows. Too many ingrown thank yous. Perhaps it is they, and not Newton, that explain my spread.

So, I send forth my "Thank yous" as this 70th lap draws to a close. Thank yous to all who have been friends and fellow passengers on this full-of-wonders ride. Retirement is better, fuller, richer than we ever anticipated it to be.

Gratefully,

Steve

* * *

Retirement Reflection (June 15, 2012)

It's been a year since I walked out of my office at San Diego State for the last time. I feel a philosopher's tug toward reflection. The first thought is what a privilege it was to be associated with San Diego State and my colleagues there. There were challenges to be sure, but they were met and mastered with good spirits and mutual respect and most of all with a conviction that we were building something of importance. SDSU was responsive to leadership as many universities are not. The responsiveness was not servile, but the product of a mutual respect for governance and a concern for what was best for our students, our university and our society. Second thought: Susan and I were allowed to leave under the best possible circumstances. Too many of my presidential colleagues have been ridden out of town on a rail, or overstayed their welcome, or left feeling unappreciated. SDSU was very kind in giving us a sendoff that continues to be a pleasant memory.

So, what's happened since? Well, first and foremost, SDSU continues its progress in spite of horrid budgetary conditions. Its new president has picked up the mantel, intuitively grasped the potential of SDSU and has set off making it better. I could not have hoped for a better replacement. Susan and I started our professional lives about 50 miles from here at the University of Maine in Orono. In the 42 years since then I never had a sabbatical. Susan used to accuse me of "sabbatical avoidance." It would not be right to call this past year a "sabbatical" since I will not take these lessons back to enrich my research or my students. But the year has enriched me in numerous ways.

First of all, it has given me some quality time with Susan. One thing about a university presidency is that it provides the opportunity, if you want it, for a spouse to be deeply involved in your work. Fortunately for SDSU, and for SUNY Oswego, and for St Cloud State, for Fairfield University and for the University of Maine, Susan was always willing, if not always eager, to be involved and to provide a sounding board, so much so that few if any people knew as much about SDSU or SUNY Oswego as Susan. Most important, when our responsibilities became campus-wide, she was an extraordinary asset both for me and for the campuses we served. But, though our work often brought us together, even living "above the store," it rarely provided time to simply enjoy one another. The past year has given us an opportunity to renew our acquaintance and the pleasure of finding out that we still enjoy one another's company.

Second, this sabbatical has given me time to get to know myself again. When I first went to the philosophy department at the U of M, it's Chair said, "Steve, we look on you as a blank check." That meant, in effect, that as the junior member of a department I would fit in and do what needed to be done. Actually, I have been a "blank check" ever since. Moving from place to place not only doing what needed to be done, but becoming (chameleon-like) what I needed to be, reinventing myself as I went along.

Now I have had some time to be alone in our garden or in my shop, or kayaking and I find that there actually is a person under all that history. One of the many in jokes that Susan and I share, not to be spoken of beyond the bosom of the family, is her teasing me about my being "so glad to be me." What that really means is that I have been pleased to play the roles that life has presented. But now I am actually pleased to be not the dean, or the V.P. or the President, but just me.

Which brings me to another small pleasure: anonymity. No one knows me at the barber shop except as the old guy that stops in after working out at the Y; no one notices or cares what I pick up at the grocery store or what abomination I happen to be wearing as I emerge from the garden. This year has given me a lovely chance to get to know more of our neighbors here on the Point. There are some fascinating/accomplished/well-traveled people here.

[Digression: I once had a colleague named Erling Skorpen when I was a faculty member at U of M. He was a great teacher, "Teacher of the Year" at the University of Maine, and a good mentor. Erling had the ability to know, befriend, and be comfortable with everyone, by which I mean non-academics. I always envied him that ability, being too stiff and formal to accomplish it myself. So now, at last, I am getting to have time with non-academics and finding I like them just fine.]

A little bit sabbatical-like: I have been working on a report all year about San Diego State's best-in-the-nation improvement in graduation rates. It is a story worth telling. But truth to tell, it is also a story accomplished mostly by others about which I have been pleased and impressed to learn. That is not untypical of a university president's work. As with an orchestra leader, it is other people who actually make the music.

I have time to read: Kissinger's *Diplomacy* is excellent/edifying. I am now reading Caro's, *The Passage of Power*; I had read the previous three volumes; this one is equally fascinating and wise. We have time, and still the health, to travel: the high Arctic last summer, Boston in the fall including the John and Abigail Adam residence in Quincy (worth seeing), New Zealand and San Diego in the winter, Prince Edward Island this spring.

One final reflection, about which I hope to write more later. One can ask little more of life than to be surrounded by beauty. Susan and I have enjoyed that pleasure almost since the beginning of our lives together, but never more so than now. As I type this reflection I look out on an overcast, calm Bay, across to Mt. Desert Island and Cadillac Mountain. The trail into our woods bends to the left revealing just-blooming Siberian irises; precocious rhododendron blooms surround us; our poppies are outrageous. Our bird feeders are visited daily by goldfinches, chickadees, and purple finches. On the ground below blue jays, mourning doves and juncos scavenge. This morning a wild turkey stopped by for a snack. In short, life is good for us; we hope it is for you as well.

*   *   *

Visitors (May 2015)

One of the problems of being a widower (I do not usually use that term to refer to myself; it comes from an old-English root meaning "to be empty" and I don't feel empty), is that you are occasionally caught off guard by the sight of happy couples. They mean no harm; just being themselves. But they inadvertently remind you of your loss and the pleasure of being a couple.

So it was this morning when Herb and Cynthia dropped by. They visited briefly last fall on their way to winter along the Gulf of Mexico. Now they are headed back to northern Quebec/the tundra of Labrador/or central Baffin Island heeding the call of wild and distant places.

When they came through last fall, staying only a few days, Herb was dressed in his "off-duty" brown and grey; but now he is spiffed up in his spectacular black/white/grey/brown — a handsome devil, but just a tad full of himself. Herb's black head is actually a deep iridescent green, that you can see when the light is just right. His deep red eyes suggest a secret nightlife. Cynthia sticks with her basic grey/brown year-round. Her eyes are also red, but not quite so. Perhaps somewhat more restraint.

Doubtless you have guessed that Herb and Cynthia are Red-breasted Mergansers. They are regular visitors to Frenchman Bay and to the waters off Hancock Point. I look forward to their visits. When they get to their northern destination (Red-breasted Mergansers breed farther north and migrate farther south than other Mergansers — all the better for their frequent flier miles), Cynthia will choose the nest sight — a shallow depression on the ground lined with down; build a nest; and lay 7–10, olive/buff-colored eggs that will hatch in just over a month. She will handle the incubation on her own as well as the chick-raising. She will lead the young'uns to water after about two days. They will be on their own in two weeks and flight-worthy after only two months. So far as I can tell, Herb is hanging out at the local bar in front of a mirror.

Seeing Herb and Charlotte semi-annually reminds me of the pleasures of traveling with a companion, of spreading wings to explore distant places. I would like to think I was a better wing-man than Herb, though perhaps not so sexy. In any event, like Charlotte, Susan did the hard work in giving us two fine sons. I was mostly in the office (sans mirror). Mergansers live in Garrison Kieller's world where, "the (females) are strong; the (males) are good-looking; and all the chicks are above average" — so much so that they can fend for themselves after only two weeks.

When I looked out the window from the loft this morning as I did my Tai Chi, I spotted Herb and Cynthia; rushed down stairs to put a longer lens on my camera; slipped on my hooded SDSU sweatshirt because it was early and still cold outside; and stealthed to the shore to say "Hello" to these welcome visitors from away.

* * *

Overheard in the Jacuzzi (February 2016)

Old age confers a strange sort of invisibility. I don't know whether it is that people assume I am too old to hear or just that I am harmless. In any event, I will occasionally lounge in the jacuzzi of our condo complex in the late afternoon, a pleasure I cannot indulge in Maine. One turn of the 10-minute dial, a sea of hot bubbles, and I relax beneath a huge Torrey Pine watching the giant pine cones struggle to hold on to their waning purchase.

This afternoon, just an hour or so ago, I found two people in the jacuzzi as I approached. Closer inspection revealed them to be, I am guessing, twelve or thirteen-year-olds, one male and one female. They were deep in earnest conversation — barely looked up to acknowledge my intrusion. I am guessing they are cousins: too excited by their conversation to be brother and sister, surely not boyfriend/girlfriend. They were painfully awkward. He was wearing, as they spoke, a pair of full swim goggles. If a goose could speak it would have her voice. No matter; they were intent on figuring out the world: school, friends, relationships, parents, etc... They sat partially submerged on the steps of the jacuzzi as I settled into the deep end. His feet were above his head as he leaned back against the inside of the railing that bisected the stairs. She sat somewhat above him, shoulders hunched. Both had adult-sized bodies, but without the definition that accompanies adulthood.

Each was trying out a persona: she tried to understand the world by asking questions almost after every sentence: "When?" "Really?" "He said, "What?" He was trying to understand the world by explaining it. He would offer a theory/interpretation; she would accept it and press for more. It was clear that he had no idea what he was taking about; perhaps just happy to have an audience. Conversely, she had no idea what she was asking about; perhaps just happy to glean what little information she might. When I entered the jacuzzi their conversation was about being "held back." What did it mean? How did it happen? Why?

If they were a year younger they would have been on opposite sides of the jacuzzi and the conversation would not have happened. A year later and I suspect it would not have happened in front of me. It brought to my mind how difficult it is to be young. How strange and threatening the world can be? How little self-control is available. There may be some challenges in old age, but they pale when compared to the terror of adolescence.

When the young metaphysicians left, I was soon joined by a little girl (I took to be about four), and her mother. They were almost the opposite of the former occupants: laughing, confident, conversing in a joyful/sharing manner completely without apprehension or awkwardness. Evidently the girl and her mother had been to a birthday party earlier that afternoon. They were discussing it: the mother prompting her daughter's memories. "What was your favorite part of ...." and clarifying what they had just experienced. For instance, the daughter thought her mother had baked all the cookies. The mother explained that she had baked only some. "Did you like the little pink ones? Abby's mother made them. I thought they were delicious, did you?" "Oh, yes." Unlike the previous occupants, each knew her role and played it perfectly.

Evidently, each child at the party was allowed an amount of play money with which to "purchase" the cookies. The mother was congratulating her daughter on how well she handled the money — pointing out that some kids ran out of money. The daughter clearly appreciated the compliment and proudly explained her theory of cookie selection. They were as full of fun as the adolescents were full of trepidation.

So how is it that a confident, bubbling young girl of four turns into a fumbling adolescent of 13? Clearly, it is the addition of self-consciousness, that most precious of gifts, that screws us up at least for a while. The little girl is who she is; there is no gap between her and herself. The two adolescents find themselves estranged from themselves, adrift, puzzled, concerned to figure out the world and what it expects of them.

Now, of course, ten years down the line the situation will have reversed. The adolescents will have sorted themselves out, will be off on their individual adventures, while the little girl will have become estranged from herself and from her mother, at least for a while. She will not laugh freely and effortlessly. It will be her turn to fall into that pit that is adolescence. I wish all three of them well as they make their way to the irrelevance of old age when they too can sit, invisible, in the jacuzzi.

* * *

Attraction (March 17, 2016)

Have you ever thought about the fact that birthdays are a relatively recent human phenomenon? They cannot pre-date the Bronze age when Babylonians first discovered how to locate themselves in the river of time. More accurately, since they thought of time as a circle, the Babylonians' accomplishment was more one of finding an island in a sea of time and recognizing when it re-appeared. In any event, thanks to those Babylonians and their Roman successors, I am conscious of this being my birthday: number 74. I will not use this occasion philosophize about life (I am, after all, retired), except to say that I never expected to enjoy this much life.

I was recently watching a documentary about Shimon Perez (whom I, amazingly enough, had the pleasure of getting to know over the years), in which he mentioned having never expected to live past age 35. Given the time and circumstances in which he grew up — and the fate of his family in Poland during the Holocaust, that is not surprising. For, myself, it was my father's early death that programed me to expect one of my own. I spent much of my adolescence checking my pulse with two fingers surreptitiously wrapped around my left wrist.

I had planned to treat myself to a second (now birthday) trip to the Tijuana Estuary, this time with proper camera and fresh batteries; to a haircut in Coronado by Joe; and to a lunch at the new Cohn restaurant in Imperial Beach. But I called yesterday and learned that Joe would not be in today. Hence, I am postponing that birthday treat until tomorrow. For today I have worked out at the Y, warmed up some of my home-made chili for lunch, and am now settling in to write a bit. Something like this.... So, what does a 74-year-old think about? Having just arrived on this temporal island I am not quite sure.

A philosopher's life is full of "I wonder"(s), some metaphysical, some ethical, some aesthetic.... But these are formally structured questionings, each with a history and its own luminaries. There are also human wonderings that do not fit nicely into these categories, but that are far more "real." This afternoon I find myself pondering the mysteries of human attraction. What is it? How does it work? Why?

If you start with a simple logical schema you could argue that there are four possibilities: Both X and Y are repelled. X is attracted but Y repelled. Y is attracted but X is repelled. Both X and Y are attracted. That would suggest a 25% chance of success. But, of course, that assumes 50/50 odds for each. What are the odds of human attraction in reality? One in a hundred? Five hundred?

The simile I have in mind is that of gravity: of two heavenly bodies (well, perhaps, no longer "heavenly"), throwing themselves at one another in empty space. If the angle of approach is too steep or the speed too slow they will spiral into one another and explode. If the angle is too shallow, or the speed too great they will bounce off and continue their solitary paths through empty space. BUT if the speed and angle are just right, they will be captured by one another in a mutual orbit balancing speed and attraction — balancing the gravity that would destroy them with the speed that would separate them, each remaining itself, but each now orbiting the other. Marvelous!

In the old days the odds of human attraction were lessened by casual interaction (e.g., "There are 20 women in this Modern British Poetry class only two of whom I might be interested in asking out for coffee or 'accidentally' falling in beside on the walk from class to class"). Now a computer does that initial sorting for us. I tell it, "within 50 miles" or "woman between 60 and 70" and it runs its algorithms. This is a strange new way in which to explore human attractions, but in our increasingly isolated lives.... I am new to this process, and surely "rusty," but absent the old-fashioned opportunities to size up potential co-orbiters, this seems to at least provide a starting place.

And so, indeed, I have found several Maine women with whom I have struck up an on-line conversation. This, after passing by hundreds and surely having had hundreds pass me by — not unlike determining in class that I have no desire to pursue an orbit with that one. I have not yet met any of these women. We have merely exchanged a few emails. There is a still unspoken assumption (at least on my part) that we will meet when I get back to Maine. Perhaps that is why attraction is on my mind.

My "electron ladies" are bright and engaging, women of interest and experience with whom one might imagine an orbit. But what is it that will make the difference? What is that attraction that will "orbitize" us, if any? My widowed South African friend, Pieter, tells me that he recognized the attraction immediately when he had lunch with an electron lady and was surprised to have the restaurant owner ask for the table back after what had evidently been three and a half hours.

Is this attraction simply physical? I doubt it especially at our advanced ages. Is it personality? That seems closer to the mark. The sound of her laugh? Her life experiences? Her openness to new experiences/adventures? Her ability to orbit without crashing in? My ability to orbit without crashing in? Her capacity to be cared for and to care? Mine? I don't know. It is a mystery. I have a sense that I will "know it when I see/feel it," but it has been a long time. So, I conclude this birthday essay with a wonderment: will I be in orbit by the time I return to this temporal island next year?

P.S. And so, dear reader, adieu, adieu; I am off to the Tijuana Estuary for a belated birthday romp.

* * *

Shallow (April 2016)

I like to think I am as shallow as the next guy. When I was young I longed for a shallow relationship with a woman, pretty much ANY woman. [Digression: It might be argued, uncharitably, that I longed for a relationship with breasts. Descartes spoke of a "dis-embodied mind"; in effect, I was seeking a "dis-embodied breast," one with which I could neck in the back seat of my car. But how to handle introductions to friends???]

Of course, I could not imagine what a profound relationship with a woman might be. I had no inkling of the pleasure of glimpsing a different perspective, a different way of being in the world. I could not imagine the joy of a quite evening, just sitting together watching a favorite movie, of learning about another life and its concerns, or sharing successes and failures. Now, having experienced those things I long for another deep experience with a woman. I long not for sex, but for intimacy, of which sex is presumably a still-delightful component. I miss the intimacy that comes from genuinely knowing another person, the intimacy of trusting another person, the intimacy of not maintaining a façade, which I used to do for a living.

As I have mentioned before, I am an admirer of the anthropologist/mythologist, Joseph Campbell. He explains the relationship between men and women in traditional societies in a way that has always resonated with me. It is far different from our pre-conceptions of the male warrior and the female gatherer. In such societies, Campbell explains, it is the woman who is in charge, not the man. Indeed, the challenge for a young man is to place his life in the hands of a woman, to trust her judgment. To listen to her earthly wisdom. Some men are not up to this challenge; they fall by the wayside. In this regard to be self-directed is to be poorly directed. And, of course, the hard part is allowing yourself to be directed at all.

I long to be other-directed. To find someone so solid, so grounded, so wise, that I can follow her lead. Someone who knows me better than I know myself. I used to joke that Susan would have to tell me whether I liked the soup, whether I really wanted to vacation in Turkey (turns out I did), or wanted to cultivate a potential friendship. More importantly, because Susan knew me better than I knew myself, I would always seek her guidance about whether or not to accept a particular post, about which colleagues I could rely on, etc... And, truth be told, I was often wrong about what I thought I wanted.

Usually, the problem was that I did not really care enough, but Susan did care; she cared enough for both of us. She had thought it through. She attended to our lives. Do not misunderstand me, her decisions were not selfish, they were engaged, in a way that mine were not. Just as she built our two fine sons, leading them to experiences and challenging their impulses, showing them the world; so, too, she built our relationship and showed me the world.

It was Susan who said that we would save our money from our first year at the University of Maine so we could spend the following summer in Europe. This medieval philosopher had no hunger to see Europe's great cathedrals. Susan did. He was not curious about the French countryside, or about Rome. Susan was. It was Susan who brought art and theater into our lives. Some of this was surely just my inertia. But Susan would rouse me over my feeble protestations and we would be off to New York for the opera, or to New Zealand, or to an art gallery.

I long for someone to know me so well that she knows when I am wrong — and will tell me so. Someone who will not just laugh at my jokes, but will laugh at me when I am inadvertently foolish. I am not looking for another Susan, but for another person who is wise and caring. Susan molded me; her successor, should I be fortunate enough to find one, will inherit a more-or-less finished product. That will surely be a challenge. But I am flexible. I know that there are many ways to be in the world and many ways to be me. I just need someone who cares enough to gently nudge me/us in the right direction. That is a lot to ask of any person. We'll see if such a woman is out there.

* * *

West Texas (January 2015)

Come, ride along with me. I am headed west on Texas route 90 from San Antonio to the little town of Del Rio on the Rio Grande and the Mexican border. "Why?" For some birding, but mostly because I have never been there before. It's not a long drive, about 150 miles straight west. Sorry about the rental car. It's not much: a grey Toyota Corolla, but it will get us there and back. Once we navigate this maze of highway ribbons getting out of the airport, do 20 minutes or so on the ring-way (U.S. 410), we're on our way.

The land is flat; the agriculture mostly grazing: cattle, sheep, surprisingly lots of goats, an occasional llama and a small herd of domesticated Elk. No, really, Elk. There is enough agriculture, together with the flatness, that I am reminded of California's Imperial Valley — but without the amenities!!! Small towns are strung out along route 90 like pearls on a necklace, except that they are hardly pearls and their distance from one another is more like 10 to 12 miles. Perhaps clods of dirt on a rusted fence wire would be a better simile. In one of these dust-covered little towns I spot, but too late to turn in, a drive-through grocery with a pickup waiting outside and another in line. No need to leave the truck to get your smokes.

There are occasional groves of live oak and other trees I do not recognize (e.g. a dark green conifer), scattered across the meadows. Red-tailed hawks perch on the crossbars of telephone poles, roughly one hawk every five miles or so, their backs are uniformly turned against the western wind hence giving me a great view of their markings. Boat-tailed Grackles work the roadsides for whatever they can glean. The same weather that is freezing us in Maine is chilling these Texans. They are not happy about the 40-degree temperatures or the grey, drizzling skies.

It was about 9:30 when we left the Budget car rental. It's now after 11 and I still have had no breakfast. I am thinking an early lunch, but not in one of the many fast-food places along the way. I want some real Mexican food, the kind you cannot find in Maine or in most parts of the U.S. It's still early; some of the places look as if they are not open. Some look as if they closed years ago. Others look too authentic.

We drive on, through Castorville, Hondo, and Sabinal. I am getting hungrier by the minute. In Knippa I stop to ask a roadside Sheriff where I can get a good Mexican lunch; judging from his girth, he should know. And he does. He answers slowly in a thick Texas accent, "No food around here, I reckon," (as if it was not clear who was doing the reckoning). "Nothin' for another 30 minutes or so until Uvalde; they've got everything there." Subsequent inspection reveals that not to be true.

And so I press on, now snacking on a bag of trail mix I liberated from our meeting room in San Antonio. I was there for the annual conference of Student Veterans of America. With the exception of me, all my friends on the Board are former military. When they talk about "living off the land" it involves grubs and roots, not hotel trail mix. In any event, we have made it to Uvalde and not a minute too soon. I pull into the first Mexican restaurant I see, walk in, have my choice of tables. The waitress comes over with two menus, one for breakfast, another for lunch. Since I am not sure just what meal this is, I ask her to leave both. Hard to decide, but I finally order *enchilandas poblanas*.

While I wait, four old men, old as in about my age, wander in and sit at what I take to be their usual booth, an assumption born of the familiar welcome from the waitress and their first-name responses. They each appear to be of Mexican descent. Their conversation is in Spanish as are many in this part of the country. Each is lean, wearing jeans, a Stetson and cowboy boots, not the black, hand-tooled, high heeled ones people wear in Dallas, but real working boots with wide, low heels and just the right amount of dirt, not so much as to be rude to other diners, enough to distinguish them from wandering philosophers. What a good lunch, not only because I was hungry, but because the food is the real thing. The enchiladas were as good as I hoped, well worth the drive. And the sauce!!! Even Annie, our Mexican housekeeper in San Diego, would approve.

So, we have about an hour left to Del Rio. Have you noticed how the landscape has changed? Not much agriculture anymore, at least not so you'd notice. The land has given way to a hard limestone crust, dotted with Creosote and Mesquite, and non-tumbling weeds. Occasional gates mark the entrance to ranches; their houses, barns, etc, lay far from the road, invisible to us. We see only a tall arch with the ranch's name: "Gun Hill Ranch," or "Rolling Hills Ranch." Not a lot of traffic now, west of Uvalde, mostly eighteen-wheelers. From the look of them I would judge that most are coming or going from Mexico. What other vehicles you see are most always pickups.

So, that's Del Rio ahead; you can tell because we are just coming to Laughlin Air Force Base that lies on the eastern edge of town. You'll be pleased to know that I have put aside my usual cheapness and sprung for the finest room in Del Rio: $55. Comes with interior hallways which is good in this cool weather. With no elevator you will be pleased to know that our room is on the second floor which, as it happens, is also the top floor. Think of it as a penthouse suite. The hotel looks to have started life as a Holiday Inn, aged into Ramada, then perhaps a Howard Johnson's. It is now a La Quinta, which, as you know, is Spanish for "fifth owner."

So, the birding has not been all that great, just an excuse for an adventure. My thought, aided by some internet research was that the Amistad Reservoir, just north of Del Rio would yield great birding; in fact, not so much. The reservoir is low, as are the clouds. The wind is stiff enough to have driven most birds to ground. I park the car in the parking lot and walk a mile or so along park paths, working my way down toward the shore. Here the land is semi-open. Light beige prairie grass, about a foot-high spreads out between an occasional live-Oak. No birds to speak of, but I do flush two deer — a spring fawn, no longer spotted, and its mother. They are about 25 yards away when the previously invisible fawn bolts. It is only then that I see the mother, kneeling, frozen, watching me watching her. Finally, smelling philosopher, she nonchalantly rises and goes to find her fawn.

Once at the shore, farther away than originally intended because of the low level of the reservoir, I see mostly Coots, though I do startle a Great Blue

Heron that glides off majestically, its long wings beating more slowly than you would think necessary to keep it aloft.

So, it's a bit out of our way, but I was thinking we might take Waylon Jennings' advice: "Let's go to Luckenbach, Texas...," while we are in the area. Well, sort of in the area. We can just hang a left when we get back to Hondo and head north towards Fredericksburg. My friend, Mike Lehnert, recommends a visit with stories of the occasionally annual chicken toss and such. I think we should go, just so I can buy a souvenir patch to send to Mike.

We make an early start from Del Rio. Having scouted the hotel the prior morning, while having their pick-up, free breakfast, I have resolved to make myself some waffles for the road in their do-it-yourself waffle machine to go with the banana and the orange I bought last night. Fine idea, but the waffles, which I execute perfectly, taste pretty much like warmed-over, semi-hardened latex as I reach for them, on their Styrofoam plate on the passengers' seat, after clearing town and passing Laughlin once again.

As promised, we turn left at Hondo on Texas route 173, which puts us at last on an open two-lane highway winding through the empty Texas countryside. No eighteen-wheelers here. Speed limit is 70. Within 15 miles the countryside has changed. We are clearly in the Texas hill country. And it is as lovely as Ladybird said it was. The fields are now about 50/50 grassland and live oaks. By grassland I mean Cartwrights-riding-four-abreast-across-the-prairie-at-the-opening-of-Bonanza, grassland. And now the oaks and the grass seem to be taking turns: sometimes mostly oaks, sometimes mostly grass. Open enough that you can see the lay of the hills; textured enough that the horizon remains close-in. It's mid-January now, but in the spring when these hills are covered with bluebonnets and lupine, they must be even more lovely.

So, Luckenbach, Texas is a complete, and delightful charade. As I approach I see signs to the "Town Loop"; the signs surprise me because I did not expect Luckenbach to be large enough to have a town loop. In fact, the "town loop" is a circular driveway. Turns out Luckenbach (population: 3) is not exactly a rockin' place in mid-January. There are eight buildings, if you count the five porta-potties; otherwise three: the Post Office, the Beer Hall which is an open stand and another that I could not quite make out. More than enough for the three residents to maintain. The Post Office doubles as a general store, complete with a wood-burning stove, warm and inviting on this cold day, with two locals artfully arranged around it. I decline their invitation to join them. I am on a mission to find Mike a patch. There they are. And more. There is a sticker I can send to Matt in Afghanistan for his armored door and a Luckenbach guitar pick that will please Rick. I have my patch for Mike and one for myself. Life is good.

Another guest looks at me and says, "You just gotta come," as if to explain her presence. She and I are the only guests there. Turns out she works at the nearby LBJ Ranch. Alas, I am already 20 miles in the wrong direction and too lazy to retrace my steps. As I drive through the rolling hills, I regret not stopping at the ranch. Now we continue on the back road for another half hour, speeding through the lovely hills, absolutely alone. When I finally hitch up with Interstate 10 I am only about 30 miles from the airport and my hotel. I will catch a flight tomorrow morning for Houston, then Boston, then Bar Harbor. I am told that cold and snow await me. May have to shovel my way into the house. It's been a good trip; glad you could join me.

* * *

Lobster Fest (July 2014)

Having responsibility (i.e. being answerable) for a university is an honor and a privilege. But, like many honors it is a pleasant one to lay down, in part because there is a role to be played; no matter how good the fit, it can never be you. A person recently told me that she remembers meeting me for the first time when I opened the door of University House wearing shorts. That that is memorable says something about what she expected to see.

More fundamentally, a university president must be a bit of a cipher, revealing different facets to different audiences in different circumstances. But, of course, in reality you are not the many, sometimes contradictory, things people imagine you to be. More fundamentally still, you speak for, and hence assume the projected identity of, the university. That is to say you must often subvert your own, relatively uninteresting, self to that of the university you serve and about which people care. But you are not that university. While others may confuse you with it, to do so yourself is the beginning of the end. In any event, part of the joy of retirement is re-finding yourself, living in a world of reduced expectations and heightened selfhood.

Yesterday was our Frenchman Bay Conservancy's annual Lobster Fest. It is held at our "Headquarters," little more than a shack, at Tidal Falls, on other side of the Point. Allow me to sketch the scene. Hancock Point sticks out from Crabtree Neck that is technically an island. To the south and west is Frenchman Bay, the western border being knifed out at the top by a tidal stream called the "Carrying Place," where, in the good old days we used to launch our kayaks for the five-mile paddle home. To the North is Hogshead Bay, so-named because its shape resembles a hog's head. The eastern shore of Crabtree Neck is formed by the outlet from Hogshead Bay joining back into Frenchman Bay. It is a "reversing falls" driven by our 11–13-foot tides. When Hogshead Bay is drained by the falling tide, water flows over the rapids to the south. When it is being refilled by a rising tide, water flows north.

In any event, it is a beautiful place where seals and eagles and eiders play and where once a year we have our annual FBC picnic on the lawn.

Saturday morning, I was among 20 or so volunteers, mostly Board members, preparing for the evening's festivities. A large rented tent had already been erected; I joined the men in moving our heavy picnic tables inside and shimming them to a semblance of level. Teams of ladies arranged bouquets of donated garden blooms, and scrounged road-side wildflowers, and covered the soon-to-be-lobster-soaked tables with newspaper. Others, men and women, were readying the kitchen where lobsters and corn on the cob would soon be boiled in a huge vat.

Just as we, when expecting guests at home, see eyesores that had previously escaped our attention, so too we saw some issues and cleared away some fallen trees. Then we set up "Popup Tents" to shelter that evening's food and workers. It was all together nice, sweaty physical labor with friends.

I was back again in the afternoon to help with final preparations: set up folding tables, place easels strategically to show a property we are raising money to buy, carry pitchers of ice water from the kitchen to tables in the tent, etc... There was a controversy among the women in the kitchen over this matter. Evidently, in the past we would stretch a garden hose half way to the tent and fill the pitchers from the hose. Some ladies thought that was "gross" and ruled that pitchers would be filled at, and carried from the faucet. Veterans of previous Lobster Fests rolled their eyes when they learned of this affectation.

I joined in de-silking corn, and finally earned a skill job wrestling lobsters and corn in the kitchen both of which had to be put into separate mesh bags for subsequent immersion into the vat: lobsters for 12 minutes, corn for five. As you might imagine, the corn is pretty straight forward; lobsters less so. These are spectacularly fresh, mottled dark green critters who raise their (rubber banded) claws and arch their back as they are picked up. My job was to grab each live lobster by the back of its thorax, cross its claws behind its head, hold it (by its knuckles) pinned there, remove the rubber bands and then carefully lower the (now-unbanded) lobster tail-first into a mesh bag which might hold as many as a dozen lobsters before we pull its drawstring secure and set it aside for future cooking. One of the problems of being a university president is, as I said, that people have strange expectations; another is that they really have no idea what it is you do. Here it is clear: like my companions, I carry tables, raise tents, drag brush, carry water, clean corn and wrestle lobsters.

Soren Kierkegaard identifies three levels of human existence, three "Stages on Life's Way": the aesthetic (which he takes to be the lowest), the ethical and the religious which you perhaps know as his "Leap of Faith." The aesthetic person lives in the moment, and in the moment, pleasure is all. He/she is bound by no rules; no universal principles impede his or her enjoyment. We might think of his motto as, "Eat, drink and be merry." Kierkegaard expresses it formally as, *"elevating the individual above the universal,"* meaning that there is no standard above you and your own desires. As opposed to the ethical in which your desires are subjugated to ethical universals, (e.g. "Thou shall not steal").

Back to Kierkegaard's aesthetic: it turns out that being merry is not a simple task; it requires some thought. This wine might be good, but is that one better? This woman attractive, but... So, the quest is to make the moment perfect. As an example, Kierkegaard describes an aesthetic man hosting a banquet: the food, the wine, the service, the guests: all perfect. Likewise, the crystal, china and linins. Skilled musicians are playing just the right music under soft lighting. You get the idea. So, what is needed to make this moment perfect? To heighten the sense of immediacy? Answer: to hear as you leave, the dining hall being dismantled, the crystal, china, etc, all being crushed. Why? So that the moment might never be tarnished by the possibility of its being repeated.

I thought of Kierkegaard's banquet this morning as Tidal Falls returned to normal. The seagulls soaring, the tides running, the lawn green and fresh with no trace of a tent or of last night's festivities, a perfect aesthetic moment, complete with the vanishing banquet hall.

I have lived a life of elevating the universal, in my case a university, above myself, the individual. Many times have I censored my own desires because they could not bear the label "San Diego State." I do not regret it at all. It made me a larger person and made time my friend just as Kierkegaard said it would. Now, however, it is a pleasure to just be myself, to sit by the Falls watching the Bay rush by. To be valued for the remaining muscles in my back and for my newly-acquired skill at wrestling lobsters. People sometimes declare that university presidents are, "full of themselves." The opposite is true at least for the good ones. Now, sitting by the falls, making small talk with tourists, picking up some occasional litter, I can feel myself filling up.

* * *

Retirement: Jim and Sally (May 2013)

Two of my best friends, both former colleagues, are retiring soon. Both have served long and well. I visited each on a recent trip to the west coast. Flying back, I was listening to some favorite iTunes tracks. There is a song from the "Appalachian Journey" album that fit my reflections; it is "Hard Times" sung by James Taylor accompanied by Yo-Yo Ma's plaintive cello. You know the refrain: *"Hard times, hard times, come again no more, many days you have lingered around my cabin door, oh, hard times come again no more."*

Both my friends have known hard times. Both have worked hard and well, but have known disappointment, too. Both are completing distinguished careers amid the applause of grateful friends and colleagues, but it has never been easy. Tough times were faced; tough decisions had to be made. My version for them would go: *"Hard times, come again no more, both are ready for retirement, hard times, come again no more, but neither has been defeated by the work; indeed, they have prospered and grown in it."*

For many, retirement is a flight away from drudgery, or failure, or despair. Not so for them. Their hard times were sprinkled among many more good times. They lay down these labors not out of weariness, but because it is time for others to step forward. Their retirement is not a fleeing of hard times, but rather a willingness to set aside the good times of work for the good times of retirement. Which leads me to this thought. James Taylor's plaintive song begins not with "Hard Times" but with: *"Let us pause in life's pleasures..."* The "hard times" of which he sings are seen in the context of life's pleasures, as indeed they should be. Otherwise his song would just be a long Appalachian whine.

You cannot have the pleasures without occasional pain. I don't just mean that the experience of pleasure requires pain as a contrast though perhaps that is true. I mean, instead, what Nietzsche's Zarathustra meant when he said:

> *Have you ever said Yes to a single joy?*
> *O my friends, then you said Yes to all woe.*
> *All things are entangled, ensnared, enamored:*
> *If you ever wanted one thing twice,*

If ever you said, "You please me, happiness!
Abide moment!"
Then you wanted all back.
All anew, all eternally, all entangled, all enamored –
Oh, then you loved the world.

My friends have both said, "Yes" to life, to it all, good and bad, pleasure and pain. They have not cowered, or run away into fantasies. They have stood tall and said with Nietzsche, *"was that life, well then, once more."* So, why retire? Not out of weariness, or frustration, or cynicism, but because in the fullness of time it is time to give others their chance. Time to let others enjoy life's pleasures. Time to set down one adventure and, unafraid, pick up another.

I love them both because they are whole and complete human beings. They ask not that hard times come again no more, only that they come midst life's pleasures. I wish others had their strength and balance, their capacity to find and appreciate life's pleasures. And I wish my friends a full and rich retirement as they continue to enjoy life's pleasures.

* * *

Sick (November 2015)

When I was a kid, perhaps like you, there was something exciting about being sick: staying home from school, experiencing the household routine, being cared for, holding up in bed with comic books, etc... My mother was a nurse, so I could not pull of this scam easily or often, but when I could... You have heard me say before that one of the transitions of going off to college is learning how to care for yourself; how, for instance, to determine that you are sick; how to judge whether your illness needs a doctor's attention or just time.

Of course, having gone off to college, I was fond of speaking of this transition from the point of view of one who had transited. But now I am sick, perhaps for the first time since retiring. It is not serious, not even worth a doctor's time. I am stiff, achy, often chilled. It hurts to comb my hair. Not only do I have a temperature (what would it mean to not have a temperature?), I have a theory. When I flew back from CA on the 28th I picked up something. The delightful young woman sitting next to me has been transformed in my mind into a petri dish. Then, in my compromised state, I went in for my annual flu shot, (if you have not yet had yours, you should). That led, I surmise, to a reaction. Now I have the flu.

As I type this I am sitting in our sun-warmed loft, wearing my black SDSU sweatpants and matching hooded sweatshirt. And, of course, I am learning things, in this case that I over-estimated the lessons of going off to college. Turns out, I have been reliant of Susan to tell me when I am sick and to minister to my ailments. It is not that Susan would hover and bathe me in feminine concern, just that she would confirm that I was ill. Which she would do with the back of her hand against my fevered brow; no thermometers for her.

And, of course, being sick was often inconvenient. It is less so now. Back then I "had to" go to the office, "had to" attend that meeting. But Susan would know where the line was. She would ask, "are you sure you're up for that?" And if I did still not get her drift, she would sometimes put her foot down declaring me to be a threat to myself and to others, ordering me to bed. She also seemed to know that a warm cuddly robe, which I usually abjure, would be welcome.

I say this because I now actually have to make these adult calls on my own. As I said, I am still basically healthy, so I have little experience with this. Out comes the thermometer. So, I have officially declared myself sick, but that is only part of the process. I still have to connect the dots which I am not good at. They may run as such: IF you are sick THEN you probably should not be cleaning up the garden, even if it is a mild day. IF you are sick THEN, you will not be able to honor the breakfast with Roger at the Saltbox this Sunday. IF you are sick THEN you will not be able to go with the caravan from Hancock Point to see the theater production at Lamoine Theater, etc... Strangely, each of these consequences had to come as a hard-won insight. Sigh.

P.S. A few days of quiet reading, a bit of TV, lots of naps, some home-made soup, and I am now fully recovered. AND feeling rather adult about myself. I am also already taking "feeling good" for granted. Do we learn nothing? Ever?

* * *

Hospitality

Hospitality is one of life's gentle pleasures. The chance to welcome friends into your home, an opportunity for quiet conversation, a shared glass of wine, perhaps a bite of home-made food. An opportunity to make friends feel, at home, to anticipate their needs, to express your affection for them. Two dear friends have just visited from San Diego. She was SDSU's Provost; he Chair of Nutrition and Exercise Physiology. Both distinguished and accomplished professionals; but most of all they are good friends. They flew into Boston for a meeting and honored me with the long drive that brought them to Maine. What a treat.

Their visit, like everyone's, was an opportunity to spruce things up a bit. As it happens I was in CA for the prior five days myself and just beat them to Maine by 24 hours which means that I did not have those five days to bring the garden to its post-frost best. I mentioned sprucing up the house.

Somehow visitors always help me see the house with fresh eyes. Why are those magazines still on the table? Can I get rid of that stain on the kitchen counter? Is that a dead ant?

It is, of course a pleasure to show off this part of Maine to friends. I took them on a drive around Schoodic peninsula and its newly enhanced park services (thank you, Acadia National Park). The coast there is lovely, fully as scenic as that on Mount Desert Island without all the traffic and tourists. Then we stopped by a local restaurant, Chester Pike's, for a bite of lunch. I took pleasure in showing them "reversing falls" which is what its name implies, where our Frenchman Bay Conservancy has its headquarters (shack might be a more appropriate designation). Pushing a bit farther, I took them to see Gull Rock Pottery, here on Hancock Point.

Maine cooperated with perfectly Maine-ish weather: cool, damp and cloudy, a relief I hoped from the incessant sun they face daily. No palm trees, but freshly-leafed birches in their early-summer chartreuse. Part of the fun, let's be honest, of welcoming guests is that it gives us a chance to show off a bit of ourselves. To display some of who we are via the home we have fashioned: the paintings we have chosen, the furniture style with which we are comfortable, the bowls and dishes in which we serve food.

Most of all, such visits are a chance for extended conversations with old friends, people with whom we share a history, a mutual affection, a chance to stay up talking well into the night. It is a combination the sleep-overs we enjoyed as kids and playing house with root beer served in toy cups.

* * *

Welcome Home (November 2018)

Our Bangor International Airport is a tiny place. No need to distinguish the terminals with letters; there's only one. Back when I first discovered it in January of 1969, on a job interview with the University of Maine, it was one room, about the size of a small house. There was a hole in the wall through which bags were passed; plastic strips failed to keep the weather at bay. Now it is a real airport, one you would recognize as same: two stories, escalators, a gift shop, a tiny traveler's grill, a pub, security screening, in short, all the fixin's.

It has two other features that are less obvious. Bangor is the northern and eastern-most airport in the United States. As an abandoned Airforce base, it has a long runway, capable of accommodating very large aircraft. Together these features make it a perfect destination for troops returning from overseas postings. Beginning in 1963, think Vietnam, Mainers have greeted troops as they returned from overseas. These "Greeters" have now shaken hands and exchanged hugs with over a million troops hastening homeward.

Steph and I were at the Bangor airport this Tuesday to board a flight to Jersey City for Thanksgiving with Steph's daughter, her family and a few friends. The terminal was full of troops waiting another flight to take them home for the holiday. Imagine their impatience: an overseas tour of perhaps nine months, an interminable flight from the middle east, and now a layover in this "where-are-we?" spot, friends and loved ones so much closer, but still so far away.

As it happens, our flight was delayed by a winter storm, which brought us back to the airport twenty-four hours later for another attempt at our own Thanksgiving rendezvous. Once again, our flight was delayed. This time there were no waiting troops. But there were about a dozen greeters awaiting a military transport and its eager cargo. Rather than just sit around, I approached two of the greeters and asked if I could join them in their welcome. I was accepted warmly and told that if I did so five times I would receive an official "Troop Greeter" badge, not unlike their own.

Soon word came over the airport speakers announcing the flight's arrival at Gate 8, our one and only international gate. Did you know that returning troops do not have to pass through customs? I thought not. We divided into two lines to greet the 280–290 troops about to arrive. And then they came, fifty yards away, turning a corner from our left moving slowly down a sloping corridor toward us. We greeters broke into applause. The troops smiled and walked unsurely toward our welcome, feeling its warmth even from a distance. Mostly young, though some were career military in their 40's, mostly male, though perhaps 10% were female, all in desert fatigues, they moved forward to accept our outstretched hands.

It was not clear whether we were welcoming them or they were humoring us. In either case, it was a lovely moment. Some eager faces, others shy. Some making direct eye contact, others with eyes adverted. Some firm handshakes, others hurried and perfunctory. Each soldier, they were all Army, shook the hand of every greeter in his/her line. I confess it felt a bit like congratulating a line of college graduates: one hand after another, a brief word, grads and troops mostly of similar ages eager to get on with their lives. There were typically six greetings happening simultaneously in each of the two lines: "welcome" and "good to have you back in the States" and "Happy Thanksgiving." How young they were. How open their faces. How pleased to be home. How eager to call family and friends to tell them that they were a step closer.

It was the word, "home," that I stumbled over most. I could easily say "welcome back," or "good to have you back in the States," or even "Happy Thanksgiving." But I always choked-up on "welcome home." What powerful words. Glinda, the good witch of the south was surely right when she whispered into Dorothy's ear, "there's no place like home. There is no place like home. There is no place like home." We are all, of course, perpetually on our way home. But that is a false equivalency. For Dorothy, Oz was only a tornado away from Kansas. These troops are flying in from Afghanistan, a considerably more distant and more hostile place even than Oz. Home means infinitely more when journeying from such a place on your way to grandma's Thanksgiving dinner, to family and friends, to your own room.

So it is that we welcome them home, wish them well and mutter "thanks for your service," even when most of us have as little idea of what that service entails as we do of Oz. As we left for our own Thanksgiving reunion these troops traveled onward toward their own. Their thankfulness at being home was palpable; so, I hope, was our gratitude for their service.

* * *

Sea Jewels (April 2015)

One encounters few obnoxious people in Maine. Perhaps that is because there are only 1.3 million of us spread out over 35,385 square miles. In any event, I encountered one a few days ago. She has left a nasty taste in my mouth. I am turning to you, dear reader, as a way of exorcising the experience.

When Susan died we had her remains cremated as she had wished. Cremation is one of those many things about which most of us have little knowledge until we know more than we want to. Surprisingly, at least to me, a funeral home transports the body to the crematorium where family members are not welcome. The resultant ashes are then sent to you in the mail, inside a plastic bag, inside a cardboard box. Ashes, being actually mostly ground bone, are surprisingly heavy. I had already determined that I, together with sons Rick and Matt, would scatter Susan's ashes in Frenchman Bay. This is, incidentally, illegal. By law, ashes must be committed to the deep at least three miles off-shore.

How to carry ashes in kayaks on a rough and windy Bay in mid- October? I bought some Mason canning jars and separated Susan's ashes into three parts excepting a handful that I placed near a pre-existing "Weber" marker. Then the three of us paddled out to the center of the Bay. Spoke a few words of appreciation for a spectacular woman, great wife and mother, and each gently released the contents of our Mason jar into the waters. You all know me to be a sentimental man. And, of course, sentiment takes strange forms. In this case I did not want to litter the bottom of the Bay with Mason jars and lids, but on the other hand I did not want to have these three Mason jars gathering dust on a shelf in the garage. Instead, I suggested that we shatter our jars on the beach where they would, not inappropriately, become "sea jewels." And that we did.

Now the encounter: last Wednesday afternoon, while working through the mail, I looked up from the kitchen table to notice a woman and her dog walking on our beach. I knew immediately what she was doing: collecting sea jewels. I pulled on shoes and a jacket and headed down to the beach.

"Who are you?" I asked.
She answered.
"What are you doing?"
"Collecting sea glass," she answered.
"I wish you wouldn't. My wife died last fall and we shattered her urn on the beach (I did not want to explain Mason jars). I had hoped to have that remembrance of her here on our beach."
"I have a perfect right to be here," she responded.
"I know that." (In Maine, as in most coastal areas, land owners own down to the high tide mark. The intertidal belt is open to walkers, fishermen, clam rakers, duck hunters, etc).
"I know you have the right; I just ask that you not exercise it here on this beach."
"I can walk this beach and I intend to. You can't stop me."

After a few more iterations it became clear that conversation was useless. I turned, climbed back to the house and left her to her gleaning. But I was stupidly annoyed. I say "stupidly" so because I knew she had the right to be there; because they were just shards of light-green glass; because this was not Susan but now-broken jars that had momentarily held her ashes. Grow up.

Two days later, as if to make her point, she was back, this time with a friend scouring our beach for more sea jewels. I did not bother to confront them. She was right; I was wrong. If I had wanted to preserve those shards of glass I should not have done so in a public space. My mistake. But, acknowledging that you are wrong is not the same thing as getting over it. The unpleasant exchange we had has continued to bug me.

Late yesterday afternoon, I climbed down to the deserted beach, thinking I might find a few "Susan jewels" to add to a box of sea jewels and other beach flotsam I have on the hearth. Unlike the scavenger, I knew where to look. But no worn glass. Then I knelt down and gently brushed the surface layer of stones/shells away. There they were; Susan jewels, now worn a translucent light green. I picked up a couple and left the rest to their fate. I suspect they will be there long after scavengers have hunted and I have gone. And that pleases me.

I share this experience with you because I suspect much of life is this way. We too easily fixate on the past, too easily see our own point of view rather than another's, too easily forget what is real, confusing it with sentiment or nostalgia. In any event, I have let this nasty lady slip from my mind like ashes descending into the deep and have, thanks in part to sharing this story with you, moved on.

* * *

Mothers and Daughters (December 2016)

Yes, I know, I do not have a clue, but not knowing what I am talking about has never stopped me before, why should it now? What follows is not philosophy; it is merely an observation humbly offered at this holiday season. I think most would agree that the relation between mothers and daughters is far more complex/fraught than that between fathers and sons? Why?

For starters, most fathers and sons pursue completely different work/careers. In my case sons Rick (law), and Matt (third world economic development), are engaged in activities about which I know little or nothing. I admire and respect their work. I am proud of them and of what they are accomplishing. But I have little to offer except moral support and my best wishes.

The situation with mothers and daughters is different because, in addition to everything else, they are both typically "home makers." That might not be fair, but it is true. I have no thoughts to offer about how Rick prepares a brief, or how Matt develops a crop in Afghanistan. However, mothers because they and their daughters have this extra responsibility/burden of home making, do share an experience and do have opinions as to how things ought to be done.

In the case of Thanksgiving: how the table ought to be set, how long the turkey ought to cook and at what temperature, how much cinnamon ought to flavor the pumpkin pie, etc... When the daughter departs from these traditions it seems as if it is a criticism of the mother and her ways. Nothing Rick or Matt do is remotely a critique of my understanding of Kierkegaard.

But, of course, the married daughter now has two mothers, two prescriptions as to how meals should be prepared and how long the turkey carcass can remain on the counter. And she has a husband who, at least with regard to some things, likes the way he knew them when he grew up. Conversely, if/when the mother tries to pitch in, her efforts can seem to the daughter as a critique. Men do not typically suffer from such implied comparisons because they do not typically engage in the same work and, importantly, they are not typically both present as the work is done.

Thanksgiving dinner is, of course, just an instance of this tension. By and large it is trivial and inconsequential. But, unfair as it might be, women also commonly assume a primary role in raising children. What of the kids and how they are being raised? Now THAT matters. Bedtime? Allowances? TV? Picking up rooms? Homework? Each of these, in any family, is the result of a negotiation between fathers, mothers and the children themselves. The result will surely be a departure from the way in which the mother raised her children including her daughter.

But, of course, while there might be an old way, there most certainly is not a right way. When Susan and I were raising Rick and Matt we were confident that we had broken the code with the help of Benjamin Spock and his all-knowing, *Baby and Child Care*. We had moved beyond the benighted superstitions of our elders into a brave new world. Problem solved. But, of course, our children raise their children in ways completely unimagined by us and it works just fine. The key is love, attention and support, all the rest is just passing fad.

* * *

Rabbi Ben Ezra (September 2015)

From the time I was in high school, (I was introduced to it at Cranbrook.), one of my favorite poems has been Robert Browning's, "Rabbi Ben Ezra." You surely remember the opening lines: *"Grow old along with me! The best is yet to be, the last of life, for which the first was made...."* Makes you kinda wonder what he was smokin'.

There is, if you are among the lucky, as I surely am, an undeniable sweetness to these "golden years": the leisure, the freedom to be who you are, (without reference to assumed roles or responsibilities), the memories. But it is certainly not the best of life (one would have to pass well into senility to imagine it is), nor is it and this is my point, the purpose for which life is lived.

Browning to the contrary notwithstanding, old age is not the end and youth the means toward it. It is rather the opposite. The purpose of life if such there be, is not the jigsaw puzzles, ocean cruises, and gardens in which my elderly friends and I indulge, pleasurable as they may be. Indeed (it is easier to say this at 70 than at 20), the purpose of life is not pleasure at all.

What then? Well, it is more doing than remembering; pushing the human march forward. It is discovery, innovation and passion. It is more about building than about residing, more about the journey than the destination. Indeed, this is why I have not joined AARP in spite of the promotional incentives; it seems so selfish, so self-centered. As if it were founded by Browning with the thought that, "It is all about the elderly." "Let us lobby on your behalf." "Against whom?" "Well, the others." "Who might they be?" "The young, of course."

Imagine an entire life of this retirement leisure. It is not a pretty picture: self-indulgent in the extreme. It is particularly unseemly when seen to be sucking life/resources from the young. I doubt that any of us would consciously choose that. The most striking thing about life is its kinetic energy, its movement, striving. That is what is to be celebrated, supported, encouraged.

The struggles of youth were not intended toward finding our way to a rocking chair. I doubt that any of us were eager to get past our youthful chores/duties/responsibilities so that we could have none. I loved my work, every minute of it. I know that sounds extreme, but I side with Nietzsche in believing that you cannot love/embrace part of life without loving/embracing it all. Youth was not about old age; it was about doing and loving and building and learning and competing and.... Indeed, when I was young I never imagined I would get to 45, (My father died in his early 40's.); I literally could not imagine being 73. If I had been able to imagine it I am quite sure I would not have imagined it as "the best."

I know I have been lucky; that life has treated me well. I know that some people have a terrible, shipwrecked youth. But Browning sounds like someone for whom the agonies of middle school are all about making it to high school, which in turn is about making it to college or to a job, which in turn is about making it to the suburbs and a white-picket fence, which in turn is about making it to the retirement home. How sad. One moment of life is not for another. Each is to be lived and hopefully savored in and for itself.

Now, of course, Browning has another theme, another axe to grind: that God knows best. Old age must be good, else what's the point. You get a sense of this in the second half of his opening stanza:

> *Our times are in His hand*
> *who saith "A whole I planned,*
> *youth shows but half; trust God: see all,*
> *nor be afraid!*

or in his conclusion:

> *My times be in Thy hand!*
> *Perfect the cup as planned!*
> *Let age approve of youth, and death complete*
> *the same!*

I do not believe, *"(Our) times be in Thy hand."* On the contrary, I take them to be in our hands and in particular, not in these wrinkled, spotted old hands, but rather in the hands of our youth. Their strong, caring, perhaps naïve hands hold our future. If perfection is to be found, it is they who will attempt it. Those hands were once our own. We never imagined that old age was our purpose. To change the world, at least to make it better was our purpose. I don't think my generation acquitted itself particularly well in that regard, but we relished the chance to enter into the lists.

Browning captures the spirit of youth in his, *"Mine be some figured flame which blends, transcends them all!"* Which is to say, youth wants it all, does not want (as life requires) to choose. Strangely, old age grants youth's request, at least in this regard, in that choices contract. It is not that one has embraced them all, but rather that the "all" is now circumscribed. Surely, that was not the purpose of the race, not why we ran.

Browning would have done better had he written:

>*Grow old with me.*
>*Youth are yet to be.*
>*They're why we stay.*
>*To help them on their way.*

Acknowledgments

What to do when you contemplate publishing a modest collection of essays but find yourself with 165 of them spread over 863 pages. Clearly, that will not do. Friends to the rescue. But not just any friends; friends whose judgment and honesty you trust. Here are their names: Georgia and Mark Munsell, (friends from Maine and San Diego); Seth Mallios, (a faculty colleague from San Diego State); and my niece, Ashley Weber, (an accomplished writer in her own right). It was their job to help me cram the proverbial 10 pounds of potatoes into this five-pound bag. Then, as the manuscript began to assume a shape I needed someone to help me with the proofreading: brother Roger Weber (retired journalist) brought his careful attention to detail to the rescue.

Finally, my gratitude to San Diego State University Press not only for its decision to publish these essays but for its help in doing so. In particular, thanks to Editor, Dr. William A. Nericcio, to University Historian, Dr. Seth Mallios, and to special editing consultant and recent University alum, Ralph Villanueva.